DIGITAL FINANCE

The internet is dramatically transforming the way business is done, particularly for financial services. *Digital Finance* takes a thoughtful look at how the industry is evolving, and it explains how to integrate concepts of digital finance into existing traditional finance platforms.

This book explores what successful companies are doing to maximize their opportunities in this context and offers suggestions on how to introduce digital finance into a firm's structure. Specific strategies for a digital future are presented, alongside numerous case studies that explore key attributes of success. In recognition of the rapidly evolving nature of finance today, *Digital Finance* is accompanied by a website maintained by the author (PerryBeaumont.com), as well as links to other content with insightful articles, analyses, and opinions.

For both practitioners and students of finance, *Digital Finance* provides a rich context for a better understanding of the landscape of finance today, and lays the foundation for us to process and create the financial innovations of tomorrow.

Perry H. Beaumont, Ph.D., serves as Head of Data Science and Actuary at Distinguished Programs (a national insurance program manager) in New York City. Perry is also a lecturer at Columbia University, and has published books, articles, and blogs on a variety of finance topics.

DIGITAL FINANCE

Big Data, Start-ups, and the Future of Financial Services

Perry H. Beaumont

Routledge
Taylor & Francis Group

LONDON AND NEW YORK

First published 2020
by Routledge
2 Park Square, Milton Park, Abingdon, Oxon OX14 4RN

and by Routledge
52 Vanderbilt Avenue, New York, NY 10017

Routledge is an imprint of the Taylor & Francis Group, an informa business

British Library Cataloguing-in-Publication Data
A catalogue record for this book is available from the British Library

Library of Congress Cataloging-in-Publication Data
A catalog record has been requested for this book

ISBN: 978-0-367-14677-1 (hbk)
ISBN: 978-0-367-14679-5 (pbk)
ISBN: 978-0-429-05304-7 (ebk)

Typeset in Bembo
by Integra Software Services Pvt. Ltd.

This book is lovingly dedicated to my sons, Maxwell, Jean-Philippe, and Nicholas

CONTENTS

FIGURES

TABLES

FOREWORD

We are presently within a new competitive era for financial services, which may prove to be more dynamic than any that preceded it.

While rivalry thins profit margins across many traditional lines of business, technologists are rapidly innovating to grow the top line via improved user experiences or to improve the bottom line through more efficient processes. At the same time, the regulatory environment is such that proposals for meaningful changes in product offerings or pricing strategies can be slow to work their way through the necessary approvals. Additionally, in areas of financial services such as insurance, phenomena like global climate change are placing stress on the traditional means of assessing and pricing risk such as standard underwriting practices and actuarial science.

In brief, the dichotomous mix of financial services that has existed for centuries, and the modern-day challenges these services now confront daily, make for a business environment that continuously requires us to come up with new, creative ways of thinking to address challenges within technology, the economy, and the environment.

At our firm, Distinguished Programs, we are committed to understanding our data more deeply, so we can make better decisions through data-driven, actionable insights. From gathering customer-focused insights via our internet portals, to surfacing risk correlations buried deep within data patterns identified with advanced statistical tools, we embrace quantitative methods as critical for any company looking to maintain a sustainable strategic position.

As a welcome addition to this conversation, *Digital Finance* offers the financial services industry its first comprehensive framework for better understanding these complex and inter-related themes. With practical examples, helpful definitions, and historical context, *Digital Finance* provides readers with real-world and theoretical foundations that show us where we are today, and where we're heading.

As we collectively find our paths forward in this new era, collaboration will be essential to success. Collaboration, that is, not only in the context of building bridges between traditional business practices and new functions, but also in the way of strengthening personal ties. Collaboration and personal connection is essential in our firm's relationships with our carriers and our valued customers. While this journey may seem aspirational, we embrace it wholeheartedly, as we embrace partnership with those who wish to take the journey with us.

Wherever your particular journey might lead you, *Digital Finance* can help you along the way. I commend it to you, and trust you'll find it as insightful as I have.

James Flynn
President, COO
Distinguished Programs
New York, New York

PREFACE

While there is so very much that the digital world enhances, for example the unprecedented amount of readily accessible resources with which to collect and analyze data, and the facilitation of insights for real-time decision-making, there are attendant dichotomies at play as well:

- Fundamental tenets of economic theory, as well as intuition, tell us that information helps to reduce uncertainty; however, lower bounds of stock market volatility have not declined in recent years but rather have held to the same minimum levels that had predominated for decades, and indeed, some measures of market volatility are increasing
- As the role of data in business has steadily risen, the transparency of methods pertaining to data applications has steadily declined
- While companies at the forefront of the active use of personal data as a core element of business strategy and development are generally headquartered in the United States, the greatest oversight of, and largest fines pertaining to those US companies have often emanated from Europe
- Balance sheet and income statement metrics, which have been referenced for over 100 years by analysts to help explain firm valuations (as reflected in stock prices), have declined precipitously in their explanatory powers.

All of these developments, and many more, are explored within *Digital Finance*, along with practical strategies that can be implemented by any business to better navigate the unchartered waters of our evolving global economy.

Figure P.1 provides a schematic of how this text has been organized at a high level, and may help the reader as a roadmap of sorts for the topics that are covered and the context of their relevance.

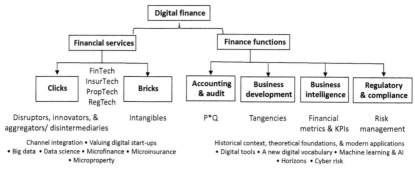

FIGURE P.1 Overview of digital finance

***

This text has truly been a tremendous amount of fun to prepare, and it is my sincere hope that readers will find it an equally pleasurable experience to explore the various themes and ideas set forth in it. While many ideas are presented alongside suggestions of related theoretical underpinnings, there are several other thoughts that are shared in a much more serendipitous way; that is, I opine about certain topics that strike me as being of interest and that I wish to share with others. Given the extent that I have read, lectured, written, and conversed on all of these topics and in a variety of contexts, it can be challenging at points to precisely delineate where one stream of thought may begin to comingle with another, though I have painstakingly attempted to share applicable citations where appropriate, and will certainly provide updates with any applicable additions or corrections in future editions. As always, I wholly accept responsibility for any errors as being my own.

Many persons have served as inspiration, support, and encouragement throughout this process, and I am very grateful to each and every one of you. In particular, to Ivan Blum for his detailed and thoughtful review of every chapter, and to those students of mine at Columbia University who were eager to get an early look at the development of the text and provide helpful suggestions; I am very appreciative of the comments shared by Ai Kato and Wanting Miao. As for the comments of anonymous reviewers during the vetting process of the book, your candid insights and suggestions have made this into a stronger work. To Christiana Mandizha and Kristina Abbotts and the entire team at Routledge, your encouragement has meant more than I think you will ever know, and it has been a great pleasure to work with you all. And for the support, encouragement, and love of my family, thank you Aly, Max, Jack, and Nicky ... you are my inspiration, joy, and happiness.

Perry H. Beaumont, Ph.D.
New York, New York

The filming of A Luminante documentary, "Data Science Pioneers - Conquering the Next Frontier", Luminante Film

GLOSSARY

There is perhaps a certain degree of subjectivity involved when determining what deserves to be defined here, and the absence of any particular term should not be construed as a reflection of its not being important. Rather, the particular role of this Glossary section is simply to help highlight some of the more commonly used words in the context of digital finance, and especially those that may have multiple meanings, or that are being referenced for the first time in this text. A cross-referencing of these words with certain online sources or in relation to other writings will no doubt result in definitions that differ in one way or another from those provided below, and such is the paradigm of newly evolving ideas. As for numbers, M denotes million while B denotes Billion.

Ability to pay Valuation method; assesses the capacity of a business to generate cash flow, with consideration of how those might be balanced against costs.

Aggregator An aggregator is an entrant that facilitates user access to a variety of potential solutions within a sector, while a disintermediator does the same with respect to a single solution.

App A venue, typically for mobile devices, that facilitates an interaction of some sort; a game, a lookup of a train schedule, news, an ordering of a good, service, or other; it may be free or require payment.

Application Programming Interface (API) Coding that is typically contained in within a single file and that can be downloaded to assist the user with accessing either data, an operating system, an application, or a related service.

Berkus method valuation method Assesses five factors for potential success.

Big data Generally a reference to all manner of digital data, which can consist of anything that can be put into an email inclusive of attachments (text, numbers, photos, images, sounds, and more).

Book Value   Valuation method; sums the value of a company's tangible assets.

Brick   A company that operates predominantly offline; there can be reasonable differences of opinion as to how "predominantly" is meaningfully defined (e.g., in terms of the amount of revenue generated offline versus online, revenue per employee in relation to online companies, ability to offer the product or service in person or offline, and so on).

Brick in Click's clothing   A company that truly functions more as a Brick yet has established itself online as a Click. For example, there are InsurTechs whose "storefront" is an online presence, yet with personnel and operations that closely mirror the profile of a Brick enterprise.

Capital Asset Pricing Model (CAPM)   A framework for helping to identify an appropriate return for an investment, taking into consideration the time value of money and the risk level of the investment as measured by standard deviation of returns.

Channel   The venue whereby a firm engages with a customer. A firm might have a single channel, as with a Brick that only deals with customers from a physical location, or a Click that only engages with customers from a web portal. Firms can also operate with multiple channels, such as the web, a physical location, by phone, or various combinations of these and other venues.

Click   A company that operates predominantly online; there can be reasonable differences of opinion as to how "predominantly" is meaningfully defined (e.g., in terms of the amount of revenue generated online versus offline, revenue per employee in relation to Bricks, ability to offer the product or service in person or offline, and so on).

Cloud   Generally regarded as a shared server environment enabling users to benefit from the functionality that a server offers yet without having to incur the expense or maintenance that would be associated with a private server.

Comparable Transactions Method   Valuation method; reference to a rule of three per financial metrics of a similar company.

Computer   Typically a desktop or laptop.

Cost Approach   Valuation method based on what it might cost to acquire all the elements of a business in the marketplace.

Cyber   Relating to the nature of computers; for example, cyber security refers to safeguarding computers from viruses or hacking.

Digital   A reference to any type of information that can be captured electronically; one way to think of this is as follows: if it is something that can be sent via email, either as text or an attachment (such as a photo, image, video, sound, or other), then it is digital.

Digital finance   A reference to any type of financial information that can be captured electronically, along with business models and processes in any way related to generating, analyzing, or otherwise making use of digital data.

Digitization   The process of creating information in, or converting it into, a digital format.

Direct Public Offering (DPO) When a firm first sells shares of equity directly to the public without an investment bank (or multiple investment banks) serving as an intermediary between the firm and investors. The stock becomes listed on an exchange (e.g., the New York Stock Exchange).

Discounted Cash Flow (DCF) Valuation method; sum of anticipated future cash flows on a present value basis.

Disintermediator An aggregator is an entrant that facilitates user access to a variety of potential solutions within a sector, while a disintermediator does the same with respect to a single solution.

Disruptor Entrant offering that tilts the way a sector has been defined and perceived up until that moment, with important competitive implications for features, pricing, distribution, or market share.

EBITDA Earnings before interest, taxes, depreciation, and amortization.

Ecosystem A reference to supportive and interrelated functions, software applications, persons, or other elements that mutually comprise a collective approach to a business or business function(s).

Efficient Market Hypothesis (EMH) The idea that market prices of securities always reflect all available information, which would hence make it difficult to beat the market on a risk-adjusted basis since any price movements ought only to be reflective of new information. A challenge to this theory is that sometimes entire markets tend to move sharply up or down to a degree that would not seem warranted by any new information coming to the fore on those particular days.

Finance At a corporate level finance can be thought of as types of business (banking, insurance, investments) as well as a reference to business functions (accounting, cash management, reporting). At the personal level finance can be thought of as retirement planning, saving, budgeting, and so on.

Financial metrics For the purposes of this text, financial metrics is defined as any measure that references something from a company's balance sheet or income statement (e.g., quick ratio, EBITDA)

Financial services A reference to banking, insurance, investments, and regulatory activities. Activities can include accounting, marketing, legal, trading, management, sales, and more.

FinTech A firm involved in some aspect of the finance industry (though typically banking or investments, or something akin to a banking or investment offering), and of which a predominant aspect of its business model is digital. There can be reasonable differences of view as to how "predominant" is measured and interpreted.

First Chicago Method Valuation method; a weighted average of three valuation scenarios based upon high, medium, and low probabilities.

Follow the energy The first law of thermodynamics, also known as the Law of Conservation of Energy, holds that energy cannot be created or destroyed, but it can lessen in one area only to become greater somewhere else. Applying this to other fields can help lead to new thinking, as with transformations of risks in the insurance industry. For example, in the case of declining revenues from insuring risks of slips and falls due to Clicks replacing Bricks, new opportunities could be found by insuring the safe and timely delivery of undamaged goods sold by online firms. There is also the case of how driverless cars of the future will be insured for the proper writing of computer code directing the car's every action as opposed to the insuring of human drivers today.

Football field chart   Often constructed with a listing of various valuation methods along the vertical or y-axis (as with DCF).

FreeAlt   A business model whereby there is a free component (email accounts, search, social media platform, or other) where those users are leveraged for supporting a revenue stream generated by an alternate source (advertisements or other). See also Freemium and Razor and Blade.

Freemium   A business model whereby there is no charge for basic usage, and add-on costs for extra features. See also Razor and Blade and FreeAlt.

Herfindahl–Hirschman Index (HHI)   A measure of a firm's market share in relation to other firms as a means of gauging industry competitiveness. An industry with a high HHI value would be suggestive of high concentration or a structure characterized more by monopoly or oligopoly than by competition.

High touch   A firm or industry characterized by a high degree of direct human interaction with customers, sometimes reflected in a low revenue-per-employee ratio.

Incumbent   A firm presently established in the marketplace.

Information dichotomy   The idea that the ubiquity and ease of evaluating complex information helps with better understanding our past, yet these same information attributes pose a significant challenge with accurately forecasting the future owing to the speed with which changes can evolve in response to new information flows as well as difficulties with parsing noise.

Innovator   Entrant offering that builds upon of some aspect of a sector in a unique way that is seen as offering a value-add in features, pricing, or distribution.

InsurTech   A firm involved in some aspect of the insurance industry (or something akin to an insurance offering) of which a predominant aspect of the business model is digital. There can be reasonable differences of view as to how "predominant" is measured and interpreted.

Key Performance Indicator (KPI)   For the purposes of this text, a KPI is a measure that references something other than what is commonly reported on a company's balance sheet or income statement (e.g., time a user spends on a webpage, or active number of users of a website).

Knowledge capital   Regarded as an "intangible asset" of a firm and comprising the organization's knowledge, relationships, procedures, unique techniques, and innovations; the full suite of knowledge captured within the company.

Liquidation value   Valuation method; based upon the sale value of company assets

Low touch   A firm or industry characterized by a low degree of direct human interaction with customers, sometimes reflected in a high revenue-per-employee ratio

Microfinance   A reference to finance-related goods and services predominantly offered online and within developing countries.

Microinsurance   A reference to insurance-related goods and services predominantly offered online and within developing countries.

Microproperty   A reference to real estate-related goods and services predominantly offered online and within developing countries.

Mobile device   A mobile phone, tablet, pad, or related hardware (e.g., Kindle).

Modern Portfolio Theory (MPT)   A framework for thinking about investments in the context of risk and return, whereby these values are calculated with reference to the prices of the assets being considered. It is sometimes referred to as a mean-variance approach, with an evaluation of the average return of assets in relation to their variability, and with each calculated using historical prices. The general idea is that assets with greater risk (price variability) ought to have a higher expected return to compensate for that greater risk. Sometimes the choice of how much history is used to calculate means and variances can have an important impact on the results obtained.

Multiples method   Valuation method; an attempt is made to estimate a firm's value in relation to other companies on the basis of some multiple of a financial metric (e.g., EBITDA, book value, or other).

Operating system   Software that supports the basic functions of a computer or mobile device.

Physical store   An actual place where goods or services can be purchased by consumers who visit the establishment; it may be the case, however, that consumers can call or email (or text or use an app) to request a drop-off or shipment from the store. Also may be referred to as a "Brick."

Platform   A computer's operating system, as with a Dell computer running Windows XP using a Windows platform, or a Mac running on the Macintosh platform.

Point of sale   The moment when the sale of a good or service is completed, online, by phone, in person. When a P*Q is achieved. Point-of-sale details can be helpful in evaluating whether a firm is more Click or Brick, or how purchase behaviors compare with return behaviors, or other considerations.

Predictive analytics   The use of data and models to identify relationships (correlations) with historical patterns so as to anticipate future possibilities.

Pre-money   A term typically used for start-ups to denote a situation where no money has yet been invested in the venture other than the resources provided by the founders.

Pre-revenue   A term typically used for start-ups to denote a situation where no revenue has yet been generated by the venture.

Price times quantity, P*Q   "P" refers to Price (or multiple prices) and "Q" refers to Quantity of a good sold (or multiple goods sold, or services). When a firm multiplies together all of the P and Q combinations it has generated over a period of time, it has a measure of its gross revenue. Identifying how a firm generates its P*Q can be helpful with determining what business it is in.

Private company   A firm whose equity is not traded on a public exchange. It is possible for a private firm to issue private equity to select investors under particular guidelines.

Private equity   Equity that does not trade on a public exchange, but is owned by a rather small number of investors. One advantage commonly cited with private equity is that it is not subject to the same kinds of stringent reporting requirements as publicly traded equity.

PropTech   A firm involved in some aspect of the real estate industry (or something akin to a real estate offering) whereby a predominant aspect of its business model is digital. There can be reasonable differences of view as to how "predominant" is measured and interpreted.

Public company   A firm whose equity is traded on a pubic exchange.

Razor and blade   A business model whereby there is a low fee (perhaps even below break-even) for one feature (the razor) and a premium fee for recurring use (the blades), or even no fees at all. See also Freemium and FreeAlt.

RegTech   A firm involved in some aspect of financial regulation (inclusive of banking, insurance, investments) of which a predominant aspect of the business model is digital. There can be reasonable differences of view as to how "predominant" is measured and interpreted.

Repurchase agreement, repo   A type of short-term borrowing (usually overnight) for larger institutional investors, where securities (generally notes and bonds) are sold and then repurchased at prices agreed upon when the transaction is originally consummated.

Risk Factor Summation   Valuation method; an initial base value is evaluated relative to 12 risk factors.

Scorecard   Valuation method; based upon starting with a baseline value and then adjusting that by a series of factors that sum to 100%

Server   Provides functionality for software or devices, and can be on the premises of a user or remote. Remote servers are most common, whereby users benefit from servers supported by service providers (e.g., Google and Gmail).

Shadow banking   Financial activities or functions carried out by entities that are not subject to the same regulations or oversight as traditional banks.

Social media   Any particular venue that facilitates an exchange or sharing of personal views or other information, and is generally free to participate.

Software as a Service (SaaS)   The third-party provider of a software solution might have the software installed on a server maintained by the provider (either on their premises or remotely), or in the cloud and maintained by another third party (e.g., AWS, or Microsoft Azure).

Start-up   A Brick or Click in the earliest stages of being launched; while determining when a firm has progressed from the start-up phase may be somewhat subjective, a commonly used metric is to ascertain whether the venture has attained profitability.

Technical analysis   The practice of analyzing patterns in prices (typically of equities, bonds, commodities, or currencies) and creating trading strategies based upon those.

Terminal value   Valuation method determining the end value of a firm at a particular horizon, and then calculating a present value of that amount.

Tracking equity (or target equity, tracking stock, target stock) An equity that is typically issued by a company that already trades on the marketplace, but which has an interest in carving out a particular wholly owned subsidiary to separately trade on its own.

Unicorn A company that has achieved a market capitalization in excess of $1 billion.

Venture capital method Valuation method; considers an exit value, a desired return on investment, and dilution effects.

Venue A point of engagement with another; it may be in person at a store, or remotely by phone, email, mobile device, or other, and via an app, website, or other medium.

Virtual store An online venue for purchasing good or services.

Website A venue, typically for devices other than mobile (though websites can be designed for functionality with both mobile and non-mobile devices), that facilitates an interaction of some sort; a game, a lookup of a train schedule, news, an ordering of a good or service, or other. It may be free or require payment.

XBRL (eXtensible Business Reporting Language) A machine-readable language used by firms to tag data in financial filings to regulatory agencies.

Yield management When routine adjustments are made in the price of a product or service in response to various market considerations.

PART I

Digital finance and financial services

1
INTRODUCTION

The term "finance" may refer to either the finance industry (generally speaking, banking, insurance, and real estate) and to the functions of finance (inclusive of accounting, business development, business intelligence, regulatory services, and more). In this text we address both contexts of finance, with an especially intense focus on digital considerations. By "digital" we mean online businesses ("Clicks") as well as all manner of digital data types inclusive of text, numbers, sound, or images. If it can be included in an email as a message or attachment, then it is digital, or is capable of being converted to a digital rendering. In this chapter we set a foundation for the remainder of the text by providing a multi-dimensional blueprint of what digital finance may include.

So what exactly is meant by "digital finance"?

Firstly, "digital" is a reference to any kind of data that can be captured and expressed electronically, inclusive of numbers, text, images, and sounds. If it is something that can be sent via text or email, it is digital.

Secondly, "finance" refers to both the financial industry (banking, investments, insurance, and real estate) and to finance functions within any business (accounting, budgeting, acquisitions, cash and capital management, or whatever functions management decides to delegate).

The value proposition of this book is that it represents a blueprint for students of finance (whether in the classroom or workplace) to use in order to see how things digital are designed, and by extension, how new constructs can be cobbled together. *Digital Finance* provides a context and tools for navigating our increasingly digital world, with an enumeration of specific strategies for success. Among the topics covered in this practical, how-to text are the following:

- Valuing a start-up;
- Maximizing the integration of online (Clicks) and physical (Bricks) business channels;
- Opportunistically exploring new opportunities in the digital economy; and
- Harnessing big data for targeted applications.

With the breadth of topics covered, references for additional resources are often cited to encourage readers to take deeper dives into topics of special interest (with regular updates also provided at perrybeaumont.com), and an extensive glossary has been created to facilitate clear understandings of commonly used (and misused) industry terminology.

Theories underlying various concepts are also presented throughout the text. Rather than simply presenting ideas on a standalone basis, efforts are made to link observations to a grounding in foundational principles. Modern Portfolio Theory, the Capital Asset Pricing Model, and the Efficient Market Hypothesis are just a few of the frameworks evoked in order to provide insights, and references to recent advancements in accounting, economics, and finance are routinely explored as well.

In addition to providing a survey of current and prospective issues of significance, *Digital Finance* also unveils novel perspectives along with unique strategies. For example, the concept of tangencies is revealed for the first time, and the newly evolving realities of a fundamental shift in the dynamics of global market volatility are also unveiled. The concept of P*Q is also introduced as a rubric for evaluating a company at any stage of its life cycle.

Frameworks for thinking about digital finance could include the various business functions for which it might be applicable, the technologies internal to a company where it could be used, and consideration of the kinds of third parties providing digital finance solutions that could be helpful to a firm in some way.

Digital Finance seeks to elucidate, to educate, and ultimately to motivate readers to think creatively about our digital world; opportunities to capture, and risks to avoid.

***

Nearly every company has at least one person who handles one or more finance-related duty. For particularly small firms, the person handling finance-related functions might also have other responsibilities. The person overseeing basic accounting and payroll might be the owner of the company, or an individual who also processes new business orders.

In larger companies, finance departments may include accounting, payroll, money management, risk management, strategy, and legal. The person generally overseeing these larger departments is often designated the Chief Financial Officer. In some instances, larger finance teams are also involved in some aspect of a company's operations, and occasionally finance and operations are merged into a single group.

For firms both large and small, the internet offers a variety of online tools and services to assist with finance duties, and these include the running of payroll, tax calculations and payments, expense management, employee benefits tracking, and more. The internet also facilitates various finance functions being outsourced altogether, as in the case of NowCFO.com and others.

In addition to the corporate functions of finance, there is also the finance industry.

The finance industry encompasses products and services related to the flow of money, and Table 1.1 helps illustrate a few of the ways in which we can categorize various products and services.

In each of the examples cited in Table 1.1, there is a function related to the flow of money. Banks take inflows of money (deposits), and lend outflows (loans) at a rate of interest. Insurance companies take inflows of money (premiums) and pay outflows (claims) when there is an insured event. Investment brokers take inflows (investor cash) to purchase assets (stocks and bonds). Sometimes these products and services can cross lines. For example, insurance companies might seek to remove or reduce potential claim liabilities from their financial statements by bundling insurance policies together and selling them as asset-backed products via investment banks.

For each category exhibited in Table 1.1 there is a Click (online) equivalent, and these are presented in Table 1.2.

TABLE 1.1 Finance industry products and services

Banks	Investment banks	Insurance companies	Asset management	Investment brokers	Accounting/audit
Take in deposits, lend	Mergers and acquisitions, capital raising	Risk transfer	Investing	Facilitate transactions in stocks, bonds, and other products	Record/evaluate flows of funds for internal and external reporting purposes

TABLE 1.2 Examples of online equivalents in financial services

Banks	Investment banks	Insurance carriers	Asset management	Investment brokers	Accounting/ Audit
Radius, Chime	Fundable, Crowdfunder	Lemonade, Metromile	Betterment, SwellInvesting	SogoTrade, TradeStation	Xendoo, Botkeeper

For clarity, the fact that a Click solution is cited in Table 1.2 does not necessarily mean that it has identified a successful business model in relation to its Brick equivalent. As we will see in Chapter 2, "FinTech, InsurTech, PropTech, and RegTech," some Clicks have yet to reach profitability.

***

One of the more exciting aspects of digital finance is how certain markets that were once viewed as being the last place one might expect to see new offerings are now often among the very first. With developing market economies, for example, the simple introduction of mobile phones has transformed business in dramatic ways. The ease of transferring money electronically has made for an explosion in the availability of credit to places and people looking to undertake new and innovative projects.

Companies involved with microfinance have seen a real transformation in the way business is done. Simply put, microfinance involves bringing financial resources to remote parts of the world where small investments can go a long way. A modest loan to a fisherman in Malaysia can facilitate payments toward the purchase of a boat, saving on costly lease payments. With monthly installments paid from fishing proceeds, the loan is eventually paid; this permits the fisherman to secure a second boat and creates the need for even more labor. Microfinance has been particularly successful with helping to launch ventures for women in developing countries, with some studies suggesting that it can go a long way to help reduce gender inequality in developing countries.[1]

It has been estimated that 2 billion people in developing markets lack access to a bank, and that 200 million small businesses have challenges with obtaining credit, estimated to an aggregate need of about \$2.2 trillion.[2] Further, mobile networks reach about 90% of people in emerging economies and nearly 80% of adults have a mobile phone subscription, and it is estimated that greater adoption and use of digital venues could increase the Gross Domestic Products (GDPs) of all emerging economies by 6% (or nearly \$3.7 trillion) by the year 2025.[3]

The digitization of money not only facilitates its transfer from one source to another, but does so in a fashion that is relatively secure and which reduces concerns such as the need to watch money stockpiles, or the need for people to monitor cash reserves rather than engage in more active labor activities. Digitization also permits robust tracking of commercial flows, helping to identify areas that are active and underserved, or inactive and perhaps in need of financial resources. Transaction records maintained by financial institutions can also help government authorities with monitoring taxable events, with commercial infrastructure potentially benefitting from improved roads and services.[4]

***

A game-changing dynamic with things digital pertains to how customers have very much evolved to become participants in the development of business strategies. The notion of "focus groups," or having a collection of people meet and provide feedback on a company's product or marketing ideas, seems almost quaint today. Company websites are now collecting information from the user's every click, mapping their entire journey from how they arrived to the site (e.g., via a search or directly) through to final checkout. It is simply a very different paradigm when compared to that of Bricks. And because of this, companies with a presence in both the worlds of Clicks and Bricks are realizing that strategies uniquely tailored to each venue can pay handsome dividends. Further, successes and lessons from one domain can help inform decision-making in another. The immediacy of online responses to particularly successful price points provides helpful information that can be passed from Clicks to Bricks. Where online users are able to access information about the in-store availability of products, this is helpful data that can be passed from Bricks to Clicks. Regrettably, many multichannel retailers have siloed structures whereby Bricks and Clicks work independently.[5]

Examples of Click and Brick collaborations that might be helpful to consumers include the following:

- Click site can check product availability at a Brick.
- Click site can reserve products at a Brick.
- Click purchaser can receive a credit if the item appears at a lower price at a Brick within X days of purchase, and vice versa.
- Click purchase can be returned at a Brick, and vice versa.
- Click users can purchase a product at a Brick yet at a Click price, and vice versa.
- Click can have a purchase shipped to a Brick for pickup (perhaps the user lives at a location where deliveries are difficult).
- Brick purchase can be shipped to a user under Click terms and conditions (free shipping, applicable discounts, or other).
- Brick loyalty rewards are handled in the same way as Click purchases, and vice versa.
- Observing the patterns in specific product purchases at Clicks may be useful to Bricks (from intra-day to time of year), and vice versa (where late-night online purchases may suggest value in later store hours).

Relevant questions for establishing an appropriate business strategy including Click and Brick considerations include the following:

- Do customers value integration?
- Does integration contribute to a competitive advantage?
- How does integration affect Brick versus Click customer retention, purchase intention, frequency of use with physical or online venues (or both)?
- What is the dynamic of cannibalization risk among channels?[6]
- To what extent can customer differentiation strategies be successfully applied on both an intra- and inter-Click and Brick basis and be effective?

- Is there a familiarity aspect for customers with either Click or Brick venues that could be important?[7]

While these questions are somewhat practical in nature, academics have evaluated potential responses for theoretical contexts by using game theory constructs. That is, scenarios can be played out using models and under sets of assumptions that can help to reflect real-world situations, as with factors relating to asymmetrical information, the setting of optimal price levels, cost structures, and so forth.[8]

There is also the consideration that for some consumers, certain types of transactions just may not lend themselves to being consummated online, or at a physical store. In the case of Microsoft operating-system software, it's difficult to see why anyone wouldn't just download an upgrade directly to their laptop.[9] With an automobile, even if a purchase is made online and with personal delivery, it would be unusual for a buyer to forego some sort of test drive beforehand. The following product and service considerations may come into play when evaluating the viability for a company's having both a Brick and a Click presence:[10]

- Homogeneity: A product that is non-differentiable and easily substitutable may be ideal for both Clicks and Bricks (e.g., books).
- Customizability: If a great deal of customization is required, Bricks may have the advantage, with buyers wanting high-touch customer service to ensure specifications are closely followed (such as a piece of custom jewelry).
- Deliverability: If an item can't be left in a mailbox or on a front porch, Bricks may have the edge (e.g., a puppy).
- Serviceability: Clicks and Bricks may be able to coexist as venues when service requirements are minimal (e.g., clothing).
- Complexity: Items that are pre-assembled and ready to use are maybe likely to have success with both Click and Brick platforms (e.g., a doormat versus patio doors).
- Durability: Products that require ongoing repairs or servicing may be more likely to be purchased from a Brick, where a personal relationship is seen as helpful (e.g., a chainsaw).
- Services involving data: Anything that can be shared on a form or included in an email attachment can be done via Brick or Click (e.g., taxes, insurance applications, loans).
- Services involving video or sound: A service that is reliant on a visual or voice can perhaps be provided either by Click or Brick (e.g., teaching).
- Digital: If the product or service is anything that could be sent via an email – as content as or an attachment – Clicks would likely be in the dominant position.

- Rent versus buy: A rental is probably more likely to be a Brick so as to permit the buyer to ask questions about the item being used, and to facilitate a quick pickup when needed and speedy return when done (e.g., a power washer).

Figure 1.1 presents ideas related to engagement venues and a firm's ability to control its message.

In brief, not every Brick needs a Click, and for Bricks with Clicks, a holistic approach to optimizing channel effectiveness could be very effective. A common term used to describe this is "channel integration," and it comprises analyses related to providing Bricks locations with access to and knowledge of the online side of the business, and providing the online business with access to and knowledge of the Brick side.

Increasingly, however, there are layers to the Clicks aspect of a business. "Online" does not only refer to a company's website as accessed from a laptop, but also the different ways in which users seek to engage with the company via mobile devices (phones or tablets) as well per social media (Twitter, Instagram). An advertising campaign on YouTube (e.g., a promotional video) can be tracked in relation to sales responses at Bricks versus Clicks in order to evaluate the effectiveness of respective venues.

Table 1.3 presents various businesses and the respective online platforms that are of particular relevance for their customer engagement. While general thinking today tilts toward the notion of treating everything online as one aggregated channel, without much active consideration of each venue as a separate line of customer engagement (e.g., the website versus the mobile app, versus the Twitter or Instagram accounts), this too can be expected to change and evolve over time.[11]

"Outbound" activities involve attempts by a company to reach out to a target user (as with a tweet or sending of an email) while the "inbound"

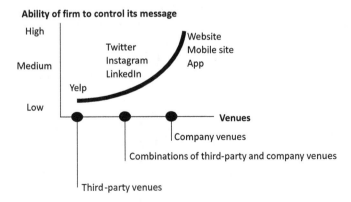

FIGURE 1.1 Engagement venues and ability to control message

TABLE 1.3 Online venues

Company	Brick (B), Click (C)	Service	Platform	Comments
Lyft	C	Driving	Mobile	Order and tracking
Starbucks	B,C	Coffee	Mobile	Order placement for pickup
Workday	C	Employee management platform	Website, mobile	Mobile phone photo of receipt can be uploaded to website platform
CNN, Fox News	B	News and commentary	Website, mobile, social media	The Brick side of the business (cable news services) offers extensions of its offerings via mobile devices and tweets
GAP	B,C	Clothing	Website, mobile	

activities of a user (or potential user) seek out a company at its website or by downloading its app. Certainly a user could tweet about their experience with a company, and this would be a third-party "outbound" action that might influence how others view the company. While many of these types of third-party entities are simply customers who want to share their experiences, in some cases they might be social influencers who are compensated in some way.

Social influencers can operate in a variety of ways, from providing endorsements on Facebook or YouTube, to writing comments that they opportunistically insert into online user forums or blogs. While it could often be desirable to know whether a given set of comments has been provided by someone who was compensated for doing so, this disclosure may not always be provided.[12] There are a variety of social media venues that can be used by social influencers and others to support a firm's message, and a partial list of these includes the following:

- Collaboration projects (Wikipedia)
- Blogs and microblogs (Seeking Alpha, Twitter)
- Content creation and sharing (YouTube)
- Networks (Facebook, LinkedIn)
- Virtual social worlds (Second Life)
- Bookmarking sites (Reddit).

Each of the venues presented is unique in terms of its content, audience, and type of engagement, and as such they all represent unique opportunities to tap into new customer connections and grow market share.

***

Certainly one important distinction between Clicks and Bricks in the context of pricing strategy is the agility of Clicks, which can alter their prices on a second-by-second basis. The changes can be made in response to any number of considerations, including the following:

- Pattern recognition of previous purchases made by the same user (or similar user profiles), where tipping points between price levels and purchase decisions are known; perhaps even the difference made by marking a product at $3.49 versus $3.99, or enabling the customer to buy two for $5.95.
- An internal marking-down of price in recognition of the user's having historically returned fewer products after purchase.
- An internal (or visible-to-user) marking-down of prices as additional products are loaded into a shopping cart.
- Special incentives just before final checkout, e.g.:

  o An opportunity to sign up for a credit card in order to receive an additional 20% price reduction
  o The information that shoppers who purchased "X" also bought "Y" and "Z"
  o Informing the customer that if they add "X" to their order, an additional discount will apply.

In addition to the above micro (or consumer-level) considerations with price changes, macro factors can be important as well, and might include the following:

- Responding to a competitor's decision to reduce particular prices.
- Reacting to a seasonal development (abnormally warm or cold weather).
- An unanticipated acquisition of goods that need to be sold as quickly as possible.

An issue that Clicks need to be aware of in such contexts, however, is that users may be willing to make their concerns known using social media or other venues if they perceive unusual price favoritism or suspicious price targeting.[13]

Fascinating studies related to pricing strategies for Clicks versus Bricks continue to be published, and in many instances we can recognize a marked evolution in conclusions from one time period of study to another; there appears to be a learning curve that is being traced out in the marketplace on a real-time basis, generating benefits for those who stay attuned to insights. Examples of interesting questions and contexts from these studies include the following:

- Economic theory seems to suggest that price dispersion can be expected to prevail more among heterogeneous products than among homogeneous ones, aided in part by the greater level of consistency in the information provided to describe homogeneous products (and, hence, lower search costs per time and effort involved). In a 2018 study of the book industry, results supporting the opposite conclusion were obtained.[14]
- For many companies that are both Click and Brick (e.g., Walmart, Best Buy, Target, and so on), the prevailing sentiment might be that a centralization of pricing decisions is desirable, whereby the price of a given good at a physical store would naturally be the price posted online. Such an approach, however, could represent a missed opportunity to achieve greater revenues via price differentiation.[15]
- A recent example of a Click seeking to tap into a Brick would be Amazon's launching of "curated" stores, in which they are carving out a niche of unique boutique-like products available within specially accessed locations on their website. The concept harkens back to the time when towns had boutique stores specializing in women's or men's clothing, and the butcher, baker, and cobbler each had their own storefront.

What is the tipping point in a scenario in which a consumer will purchase an unknown brand at a Brick (because the consumer can see, touch, feel, and try on the merchandise) but will not purchase an unknown brand at a Click (because they cannot access the product)?

- Does it come down to the brand of the venue as opposed to the brand of the merchandise (i.e., the branding of the particular Brick or Click)?
- Does the return policy carry the day?
- Are there demographic considerations, in that brand may simply not mean as much to younger generations?

★★★

With Uber not owning any cars, Airbnb not owning any real estate, and Alibaba not owning any inventory, these Click leaders can offer unique lessons to their Brick counterparts.

Notes

1 For example, see "How microfinance reduces gender inequality in developing countries," (2017, March 2), *The Conversation*. Retrieved from https://theconversation.com/how-microfinance-reduces-gender-inequality-in-developing-countries-73281.
2 James Manyika, Susan Lund, Marc Singer, Olivia White, and Chris Berry (2016), *Digital finance for all: Powering inclusive growth in emerging economies*, McKinsey Global Institute (MGI).
3 Ibid.

4 In the United States and other developed countries, financial institutions routinely provide government entities with information related to various types of cash flows, such as interest and dividend earnings, currency transaction reports, the receipt of two payments or more totaling $10,000.00 or more over the course of 12 months from the same payer, and others.

5 See Santiago Gallino and Antonio Moreno (2014), "Integration of online and offline channels in retail: The impact of sharing reliable inventory availability information," *Management Science, 60*(6), 1434–1451, and see D. Rigby (2011), "The future of shopping," *Harvard Business Review, 89*(12), 65–76 as well as the survey performed by the Aberdeen Group (2012), "The 2012 omni-channel retail experience," at https://www.aberdeen.com/opspro-essentials/the-omni-channel-effect-how-retail-distribution-and-manufacturing-are-evolving/.

6 Cannibalization is the notion that a firm develops a new product or service that somehow detracts from the revenue or success of an existing line of business, with an overall lowering of corporate earnings.

7 The notion of familiarity here deals with how comfortable customers may feel about doing business with an entity they do not know; that is, whether people feel less comfortable providing their payment information online for a particular transaction than they would making a payment in person for a product they can touch, at a Brick.

8 Examples of reference papers dealing with these topics include:
Wei Yan, Yu Xiong, Junhong Chu, Gendao Li, and Zhongkai Xiong (2018), "Clicks versus Bricks: The role of durability in marketing channel strategy of durable goods manufacturers," *European Journal of Operational Research 265* (3), 909–918; Chen Fan, Yongmei Liu, Xuehua Yang, Xiaohong Chen, and Junhua Hu (2019, July), "Online and offline cooperation under buy-online, pick-up-in-store: Pricing and inventory decisions," *Journal of Industrial & Management Optimization 15*(3) (July 2019), 1455–1472; Tao. Shi, Qian Chen, and P.U. Rong-rong (2018), "Game analysis on return costs of dual channel supply chain considering service," 2nd International Conference on Education, Management and Applied Social Science (EMASS 2018), *DEStech Transactions on Social Science, Education and Human Science,* emass (2018).

9 While perhaps difficult for some to believe today, there was a time when Microsoft software upgrades were purchased at a store or ordered by phone, and were uploaded from multiple disks.

10 Here the focus is on products and services, and not experiences (such as hotels, resorts, activities, and so on).

11 This is to say that while certainly some firms may be actively seeking to cross-maximize messages, data, and results across all of their online platforms, it is rare at this point in time.

12 A more narrow definition of a social influencer might be to describe such a person as someone who is recognized as having an established credibility in a specific industry, has access to a large audience, and can potentially persuade others.

13 There is the instance of Amazon's engaging in a price-differentiating experiment involving DVDs, where users shared their experiences online with negative publicity accruing to Amazon. See Linda Rosencrance (2000), "Amazon charging different prices on some DVDs," *Computerworld*, September 5.

14 Jifeng Luo, Han Zhang, and Haizheng Li (2018), "Pricing strategies in online book industry: A comparative study," *Information Systems and e-Business Management, 16*(4), 791–816. In one time period studied, a rather heterogenous set of prices was observed, while in a later time period prices were found to be more homogenous.

15 Rojers P. Joseph (2018), "Digital transformation, business model innovation and efficiency in content industries: A review," *The International Technology Management Review*, 7(1), 59–70.

Bibliography

Aberdeen Group (2012). The 2012 omni-channel retail experience. Retrieved from https://www.aberdeen.com/opspro-essentials/the-omni-channel-effect-how-retail-dis tribution-and-manufacturing-are-evolving/.

Allen, F., Demirgüç-Kunt, A., Klapper, L., & Peria, M.S.M. (2016). The foundations of financial inclusion: Understanding ownership and use of formal accounts. *Journal of Financial Intermediation, 27*, 1e30.

Barbesino, P., Camerani, R., & Gaudino, A. (2005). Digital finance in Europe: Competitive dynamics and online behavior. *Journal of Financial Services Marketing, 9*(4), 329e343.

Beck, T., & Brown, M. (2011). *Use of banking services in emerging markets, household-level evidence.* (CEPR Discussion Papers 8475). London: Centre for Economic Policy Research.

Cecchetti, S., & Kharroubi, E. (2012). *Reassessing the impact of finance on growth.* (BIS Working Paper 381). Basel: BIS.

Demirgüç-Kunt, A., & Klapper, L. (2013). Measuring financial inclusion: Explaining variation in use of financial services across and within countries. *Brookings Papers on Economic Activity,* 2013(1), 279e340.

Fan, C., Liu, Y., Yang, X., Chen, X., & Hu, J. (2019, July). Online and offline cooperation under buy-online, pick-up-in-store: Pricing and inventory decisions. *Journal of Industrial & Management Optimization, 15*(3) (July 2019), 1455–1472.

Gallino, S., & A. Moreno (2014). Integration of online and offline channels in retail: The impact of sharing reliable inventory availability information. *Management Science, 60*(6), 1434–1451.

Gomber, P., Koch, J.A., & Siering, M. (2017). Digital finance and FinTech: Current research and future research directions. *Journal of Business Economics, 67*(5), 537e580.

How microfinance reduces gender inequality in developing countries. (2017, March 2). *The Conversation.* Retrieved from https://theconversation.com/how-microfinance-reduces-gender-inequality-in-developing-countries–73281.

ITU. (2016). *The digital financial services ecosystem.* (Technical Report). The International Telecommunications Union.

Joseph, R.P. (2018). Digital transformation, business model innovation and efficiency in content industries: A review. *The International Technology Management Review, 7*(1), 59–70.

Ketterer, J.A. (2017). *Digital finance: New times, new challenges, new opportunities.* (IDB Discussion Paper No. IDB-DP-501). Inter-American Development Bank. Retrieved from https://publications.iadb.org/handle/11319/8199.

Kollewe, J. (2018, June 18). UK debit cards transactions overtake cash for the first time. *The Guardian.* Retrieved from https://www.theguardian.com/business/2018/jun/18/uk-debit-cards-transactions-overtake-cash-for-the-first-time.

Luo, J., Zhang, H., & Li, H. (2018). Pricing strategies in online book industry: A comparative study. *Information Systems and e-Business Management, 16*(4), 791–816.

Manyika, J., Lund, S., Singer, M., White, O., & Berry, C. (2016). *Digital finance for all: Powering inclusive growth in emerging economies.* McKinsey Global Institute (MGI).

Rigby, D. (2011). The future of shopping. *Harvard Business Review, 89*(12), 65–76.

Rosencrance, L. (2000). Amazon charging different prices on some DVDs. *Computerworld,* September 5.

Scott, S.V., Van Reenen, J., & Zachariadis, M. (2017). The long-term effect of digital innovation on bank performance: An empirical study of SWIFT adoption in financial services. *Research Policy, 46*(5), 984e1004.

Shi, T., Chen, Q., & Rong-rong, P.U. (2018). Game analysis on return costs of dual channel supply chain considering service. 2nd International Conference on Education, Management and Applied Social Science (EMASS 2018). *DEStech Transactions on Social
Science, Education and Human Science*, emass.

TSYS. (2016). US consumer payment study. Retrieved from https://www.tsys.com/
Assets/TSYS/downloads/rs_2016-us-consumer-payment-study.pdf.

Yan, W., Xiong, Y., Chu, J., Li, G., & Xiong, Z. (2018). Clicks versus Bricks: The role of
durability in marketing channel strategy of durable goods manufacturers. *European Journal of Operational Research, 265*(3), 909–918.

2

FINTECH, INSURTECH, PROPTECH, AND REGTECH

FinTech (Financial technology), InsurTech (Insurance technology), Prop-Tech (property technology, or commercial real estate technology) and RegTech (regulatory technology) are all financial services designations for firms that may have a particular edge in relation to traditional financial entities. In some instances a tech may truly have some type of value-add in relation to Bricks, though in some cases a tech might be more of a Brick in Click's clothing, attempting to showcase tech abilities that Bricks already have. We explore what Techs are doing unique to Bricks, and suggest some metrics that can be used to help delineate techs from traditional firms (or Clicks from Bricks). In the digital world, loans can be obtained online, along with insurance policies and a variety of property rentals or leases. The tech domains of digital finance are generally thought to consist of FinTech (finance), InsurTech (insurance), PropTech (property, sometimes referred to as CRETech for commercial real estate), and RegTech (regulatory), and for each of these there are a variety of sub-classifications, such as disruptors, innovators, and aggregators/disintermediators. In some instances there are Clicks looking to do exactly what Bricks are doing except for being online, while in other cases there are Clicks who are truly innovating with solutions that cannot be easily replicated by Bricks. It can be meaningful to make distinctions between solutions that are merely offering a digital alternative and those venues that are creating new opportunities.

A somewhat basic question in the context of XTechs (a collective reference to all Techs, FinTech, InsurTech, PropTech, and so forth), is "what makes a firm an XTech versus a traditional firm"?

We can't really say that the fact that a firm uses online venues automatically qualifies it as a Click. The only way to get a Starbucks coffee is for someone (yourself, or a delivery person) to show up at a Starbucks location and purchase a coffee. Yet Starbucks participates in social media, accepts electronic payments, has apps for pre-orders, and facilitates the electronic sending of store credits. Yet despite these *bona fide* online practices, Starbucks is probably better characterized as being more of a Brick than a Click. Why? Because Starbucks can't send you the desired deliverable (a coffee) as an attachment via text or email.

Is there a single distinguishing characteristic of a firm that permits it to be best labeled as a Brick rather than a Click?

- Is it best defined by point of sale?

    o What about an online purchase of a physical product (shoes) versus an in-store purchase of something that can be used online (gift card)?

- Is it best defined in reference to the particular good or service under consideration?

    o Is the purchase of an eBook always a Click transaction regardless of how it is ordered (online or with the assistance of a physical book store clerk)? Or is the remote unlocking of a car door always a Brick transaction regardless of whether it is done in the car lot of an auto dealer or on the side of a road via OnStar (using satellite technology to open a car door remotely)?

- Ought the designation of Click be reserved only for those particular situations where a transaction can be entirely consummated from start to finish online (e.g., buying or selling stocks), or would 51% be good enough? If 51% is good enough, then 51% of what? Gross revenues online versus gross revenues not online? Customer engagements? Number of products or services sold?

It would be reasonable to think that on the basis of comparable sales metric comparisons (e.g., volume of sales per number of units sold) anything that Bricks could do (e.g., sell clothing) could be done by Clicks with fewer people, but not vice versa. The assumption underlying this assertion is that the online site itself represents the ability to have key tasks performed electronically in place of by people (or why else have a web presence anyway?). Figure 2.1 presents key attributes of Bricks and Clicks.

One interesting offline–online proposition in this regard would be the following:

> Anything that has never previously been online can have key aspects of its product cycle successfully brought online with a comparable level of

Clicks	**Bricks**
• Speed	• Engagement
• 24/7	• Appointments may be available
• Anonymity	• Social
• Consistency of experience	• Serendipitous
• Impersonal	• Personalized

FIGURE 2.1   Bricks versus Clicks: Key attributes of respective venues

success, but not everything originally created as an online offering can have key aspects of its product cycle brought offline with a comparable level of success.

For examples pertaining to this proposition in the area of fine dining, we can consider the following three scenarios:

1. Restaurants: it is simply not possible for a fine dining establishment (offline) to offer its full dining experience virtually (online), but it can offer an online takeout menu to reach a new market segment.
2. Restaurant reviews: for years, Zagat existed as a published reference guide (offline) for fine dining experiences, and while today there are online Zagat reviews available there are also many other online venues where one can learn about user experiences related to restaurants (Yelp).
3. Restaurant reservations: prior to the development of the internet, a person wanting to know which restaurants had a last-minute cancellation would have to call each establishment and inquire about table availability (offline). Today OpenTable serves an important role with the aggregation of multiple availabilities into a single venue (online); is hard to imagine this being replicated with any great success in offline.

There are also originally created online venues that can really only exist online, as with the $100 billion global online gaming industry.[1]

A reason for companies to think about these various constructs, especially in the case of start-ups, is to help determine just what type of business model would be most appropriate, bearing in mind attendant considerations related to resource needs, and especially employees. For many high-touch businesses, payroll is the single largest business expense. For more technology-oriented lower-touch businesses, the contribution of payroll to expense is relatively small. Figures 2.2, 2.3, and 2.4 present business model examples for insurance, banking, and real estate.

Figures 2.5 and 2.6 illustrate possible cost profiles relating to Clicks and Bricks. The relatively high and flat infrastructure cost profile for Clicks suggests that whether there is one user or 100,000 users, the online solution needs to be fully in place on day one to accommodate everyone. By contrast, the relatively low and curved infrastructure cost profile for Bricks suggests that users can be accommodated in more of an

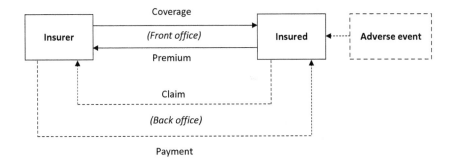

Dollar value of Insurance exposure may be less than, equal to, or greater than amount of premium

FIGURE 2.2 An insurance business model: Property coverage

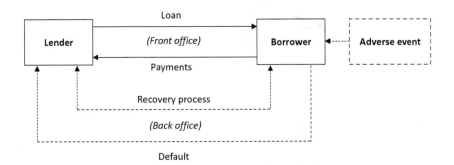

Dollar value of bank exposure is less than or equal to remaining value of loan

FIGURE 2.3 A business loan model

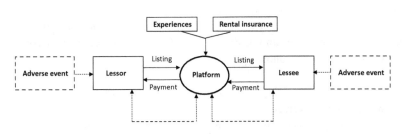

Responsibilities might reside with the lessor, platform, and/or lessee, and dollar value of exposures can vary depending on the adverse event

FIGURE 2.4 A Click real estate business model

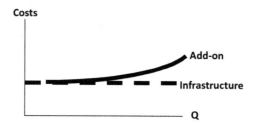

FIGURE 2.5 Example cost structure for Clicks

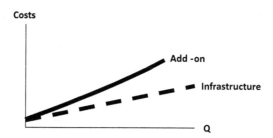

FIGURE 2.6 Example cost structure for Bricks

evolutionary manner, and with additional resources added as demand grows. Clearly, there are a number of possible scenarios.

If you are operating your business via an online portal that has a revenue-to-employee ratio comparable with Bricks for your industry sector, then perhaps you are not a Click no matter how much technology you may be using. Perhaps you are essentially a Brick in Click's clothing.

To take this a step further, if you believe you are a Click but are not able to get your revenue-to-employee ratio to more than the average of Bricks in your industry sector, then you'll perhaps find it a challenge to survive, especially if your profit margins are comparable with Brick profit margins, and particularly if those profit margins are already squeezed.

If your employee-to-revenue ratio as a Click is lesser than that of industry averages for your sector among Bricks, then factors of importance to your success would include the following:

1. Your ability to quickly move your ratio to something sustainably larger than the Brick average
2. Your having something that is perceived to be of a greater value than the revenue-to-employee ratio, such as:

    a. Valuable intellectual property underlying the business that could perhaps also be replicable with new opportunities

    b. Market share generation capabilities to capture especially desired demographic segments for use with cross-selling other products.

As an example relevant to the above, perhaps a Click is able to establish itself as the early go-to solution among millennials, with the incurrence of a low revenue-to-employee ratio being the cost of identifying the attributes of success with reaching that market. Once those attributes are identified, they can then be used to seek out and establish new opportunities.

In sum, there is likely no one single all-encompassing metric to arbitrate whether a firm is definitely a Brick or a Click. Perhaps a more relevant objective here would be for firms, and investors, to think critically about what their true edge is (or could be) in relation to both Bricks and Clicks, and to place less priority on making a case that the firm is more Click or Brick and more on exploring how it is going to be profitable in a competitive environment, regardless of how it might be labeled.

FinTech

The finance industry in particular has made tremendous inroads to things digital by addressing a variety of product and service needs in ways that can be facilitated via electronic venues. For example, consumers can use online banking to transfer funds, receive paychecks, and pay bills. PayPal is an interesting FinTech in that it is very well known as a venue for facilitating financial transactions, yet does not have a US banking license. Despite this, PayPal offers FDIC insurance on deposits, a debit card to withdraw cash at ATMs, and the ability to have direct deposit. PayPal achieves this by engaging in special relationships with actual banks. In an early 2018 announcement, PayPal touted a deal between itself and M-Pesa, a mobile money venue in Kenya, and the ability for M-Pesa users to link their accounts to PayPal to facilitate the purchase of products and services outside of Kenya. Others are also apparently looking to dabble in the banking sector, as with Square and Amazon, and TransferWise is already offering bank services in the way of free currency conversions, and the free digital prepaid debit card company Monzo recently offered to transition its UK users to full bank accounts.

PayPal is an example of a FinTech company dating from before the term "FinTech" even came into common currency. As a popular online payment system, PayPal solved the challenge of two parties making and receiving payments at any time, enabling them to do so from any device with internet access. Although PayPal very much functions like a Brick bank, it is not technically one. And by "technically," we mean in the sense of needing to conform with U.S. regulatory registrations and filings of traditional banks, because it is registered as a bank in Luxembourg. Table 2.1 provides a listing of banking functions carried out by Clicks and Bricks.

Since the launching of PayPal, other payment venues have evolved, such as Venmo, Stripe, Dwolla, Zelle, M-Pesa, and others. Other FinTech firms have

TABLE 2.1 Banking functions by Bricks and Clicks

	Banks	Investment banks	Insurance companies	Asset management	Investment brokers
Traditional roles of Bricks	Take in deposits, Lend	M&A, capital raising	Risk transfer	Investing	Facilitate transactions in stocks, bonds, and other products
Click alternatives	Synchrony, Lending Club, Kickstarter	Starter, Halo, DPOs (Direct Public Offerings) instead of IPOs (Initial Public Offerings)	Bikelane, Lemonade, Metromile, Sureify	Betterment, Mercatus, Kantox	Ally, Robinhood, E-Trade

also been launched, generally taking brick-and-mortar functions of traditional banks and investment banks, and bringing those functions online.

Table 2.2 provides examples of online firms who provide a variety of finance-related functions.

InsurTech

There are a few different ways to be involved in the insurance industry, and they are as follows:

- Carrier: sells policies to generate premiums, and generally retains the responsibility to make claims payments
- Reinsurer: agrees to take on responsibility for certain claims payments from carriers in exchange for a portion of policy premiums
- Broker: sells carrier policies to generate premiums, and may not retain the responsibility for making claims payments
- Managing General Agent (MGA): An insurance agency or business entity with authority provided by an insurance carrier to administer insurance programs and negotiate contracts on behalf of the carrier; the MGA serves as an intermediary between carriers and agents and/or the insureds, and in some cases may share in the claims of policies
- Aggregator: Provides an online venue for insurance shoppers to compare and contrast carrier features and pricing, with links to sites where a purchase can be made
- Risk transferor: Provides a vehicle (often in the form of a structured bond) whereby policies and their respective premiums are aggregated into pools

TABLE 2.2 XTechs in relation to Bricks

Core offering: Loan

	FinTech	Brick
Engagement	Online	Physical location, email, phone
Value proposition	Speed, Multiple lenders, 24-7	Personal situations considered
P*Q	Price (P) of loan may be greater, and loan size (Q) may be smaller[1]	Price (P) of loan may be lower, and loan size (Q) may be greater[1]
Delivery	Electronic transfer	Electronic transfer

Core offering: Auto insurance

	InsurTech	Brick
Engagement	Online	Physical location, email, phone
Value proposition	24-7	Opportunity for real-time questions and clarifications
P*Q	Generally little material difference from Bricks	Generally little material difference from InsurTech
Delivery	Electronic transfer	Electronic transfer

Core offering: Lodging

	PropTech	Brick
Engagement	Online	Physical location, email, phone
Value proposition	Current user-rated experiences with detailed photos and descriptions of actual surroundings	Known brands, standardized offerings, amenities
P*Q	Generally a wide range of prices and growing availability of options	Generally a narrow range of prices and limited number of rooms
Delivery	Check-in experience can vary	Check-in experience fairly routine

1 https://www.valuepenguin.com/average-small-business-loan-amount

and sold to investors; the fewer claims payments that are issued, the greater the profitability of the investment.

For a working definition of InsurTech, we can say that it is a reference to the use of technology and related innovations to create venues for the maximization of revenues or minimization of risks within the insurance industry. Maximizing revenues might include the creative use of social media to tap into new markets for the generation of insurance premiums, and minimizing risks could include the use of home-monitoring devices to signal when a danger may be imminent.

In some industries there is also the notion right at the start that there will be losses. For example, insurance companies and asset management firms are in lines of business where losses are not only possible, but are very much expected. An insurance company desiring to sell policies where no claims would ever be filed would likely find a dearth of customers wanting to pay for the particular coverage. Insurance for the Zombie Apocalypse, anyone?[2] The reality is that consumers want insurance to cover adverse events that could, and do, actually happen, and in such instances claims payments are inevitable. With proper pricing, risk management, and a bit of luck, premiums collected on the sale of policies will exceed claims dollars paid out, and profits will be generated.[3]

In 2018, some insightful articles appeared on LinkedIn related to the Insur-Tech sector.[4] The authors were Matteo Carbone and Adrian Jones, and they examined the public regulatory filings of various InsurTechs for the full year of 2017. Each of the start-ups they examined was seeking to build a carrier business model (i.e., selling policies to generate premiums, and retaining responsibility to make claims payments).

Among their findings were the following:

- Mediocre underwriting results
- Cash burn of about $15 million a year
- Focus on customer acquisition costs and back-office expenses seeming to matter more than achieving efficiencies from digitization
- Reinsurers supporting InsurTech lost money as well, and
- Start-ups that seemed to do better were in markets not targeted by incumbent Bricks.

So, here's the thing ... these InsurTechs were not pursuing models related to freemiums, razor and blade, or free offerings offset by other revenue streams such as third-party ads. If they were, a case might perhaps be made that they were simply in need of time to generate positive cash flow from the losses one would expect to be incurred in initial phases of operation. Rather, the InsurTechs studied by Carbone and Jones seem to have been unprofitable in the old-fashioned way: with operation costs far in excess of revenues.

In light of these findings, it's quite reasonable to ask where all this is heading. In many instances, the investors in these start-ups have good track records with other investments they have made. Possible answers include the following:

- The losses represent the kind of sunk costs often involved with establishing a new business model (i.e., the selling of insurance exclusively online), and positive returns may soon follow.

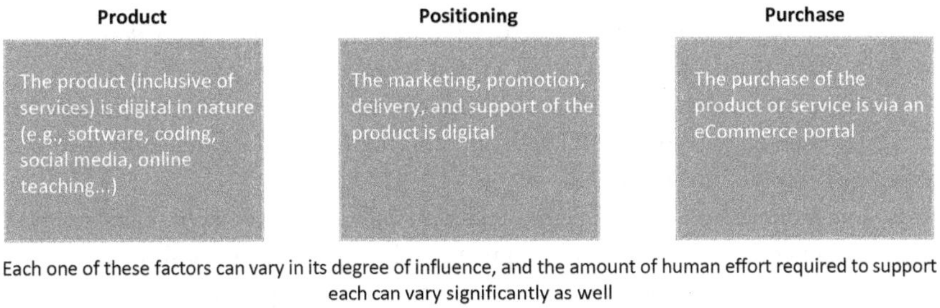

Product	Positioning	Purchase
The product (inclusive of services) is digital in nature (e.g., software, coding, social media, online teaching...)	The marketing, promotion, delivery, and support of the product is digital	The purchase of the product or service is via an eCommerce portal

Each one of these factors can vary in its degree of influence, and the amount of human effort required to support each can vary significantly as well

FIGURE 2.7 Ways to be a "Click": The three Ps

- The bigger picture here is not about building an insurance business, but is instead about building a venue for the selling and administration of insurance. Accordingly, the end goal is to find an insurance company who will acquire the InsurTech's technology and use it to develop online opportunities. Perhaps as part of the sale the InsurTech will include whatever book of business it had developed over the course of its existence. In this regard, InsurTech companies have something in common with firms who operate on a subscription-based model. Notably, if someone has something they need insured in one year, then perhaps the chances are pretty good that they will need insurance in year two, and three, and so forth. In brief, renewals can grow to become a large portion of an insurance entity's book of business. Arguably, it is the first sale that takes the most time and effort on the part of a salesperson, with subsequent renewals requiring a fraction of the initial time and effort. Under this scenario, valuing an InsurTech's book of business could involve calculating the present value of a series of potential future cash flows, not unlike the valuation of a bond.
- In the near future investors may conclude that their InsurTech experiments simply have not worked out as expected, and InsurTechs will begin to disappear. This situation may be all the more likely under a weakening economy scenario.

An interesting point to ponder with regard to many self-styled InsurTechs is whether they are truly InsurTechs at all. To phrase this in a slightly different way, what is the tipping point for an InsurTech or any type of tech to be more appropriately characterized as a Brick instead of a Click? Figure 2.7 presents ideas around ways to be a "Click."

PropTech (or CRE Tech)

With FinTech often regarded as being in first place with digital innovations, InsurTech has been widely seen as coming second and PropTech third. Nevertheless it has been estimated that venture capitalists invested $12.6 billion in PropTech in 2017 across 347 deals, or about triple the amount invested in

2015.[5] One of the first PropTechs to be valued at over $1 billion was founded in 2016, with three others following in that same year.

There are a number of interesting products and services that have surfaced in the PropTech sector (or CRETech, for commercial real estate), and a few of these are presented in Table 2.3.

As also indicated in Table 2.3, the technical offerings have applicability for both personal and commercial real estate contexts, and span the gamut of short-term non-ownership markets (Airbnb) through to long-term lease or purchase venues (Zillow) and a variety of service solutions in between (Ubitquity, Matterport, and Homelink).

As for future trends, much is expected to center around the user experience of the lessee, whether as an overnight business traveler, or as a three-year tenant of a commercial office space. When an occupant arrives at the property, lighting

TABLE 2.3 PropTech solutions

Product/Service	Solution
Airbnb	A service offering a variety of user choices and experiences with lodging
Compass	An app to identify available residential properties, and with a variety of data tools and insights
Homelink	A vehicle-based wireless control system that permits users to perform a variety of tasks, e.g., to open and close garage doors or gates, activate or deactivate a home's security system, turn on or off interior or exterior lighting, appliances, electronics, and more
Lone Rooftop	A platform that calculates where and how many people are in a building at any given time
Matterport	3D imaging technology for marketing experiences
Open source data	An increasing number of municipalities are offering free data that can be applied to insightful analyses of local real estate markets. For example, New York City reports the number of housing violations that a property receives, while Chicago cites a problem landlord list. Federal Census data can also be a rich source of real estate-related information.
Opendoor	Buys and sells homes online
Ubitquity	Blockchain technology to track and maintain real estate documentation (e.g., titles, contracts, and so on)
ULC	A drone operating service with the ability to detect hazardous gas leaks and more
VTS	An app for leasing and asset management
WhoseYourLandlord	A platform with several detailed pieces of information related to properties
Zillow	A platform that offers a variety of ways to find properties available for sale or rent and with significant details to assist with both price discovery and risk assessment

and temperature will have been electronically set to levels commensurate with preferences indicated in their user profiles, their Spotify playlists will seamlessly connect, and they will automatically be upgraded to the nicest conference room venue when it unexpectedly becomes available. Meantime, from a landlord perspective, datapoints related to occupancy, vacancy rates, energy consumption, and usage of building amenities will all contribute to the creation of optimal pricing strategies as well as ideas for improved customer offerings.

An important development in the context of PropTech generally is that many major metropolitan governments have launched open-data initiatives, with a variety of information now publicly available. From Albuquerque, New Mexico to Winston-Salem, North Carolina, close to 100 cities are reporting an appreciable amount of data on everything from building permits to locations of fire stations, with tremendous potential in terms of how these insights could help to better forecast patterns of future growth and meet anticipated needs for services.

With regard to examples of PropTech unicorns, these include Compass, Homelink, SMS Assist, Opendoor, and Airbnb. Curiously, these companies are not all based in the United States (Homelink is in China), and each of these start-ups is in a rather unique niche of the market. Compass is involved with identifying available residential properties (leveraging a network of brokers), Homelink assists with wireless connections for home devices (a property management tool), and Opendoor serves as a direct buyer of properties (with algorithms used to determine applicable prices).

Perhaps particularly deserving of note in Table 2.3 is the number potential overlaps and synergies between PropTech products and services with both FinTech and InsurTech. For example, Lone Rooftop could be used to monitor unusual patterns of persons entering and leaving buildings, which might be related to burglaries or other nefarious behavior. Or in the case of Airbnb, there could be the opportunity at the check-out page to select an option for adding on rental insurance.[6]

Meantime, trends to watch include coworking venues (WeWork), co-living (Common), the role of crowdfunding with real estate investing (CrowdStreet), and home swapping for seasonal or longer-term rentals (LoveHomeSwap).

An interesting company that combines multiple real estate functions into a single venue is Opendoor. This start-up purchases property online directly from homeowners, and with reference to a price that is determined by a proprietary algorithm augmented with any special information about the property's unique features. An estimate is then provided to the seller along with a list of items that need to be updated or repaired, and if a selling price is agreed upon then Opendoor purchases the home and then places it on the market, using remote-controlled locks and cameras to facilitate self-guided visits from potential buyers. Opendoor spans the traditional roles of brokers, bankers, and contractors.

Other digital offerings in the PropTech space include the following:

- No Agent: No Agent is an end-to-end digital property-management venue to help automate the marketing and administration of rental properties.

Recognizing that there is an important role for human involvement in the rental market, No Agent offers technology accompanied by customer service in the form of property experts.

- Clixifix: Clixifix endeavors to ease the burdens of housebuilders and commercial contractors by allowing them to manage their customer care operations online, and track defects and repairs in homes and commercial buildings. The SaaS venue permits the assigning of repairs to contractors and communication with clients and property occupants. Contractors can then provide instant updates as work is performed.

- Reposit: Reposit provides tenants with an affordable alternative to rental deposits on apartments and other rental properties. Rather than a renter providing a month's worth of rent as a deposit which is then kept for the term of the lease, with Reposit a renter pays a nonrefundable fee of one week's rent. Reposit's services include a month's worth of cover to the landlord for damages, unpaid rent, cleaning costs or any other items typically applicable with security deposits.

- Seeable: Seeable uses mobile mapping techniques to create augmented reality and virtual reality building visualization apps. Seeable's apps provide an easy and nontechnical access point to buildings inclusive of data relating to their structure.

- Pavegen: Pavegen aims to alter the way cities are built by seeking to harvest energy and data from human steps. Pavegen makes flooring that can generate renewable electricity by converting the downward force of a step into electricity via a flywheel mechanism. The most recent tile prototype was released in 2016 and can apparently generate up to 5 watts per person.

- HomeAdvisor: Offers a consumer venue on which to search for and compare various home-improvement projects and related services.

***

Prior to moving along to RegTech, it may be insightful to pause and observe that while FinTech, InsurTech, and PropTech are all substantive phenomena in their own right, they can cross over and intersect as well, as illustrated by Figure 2.8.

FIGURE 2.8   Combinations of Tech: InsurTech, FinTech, PropTech

RegTech

As suggested by Table 2.4, there are many layers to financial regulation around the globe, and a variety of solutions have emerged to help address the many reporting and compliance requirements.

By one estimate, financial institutions have paid over \$300 billion in fines since the financial crisis of 2008. Not only do regulations exist to guide firms with regard to desired conduct, but there can also be monetary consequences for alleged infringements of those rules. Table 2.5 provides a sampling of key RegTech terms to help with navigating this sector.

As shown in Figure 2.9, it can be rather complicated to follow all the linkages for respective regulatory authorities and applicable regulated entities. Even firms who are highly motivated to stay abreast of key regulatory developments can find themselves mired within a complex web of mandated expectations. In 2017 there were a total of 56,321 regulatory alerts issued by more than 900 regulatory bodies, or an average of 216 alerts a day.[7]

Since 2014, investments in RegTech–related ventures have been estimated to be in excess of \$1 billion each year.

Figure 2.10 presents various categories of regulatory requirements, and associated FinTech solutions that presently exist.

Of all RegTech developments to date, perhaps the most noteworthy might be the evolution of XBRL in the category of financial reporting. As presented in detail in Chapter 3, XBRL is a multi-dimensional reference to a programming language (eXtensible Business Programming Language), a required reporting taxonomy of the SEC (and increasingly of regulatory authorities around the world), and a searchable venue which enables the user to pull a variety of financial metrics across many firms in a straightforward way.[8]

TABLE 2.4 Regulatory contexts and RegTech solutions

Regulatory context	RegTech solution
Compliance intelligence	Ayasdi, bigstream, compliance.ai
Identity management	SOCURE, trooly
Monitoring	Corlytics, R sam, NetGuardians, OpenGamma, Droit, Arcadiasoft
Predictive analytics	onfido, MindBridge, BehavioSec, Merlon Intelligence, Digital Reasoning, Comply Advantage, neurensic
Risk identification	Qumram, LogRhythm
Secure exchanges of data	token, TrueLayer, Railsbank
Workflow	MetricStream, Archer, WorkFusion, Ripcord

TABLE 2.5 Key RegTech terms

Key RegTech Terms

AIFMD – Alternative Investment Fund Management Directive
AMLD – Anti-Money Laundering Directive
ARM – Approved Reporting Mechanism, an organization to which firms must submit transaction reporting
BCBS – Basel Committee on Banking Supervision
CAT – US consolidated audit trail
CCAR – Comprehensive Capital Analysis and Review
CECL – Current Expected Credit Loss
CFI – Classification of Financial Instruments
CIC – Complementary Identification Code
Corep – Common Reporting
CRD – Capital Requirements Directive
CSIRT – Computer Security Incident Response Team
CTF – Counterterrorist financing
CVA – Credit Value Adjustment
D-FAST – Dodd-Frank Act Stress Testing
D-SIB – Domestic Systematically Important Bank
EBA – European Banking Authority
EIOPA – European Insurance and Occupational Pensions Authority
EMIR – European Market Infrastructure Regulation
ESMA – European Securities and Markets Authority
ETD – Exchange-traded Derivatives
Euribor – Euro Interbank Offered Rate
FASB – Financial Accounting Standards Board
FCA – Financial Conduct Authority
FINRA – Financial Industry Regulatory Authority
FIRDS – Financial Instruments Reference Data System
FIU – Financial Information Unit
FRTB – Fundamental Review of the Trading Book
FSB – Financial Stability Board
FSMA – Financial Services and Markets Act
G-SIB – Global Systemically Important Bank
IFRS - International Financial Reporting Standards
IOSCO - International Organization of Securities Commissions
ISO – International Organization for Standardization
ITS – Implementing Technical Standards
KID – Key Information Document
KYC – Know Your Customer
LCR – Liquidity Coverage Ratio
LEI – Legal Entity Identifier
MAR – Market Abuse Regulation
MIC – Market Identifier Code
MiFID II – Markets in Financial Instruments Directive II
MiFIR – Markets in Financial Instruments Regulation
MMFR – Money Market Funds Regulation

Key RegTech Terms

MTF – Multilateral Trading Facility
NCA – National Competent Authority
NIS – Network and Information Security Directive
NSFR – Net Stable Funding Ratio
OTF – Organized Trading Facility
PEP – Politically Exposed Person
PRA – Prudential Regulation Authority
PRIIPS – Packaged Retail and Insurance-based Investment Products
RTS – Regulatory Technical Standards
RWA – Risk Weighted Asset
SEC – Securities and Exchange Commission
SFTR – Securities Financing Transactions Regulation
SI – Systematic internalizer
SMCR – Senior Managers and Certification Regime
SRO – Self-regulatory Organizations
UCITS – Undertakings for Collective Investment in Transferable Securities
UPI – Unique Product Identifier
UTI – Unique Transaction Identifier

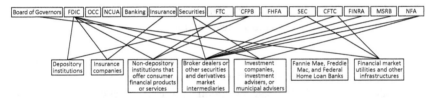

FIGURE 2.9 Regulatory bodies and corresponding businesses subject to regulation

Disruptors, innovators, and aggregators/disintermediators

A variety of catchy and thought-provoking terms are used in digital contexts, and while a few variations of definitions exist, these particular descriptions and suggestions are offered:[9]

> Disruptor: Entrant offering that tilts the way a sector has been defined and perceived up until that moment, with important competitive implications for features, pricing, distribution, or market share.

> Innovator: Entrant offering that builds upon some aspect of a sector in a unique way that is seen as bringing a value-add in features, pricing, distribution, or another dimension.

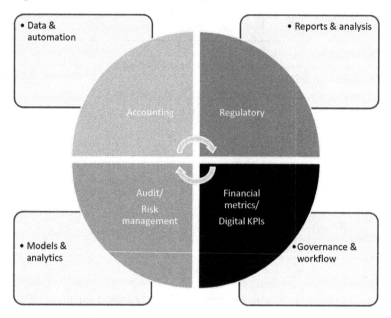

FIGURE 2.10 Responsibilities and functions related to digital finance

Aggregator/Disintermediator: An aggregator is an entrant that facilitates user access to a variety of potential solutions within a sector, while a disintermediator does the same with respect to a single solution.[10]

Examples for each of these are provided in Table 2.6. The table is certainly not intended to be exhaustive or definitive, but simply illustrative.[11]

As indicated in the Table 2.4, disruptions, innovations, and aggregations/disintermediations can involve products or services (and sometimes both), and naturally, for such subjective concepts, there can be reasonable disagreements as to which categories are most applicable for a particular company or industry.

For the purposes of this text, there is no favor, hierarchy, or prestige intended or implied with the designations of disruptor, innovator, or aggregator/disintermediator; they each represent important contributions in their own right. Having said that, some might take the position that a reflection of a company's having truly moved the needle is embodied within the market share it has grown, or the market cap it has achieved. In this regard, there is certainly a distinction that can be drawn between an Uber valuation of $120 billion relative to Expedia's at $17 billion, though those respective stories are still unfolding.[12]

It is also the case, as again reflected in Table 2.4, that one company can find itself in more than one category, with this being attributable to a firm's building upon its foundation in new and creative ways. For example, Table 2.4 cites Airbnb as a disruptor, and "Airbnb Experiences" is cited as an innovator. Airbnb

TABLE 2.6 Disruptors, innovators, aggregators/disintermediators

Disruptors	Innovators	Aggregators/Disintermediators
iPod: The iPod disrupted the way music could be enjoyed, as well as the way music was distributed to users. Mobile devices for playing music like the Walkman or portable radios faded in use, and Brick music outlets like HMV and Tower Records have closed.	Spotify: Took music downloads to a point of permitting play on a variety of platforms	Freshtunes: Permits new and established artists to provide their work online and with unique royalty arrangements
Lyft: Uber disrupted the public transportation paradigm of many cities. The business model of taxi services has come under serious threat, with dramatic reversals of fortune in that space owing to preferences for Uber drivers.	Via: Building on the concept of Lyft and Uber, Via offers fixed-rate car transportation within designated areas of Manhattan.	Bellhop: This app aggregates information across more than a dozen car ride services
Airbnb: Airbnb has disrupted the way people think about where they will stay for business and personal travel.	Airbnb Experiences: Building on the idea that people may want ideas for interesting things to see and do when they travel, Airbnb Experiences offers suggestions along with information related to bookings	Expedia: Expedia aggregates user travel choices for transportation, accommodation, things to see and do, and more.
Gateway: In 1985 Gateway was one of the first companies to offer direct-sales of PCs	GitHub: Started in 2008, GitHub offers the ability to access and download a variety of open-source models and software tools	Quandl: Launched in 2011, Quandl is a data store where many different types of aggregated data sets are available (some free, and others for a fee).
Paypal: Started in 1998 as a money transfer service	Zelle: Paypal's Venmo does not have direct integration with banks, though Zelle offers this along with money transfers that are claimed to be processed faster and with no fees for the quicker service	Square, Stripe, and PayPal: There are a variety of opinions as to the respective benefits of Square, Stripe, and PayPal as a one-solution aggregator for handling a variety of payment and needs for small and larger

(Continued)

TABLE 2.6 Continued

Disruptors	Innovators	Aggregators/Disintermediators
		businesses, with respective strengths related to ability to customize and enhance
Email: The first email to have been sent across a network is said to have been generated by Ray Tomlinson in 1971; he also applied the "at" symbol to separate usernames and a user's platform	Twitter: Twitter took the concepts of email and instant messaging and transformed them into a new venue for sharing thoughts and ideas.	Slack: A messaging and collaboration tool that aggregates a variety of communication and other functionality into a single platform

took its success as a popular venue at which to book a place to stay, then added on the innovation of people combining venues with activities. Parenthetically, this creative move by Airbnb is very much aligned with the ideas expertly set forth in the book *The Alchemy of Growth* by Mehrdad Baghai, Stephen Coley, and David White. In brief, White, Baghai, and Coley speak to the notion of three horizons representing different points in time of a company's evolution, and the need to develop ideas that build upon current (horizon 1) goals and objectives by adding subsequent (horizon 2) and future (horizon 3) plans for growth and opportunity.[13]

Valuing digital start-ups

Figure 2.11 presents a histogram of the founding year for companies presently in the Fortune 500. While the last cohort (2001–2018) is small, it is quite impressive that even this number of companies managed to get on the list in such a short period of time, with about a dozen firms making it in about the last 10 years. Something that may not be so comforting for those companies to hear, however, is that the average time period that a firm remains on the list has been steadily declining. Indeed, of those companies that were in the Fortune 500 in 1955, 10 years later about 375 firms were still there.[14] By contrast, of the companies comprising the Fortune 500 in 1995, 10 years later there were fewer than 300 firms remaining. In a word, the Fortune 500 has been increasingly characterized by churn, and the phenomenon is observable with the S&P 500 as well. The average tenure of companies in the S&P 500 in 1965 was 33 years; this narrowed to 20 years in 1990, and is projected to shrink to under 15 years by 2026.[15] So while many firms today seem to emerge as overnight success stories, longevity appears to be increasingly elusive. Though before a firm can make it

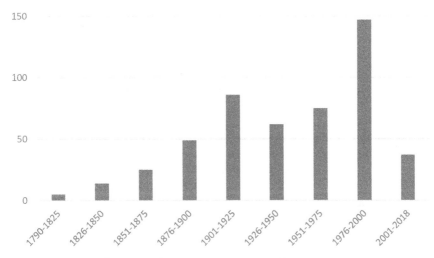

FIGURE 2.11   Founding year of companies in Fortune 500

to either the Fortune 500 or S&P 500, it first needs to get itself launched. To achieve this many start-ups need capital to get the ball rolling, and how much capital a start-up can attract, and at what cost, can be a tricky matter to determine since these considerations typically tend to be tied up in the question of what the start-up is worth.

A significant challenge with valuing a start-up is that it can take the venture some time to become profitable; that is, it can take a while to achieve a meaningful market presence along with a sustainable and profitable market share. An additional layer can be added to this dynamic when the venture first seeks to establish a market presence, and then seek to add a revenue model on top of that. For example, before Facebook, Google, Instagram and other social media sites were in a position to charge for advertising as a primary revenue stream, they first needed to establish themselves as a free (non-revenue-producing) venue with multiple users. With very little (or even zero) revenue initially, there was no basis to evaluate the company's worth in relation to traditional metrics inclusive of cash flow. For the purposes of this discussion, and anyone else desiring to use this term is certainly welcome to do so, we refer to this business model as FreeAlt. In the case of the immediately preceding examples of Google, Facebook, and Instagram, the "Free" part of the business model involves those aspects that attract users for freely offered products, and the "Alt" part of the business model refers to the Alternate way that these firms generate their revenue (i.e., advertisements or other).

As a variation of this theme, the business model for many start-ups involves a "freemium" offering (no charge for basic usage, and add-on costs for extra features), or a "razor and blade" strategy with a low fee (perhaps even below break-even) for one feature (the razor) and a premium fee for recurring use (the blades), or even no fees at all.[16] In the case of no fees being charged, the model might involve a venue where users pay nothing, and where third-party ad placements generate the site's revenues.

Some examples of razor-and-blade combinations include:

- Printers/ink
- Water filtration systems/replacement filters
- Power surgical tools/blades
- Coffee makers/coffee pods
- Game consoles (Xbox)/games
- Cellphones sold by service providers/service contracts
- Instant cameras (Polaroid)/film
- Pez dispensers/candy
- Unique pens/ink
- Website building tools and domain name/hosting
- Swiffer/disposable attachments
- Amazon Kindle/e-books
- Cellphone/apps.

Some examples of Freemium venues include:

- Slack: instant-message-style communication tool for teams
- Wistia: upload up to three videos with 200 GB of bandwidth per month
- Spotify: create playlists, save songs, and use the app on mobile, TV, or other devices
- MailChimp: if your email database has fewer than 2,000 contacts, MailChimp's "Entrepreneur" Freemium offering permits sending up to 12,000 emails a month with access to Facebook and WordPress integrations
- Box: 10 free gigs of secure storage, with a 250MB file upload limit
- OneDrive: 5 free gigs of secure storage
- Evernote: create and access up to 250 notebooks, sync across 2 devices, upload up to 60MB content of external files a month, and collaborate with other users
- SurveyMonkey: create a survey up to 10 questions long and collect up to 100 responses
- Skype: chat one-on-one via instant messaging or video with any other user anywhere
- Hootsuite: schedule posts to and monitor up to 1 profile on 3 different venues
- Buffer: attach one account on the following venues: Twitter, Facebook, LinkedIn, and Google+, also up to 10 posts scheduled to each venue at one time and with access to their link shortening/tracking, mobile app, browser extension, and gif/photo uploader
- Join.Me: share your computer screen with a colleague, make voice calls online.

Figure 2.12 provides an example of looking at revenues from sales versus revenues from advertising, and Figure 2.13 shows a perspective of revenues from sales and advertising with company examples.

With each of these situations, there may not be positive (or any) cash flows for a rather considerable period of time, making it a challenge to derive a specific idea of what a company might actually be worth as an acquisition or investment candidate in a buy-out scenario or to an angel investor. Figure 2.14

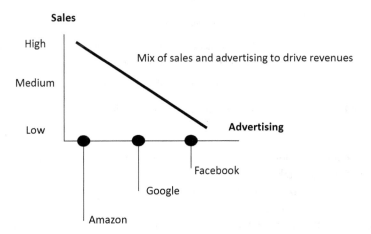

FIGURE 2.12 Revenues from sales versus revenues from advertising: The mix

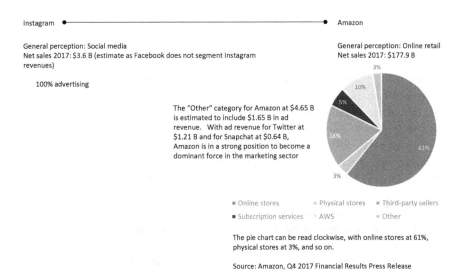

FIGURE 2.13 Revenues from sales versus revenues from advertising: Company examples

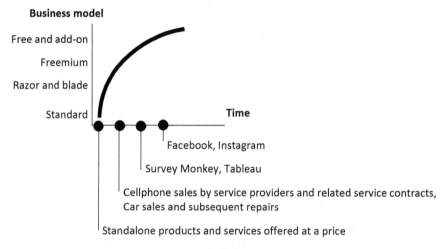

FIGURE 2.14   Timing to revenue streams by business model

offers a conceptual look at trade-offs in timing for various business models. As indicated, it could take a freemium business model longer to get to meaningful revenue streams relative to a standard business model, for which full price is paid for the product or service from day one.

In light of the different business models that can exist for start-ups, there are a variety of methods that can be used to value a start-up firm. However, even with Bricks, there is no one valuation method that has been ordained to be the best way to value an enterprise. Companies vary considerably in terms of where they are in their growth cycle, their competitive environments, the advantages they may have with patents or other forms of intellectual property, and many other considerations. It is, in fact, in recognition of these differences that companies tend to be classified into different categories. There are manufacturing companies, pharmaceuticals, retail, automotive, and of course many more. Interestingly, these labels sometimes change, and firms themselves often evolve such that they become listed under a new category.

In September 2018, for the first time in about 20 years, the S&P Dow Jones Indices group announced changes in the way it was classifying certain companies. Specifically, the following changes were made to the S&P 500:

- The Telecomm sector was renamed "Communication Services"
- Stocks were moved from the S&P 500 Consumer Discretionary sector into the new Communications Services sector
- Companies previously in the Technology and Consumer Discretionary sectors were given greater weightings

Specifically,

- Alphabet (GOOG/GOOGL) and Facebook (FB) were moved to Communication Services from Technology, with weightings of about 18% and 25%, respectively
- Disney and Comcast were added to Communication Services

These updates reflect fundamental changes in terms of the realities of what digital companies are and how they are evolving, as well as the importance of keeping pace with what lines of businesses they are truly in.

As there are different types of companies, there are valuation models that can be more useful for particular company contexts. Or, to vary this theme, different inputs or assumptions can be more applicable with certain models in order to accommodate the nuances of different types of firms.

For example, manufacturing firms have a physical inventory, but banks generally do not. Pharmaceuticals typically have many patents, though retail firms usually do not. Accordingly, one reason why multiple valuation models exist is to provide a better fit in different situations.[17]

In one sense, the answer to the question of "What is a firm worth?" could be that it is worth whatever its market capitalization value indicates, but even that may have some vulnerabilities. For example, on January 3, 2019, Apple's market cap closed at just below $700 billion, having fallen from $450 billion just six months earlier. Though market cap certainly has some desirable characteristics, for example its transparency and ease of calculation, it is disconcerting that it can reflect such different valuations over a rather short period of time for a firm and market environment that was fundamentally the same. And, of course, a problem with using market capitalization for start-ups is that they may not have shares trading on an exchange (or perhaps do not have shares of any kind) and so do not have a market capitalization value that is easily derived.

At minimum we can consider a revenue and expense framework for digital start-ups; Figure 2.15 shares a revenue and expense framework (REF), while Figure 2.16 provides a revenue and expense evaluation example.

Firms are run by people, and operate within contexts whereby a number of moving parts (also influenced by human behavior) simply do not lend themselves to having a high degree of future certainty. How the economy will be performing next year, what the political climate will be, and how regulations will evolve, are all moving targets of great importance to businesses. By extension, it is small wonder indeed that it can be quite a challenge to generate accurate price forecasts for equities on a regular basis. In fact, it can be a real challenge to come up with an indication of an equity's theoretical value right now, let alone three years from now.

While valuing a company that has been around awhile can be a unique challenge in its own right, attempting to value a company that is relatively new presents a whole new set of questions.

A revenue and expense framework (REF) for digital start-ups

1. Collect Revenue per Employee (RPE) ratios for existing start-ups and Bricks in the same industry segment(s) as the start-up under consideration

2. If the RPE of the start-up under consideration is materially lower than that of its competitors, then what is the answer to these questions:

    What is the start-up doing differently that will eventually result in an improved (higher) RPE ratio?

      Greater revenue (P*Q) via P as a result of _____ ?
      Greater revenue (P*Q) via Q as a result of _____ ?

      Possibilities for filling in the blanks above could include advancements/efficiencies via technology, distribution innovations, product enhancements, improved risk management, streamlined operations, customer service offerings, etc.

3. Collect Expense per Employee (EPE) ratios for existing start-ups and Bricks in the same industry segment(s) as the start-up under consideration

4. If the EPE of the start-up under consideration is materially higher than that of its competitors, then what is the answer to these questions:

    What is the start-up doing differently that will eventually result in an improved (lower) EPE ratio?

      Are certain employees needed only for the early phases of the operation?
      Will the need for employees decline as the start-up grows?
      Will employees with a lower cost base (e.g., commission-linked compensation) increasingly replace higher-cost-base employees?

    If a start-up's RPE is materially lower than those of its competitors, and if its EPE is materially above those of its competitors, then a serious deliberation is in order as to whether the venture is truly positioned for long-run success

FIGURE 2.15   A revenue and expense framework (REF) for digital start-ups

A factor that can make for an especially unique situation for a start-up is when it's a digital company; in such cases, oftentimes there is initially no substantive and tangible intrinsic value. If the company is making pencils, we can likely have a pretty good sense of the intrinsic value of its finished products, raw

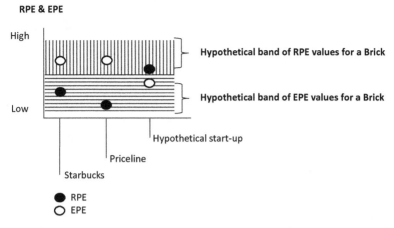

FIGURE 2.16 A revenue and expense (REF) evaluation example

materials (lead, wood, paint), machinery, and any other assets. But for a company that is offering a new venue for social engagement, there may not be much there that's tangible, other than the website or app and its underlying software. In brief, the value lies not so much in the immediacy of any finished product or inventory (there may be neither), but rather in the *hope* of something more. This is not to say that there's not a hope of something more with *every* kind of company; there certainly is. The difference here is centered more on the idea that if the hope does not materialize, then there may really not be much at all that's left with any value.[18]

For traditional companies looking to make an Initial Public Offering (IPO), a common practice is to compare and contrast. Where did the last IPO get priced for a company doing a similar thing? What are valuations of companies in the same peer group? What would the value of the company be if it were possible to sell all of its existing assets (and then adjust that for existing liabilities)? With a start-up digital company, these questions simply may not readily lend themselves to easy answers.

What to do?

There is no one reference formula available to plug in a series of variables and arrive at some magic number. But if there were, where would be the fun in that? The very process of noodling through what a company has to offer, what makes it different, why it is deserving of a particular valuation, is how real insights can be made, along with exciting breakthroughs in truly understanding what a company is all about, and its potential.

In Table 2.7 we provide a variety of valuation methods that can be used for any company, though here we provide a focus on how they can be applicable for start-ups, and digital start-ups in particular. In some instances a start-up is referred to as being in a "pre-money" situation; that is, a firm that has yet to

TABLE 2.7 Valuation methods for start-ups

Method	Description
Ability to Pay	Assesses the capacity of a business to generate cash flow, with consideration of how those might be balanced against costs
Berkus Method	Assesses five factors for potential success
Book Value	Sums the value of a company's tangible assets
Comparable Transactions Method	Reference to a rule of three per financial metrics of a similar company
Cost Approach	Based on what it might cost to aquire all the elements of a business in the marketplace
Discounted Cash Flow	Sum of anticipated future cash flows on a present value basis
First Chicago Method	A weighted average of three valuation scenarios based upon high, medium, and low probabilities
Liquidation Value	Based upon the sale value of company assets
Multiples Method	An attempt is made to estimate a firm's value in relation to other companies on the basis of some multiple of a financial metric (e.g., EBITDA, Book Value, or other)
Risk Factor Summation	An initial base value is evaluated relative to 12 risk factors
Scorecard	Based upon starting with a baseline value and then adjusting that by a series of factors that sum to 100%
Terminal Value	Determining the end value of a firm at a particular horizon, and then calculating a present value of that amount
Venture Capital Method	Considers an exit value, a desired return on investment, and dilution effects

generate sales. In other cases a start-up may be "pre-funded," or in a situation whereby it has not yet received an investment. It is also possible for a start-up to be both pre-money and pre-funded. While each of the approaches cited in Table 2.7 will be described, it may be more beneficial to consider a few different models in a valuation scenario rather than rely on the insights provided by just one in isolation.[19]

Let's consider each valuation method from Table 2.7.

Berkus

Dave Berkus estimates from his experience as an angel investor that fewer than one in a thousand start-ups meet or exceed projected revenues within the periods planned.[20] Berkus sought a new approach to valuing start-ups without having to look to a history of revenues, precisely because start-ups do not typically have much history of revenues.

The Berkus method begins with the notion that an investor believes in the potential for a new company to achieve over $20 million in revenues by the fifth year of business. This starting point is then evaluated with consideration of the following add-ons, which represent maximum values:

- If the new business is seen as being based on a sound idea, then this is worth up to $500,000 ($500k)
- If a prototype of the idea exists, up to an additional $500k can be added on
- The involvement of a quality management team can mean up to another $500k
- Having strategic relationships may add up to an additional $500k, and
- A product in hand or immediate sales opportunities could mean another $500k.

The sum of these amounts results to a potential valuation of up to $2.5 million.

Clearly, variations of the Berkus method could include different revenue targets, and varying dollar values of various add-ons.

Risk factor summation (RFS)

The RFS method considers a wider range of factors than those cited in the Berkus method, and is heavily tilted toward risk factors associated with start-ups.

Beginning with management risk, which RFS treats as topmost with a new venture, other types of risks cited for assessment include:

Stage of the business
Legislative/Political risk
Manufacturing risk
Sales and marketing risk
Funding/capital raising risk
Competition risk
Technology risk
Litigation risk
International risk
Reputation risk
Potential lucrative exit

Each risk category is analyzed with points assigned according to the following profile:

+2: very positive for growing the company and executing a meaningful exit
+1: positive
0: neutral
-1: negative for growing the company and executing a meaningful exit
-2: very negative

Starting with what is deemed to be an appropriate baseline to work from in relation to other recent pre-money and pre-revenue investments, a particular dollar amount is added on or subtracted, depending upon whether a given risk factor is deemed to be a positive influence or a negative influence. For example, if an appropriate baseline valuation is determined to be $2 million, then an additional $250,000 could be added for each +1 increment, while $250,000 would be subtracted for each -1 increment. A neutral value (of zero) would result in no incremental value being added or subtracted.

It is important to note that the baseline reference for the Berkus method differs from the baseline reference with the RFS method. Specifically, a baseline approach with the Berkus method involves making adjustments to an expectation of the new company achieving over $20 million in revenues by the fifth year of business, while the baseline approach with the RFS method involves starting with a value at which other recent applicable deals have been done and then making adjustments. The Berkus baseline starts with an end value (five years out) and adjusts, while the DFS baseline starts with a current value (at which current deals have been done) and adjusts.

Scorecard

The scorecard method is sometimes referred to as the Bill Payne method, and is similar to the RFS approach as it starts out with a baseline predicated upon a current value.[21] A series of factors (summing to 100%) are then evaluated, and weighted relative to perceptions of their relative strength or weakness with the particular company being evaluated. For example, with reference to Table 2.6, the norm for management importance is tagged at 30%, but that factor is given a strong weighting at 125% to signal particularly strong management. When combined, the 30% weight for management becomes 30%*125%=37.50%. When all values in the combined column are summed we arrive at 108.75% in this hypothetical example, and if the baseline value were $2 million then the scorecard value would be $2 million*108.75%=$2,175,000.

Comparable (or Precedent) Transactions Method

With this approach, the idea is to identify where recent investments have taken place within the industry that are comparable to the particular start-up being evaluated, and then use these as the basis for a potential valuation.

For example, if the start-up is in the financial software sector, then information related to recent investments (or sales) of financial software companies would be identified, perhaps along with particulars related to individual company metrics. Those metrics might be financial, such as EBITDA, or could be key performance indicators (KPIs) such as number of employees, number of patents filed or granted, number of active users, or other measures.[22] By comparing any

TABLE 2.8 Scorecard method

	A	B	A*B
Factor	*Norm*	*Weighting*	*Combined*
Management	30%	125%	37.50%
Size of opportunity	25%	115%	28.75%
Product or service	10%	110%	11.00%
Sales channels	10%	70%	7.00%
Stage of business	10%	125%	12.50%
Other factors	15%	80%	12.00%
Sums	**100%**		**108.75%**

Note: The "Weighting" values indicated above are hypothetical only, and will vary by how much above or below the norm a rater places the start-up being considered

one or more of these metrics with the characteristics of the start-up being considered, an investment value or range can be identified.[23]

The rationale behind citing the particular financial ratios above is that they are commonly referred to in the context of discussions related to company valuations and multiples, and respective definitions are cited in the Glossary.

As to the term "multiples," this is typically a reference to a ratio that includes an estimate of the firm's value (as with EV, or Enterprise Value) and a financial performance metric of some type (as with sales or earnings). Thus, if we have a collection of companies comparable with our start-up, and where the mean EV/sales ratio is 2.03 (where sales is an annual sales value), then we can take the start-up's annual sales value and multiply it by 2.03 to obtain a benchmark EV number.

If the start-up's annual sales were $10 million, then we obtain a benchmark EV for the start-up of $10 million* 2.03=$20.3 million. If the start-up's EBITDA multiple in relation to, say, an industry average ratio of EBITDA to number of employees were to put the start-up at a valuation of $18 million, then with a reference to these multiples we obtain a range of valuations of $18 million to $20.3 million.

Since many start-ups simply may not have a long enough track record to be able to generate meaningful financial metrics, a simple comparison with other company sales may not be the most appropriate method (and might be more meaningful with an incorporation of KPIs).

Liquidation value

The legendary value investor Benjamin Graham once commented that liquidation value measures what business owners can get out of the business, while book value measures what they have put into the business.[24] In brief, liquidation value is what a business might expect to receive if it were to immediately sell its assets. With start-ups it is unlikely that there would be much in the way of real estate holdings, and there are strong incentives to lease rather than buy, though there may be intellectual property in the way of patents or valuable copyrights. Once any positive cash flows are determined from the liquidation of assets, these would need to be offset by any obligations including debt or accounts payable. Liquidation value may not be a meaningful valuation method for many start-ups due to a lack of time available to accumulate meaningful assets.

Discounted cash flow (DCF) method

The DCF method involves making forecasts of what future receipts of cash might look like, and then bringing those into a present value number.

Reference Table 2.9 below for an example.

Even when a start-up is receiving positive cash flows, these can be difficult to forecast with much accuracy in the early growth phases of a company.

First Chicago Method

In essence, the First Chicago Method involves taking three scenarios, and weighting them with high, medium, and low probabilities that collectively sum to 100%. Generally, the same valuation methodology is used under each weighting exercise. For example, three series of DCF calculations might be performed using discount rates of 50%, 25%, and 15%, and with results of these three series being weighted by 10% (for the high), 70% (for the medium), and 20% (for the low).

The First Chicago Method could also be used with KPIs, and accounting metrics.

Venture Capital Method

The existence of different valuation methods certainly attests to the notion that there is no one single appropriate approach to use, and this is influenced in part by there being different interests and objectives with a valuation exercise.

TABLE 2.9 DCF example

	Cash inflow	Cash outflow	A-B	Discount rate	DCF
1 year from now	100	115	-15	50%	-10.00
2 years from today	110	110	0	50%	0.00
3 years from today	120	105	15	50%	4.44
4 years from today	130	100	30	50%	5.93
5 years from today	140	95	45	50%	5.93
					6.30

Generally speaking, people interested in start-up valuations would be company owners, angel investors, venture capital investors, regulators and others.

As one variation of the Venture Capital Method (VCM), we start with a posited exit value of the firm. This particular value might not necessarily be derived in any robust way, and could perhaps simply be a dollar value that a venture capitalist identifies as the sum they need to receive at exit in order to have an interest in being involved with a deal. For sake of illustration, let's say that the exit value of relevance happens to be $100 million.

> Step 1: With an exit value target of $100 million and a desired return on investment of 20X, this translates into $5 million ($100 million divided by 20) which is referred to as the post-money valuation.

> Step 2: If $1 million is invested today toward the $5 million post-money valuation for a 25% ownership, then this means that $4 million is the pre-money valuation (the $5 million post-money valuation less the $1 million investment). This $4 million, however, is pre-dilution, meaning that as more venture capitalists become involved as investors there is an increasing likelihood that more shares of the company will be issued, which will have a dampening effect on the price of shares issued earlier on.

> Step 3: If a reasonable dilution rate is assumed to be 30%, then the dilution-adjusted pre-money valuation of the company becomes $2.8 million ($4 million * (1-30%)).

Full circle, under this scenario, a venture capitalist may look to invest about $2.8 million in a firm today for an exit value expectation of $100 million (and with a desired return on investment of 20X with a dilution rate of 30%).

The VCM can be used with both pre- and post-revenue start-ups.

Cost approach

The cost approach, which is not as commonly used in corporate finance, looks at what it actually cost or would cost to rebuild the business. This approach ignores any value creation or cash-flow generation and only looks at things through the lens of "cost = value."

Ability to pay

The ability-to-pay approach looks at the maximum price an acquirer can pay for a business while still hitting some target. For example, if a private equity firm needs to hit a hurdle rate of 30%, what is the maximum price it can pay for the business? If the company will not continue to operate, then a liquidation value will be estimated based on breaking up and selling the company's assets. This value is usually highly discounted as it is assumed that the assets will be sold as quickly as possible to any buyer.

Others

There are many other valuation techniques that can be used, and these include the Replacement or All-in Method, the Rule of Thirds Method, the Cayenne Consulting "High Tech Start-Up Valuation Estimator," variations of these, and more.[25]

The wide choice of valuation methods available is testament to the different insights each can provide, and if only on that basis there can be value to considering more than one approach for the benefit of what each perspective has to offer. Within that spirit, three such approaches that could serve as complements to one another might include the Risk Summation Method, Comparable Transaction Methods, and Discounted Cash Flow. With each of these involving a different tack on approaching the same challenge, the varying perspectives offered up can perhaps bring some different yet helpful insights.

***

It took a few years for Google to become profitable.[26] Google needed time to build up the free portion of its business model (Google Search) to have a base for revenue-generating add-on businesses. The phenomenal success of Google contributes to a conundrum for many investors and others in the digital world; how much time and money should be committed to a digital undertaking before positive cash flow materializes?

At the time of writing Uber has announced that it plans an IPO in the near future with a value estimated at perhaps up to $120 billion, even though the firm has been reporting continuous losses. Twitter went into its $24 billion IPO in 2006 with a reported a loss of $79 million, and reported additional losses for the following four years. Microsoft paid $26 billion for LinkedIn in 2016 when the latter was generating losses, and Facebook paid $19 billion for WhatsApp in 2014 when it was operating at a loss with zero revenues. Table 2.10 presents 10 private FinTech firms in the United States with a greater than $1B valuation.

The business model approach of using a somewhat extended runway for getting to a point of revenue generation, let alone profitability, is a challenging notion to grapple with, perhaps last encountered with the advent of radio and television, cable, and print media, for which market share as an all-important near-term objective was so essential. In Table 2.11 we provide descriptions for various types of business models.

Whether a coincidence or integral to the process, it is certainly of interest that the emergence and proliferation of business models requiring more time and expenditure to achieve revenue and profitability exists at a time when there has also been a greater number of IPOs of companies reporting a negative earnings

TABLE 2.10 10 private FinTech firms in the United States with a greater than $1B valuation

Company	Founded	Valuation	Description
Oscar	2013	$2.7B	Simplifies purchase and use of healthcare coverages
Zenefits	2013	$2.0B	A human resources platform in the cloud
Robinhood	2013	$1.3B	Free trading of stocks and ETFs with a mobile app
Avant	2012	$2.0B	Online loans to consumers with lower credit scores
SoFi	2011	$4.3B	Student loan refinancing and other services
Stripe	2010	$9.2B	Online and mobile payment platform
Credit Karma	2007	$3.5B	Free credit scores and advice with credit cards and loans
GreenSky	2006	$3.6B	Financing for home improvement projects and contractor contacts
Prosper	2005	$1.9B	Joins borrowers and investors for unsecured loans
AvidXchange	2002	$1.4B	Automated invoicing and bill payments for businesses

TABLE 2.11 Business model examples

Business model	Description	Initial business strategy
Free and add-on	Facebook is widely known as a social media platform that is available to users at no charge, and whose revenue is generated from add-on advertising and marketing programs	With the success of earning revenue via advertising and marketing (the "add-on") being contingent on having generated meaningful demographics from the social media platform (the "free"), it is important to first build up a meaningful market share of the "free" (social media)
Freemium	SurveyMonkey allows the user to create basic programs at no charge, and with extra charges for more advanced features	Part of the reason for having the "free" in "*Free*mium" is to get users excited about using an offering, and then enticing them to upgrade. As such it may take awhile for meaningful revenues to be generated, though presumably not as long as it might take for a free and add-on model
Razor and blade	Cellphone service providers offer special discounts on devices ("razors") in exchange for multiple-year service contracts ("blades")	The structure of the razor and blade model can be relevant here, whereby the selling of an actual razor accompanies the sale of an actual blade, but the sale of car repairs can follow a year or more after the sale of the car itself
Standard	Most companies have a core offering that also happens to be their primary product(s) or service(s)	With a standard model the expectation may be that revenues will follow fairly soon after start-up

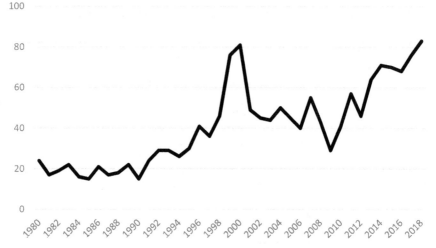

FIGURE 2.17   IPOs with a negative earnings-per-share at time of launch

per share (EPS). Figure 2.17 shows the percentage of companies with a negative EPS and the time of their IPO going back to 1980. As indicated, more recently we have been seeing record numbers of these, and it appears as though previous peaks in these ratios have been followed by significant market corrections.[27]

***

There is a webpage on the United States Department of Justice website that provides a mathematical equation: this is the expression for the Herfindahl–Hirschman Index (HHI).

The HHI attempts to capture a numerical representation of a company's particular market share in relation to its core product(s).[28] The HHI is near a value of zero when a market is characterized by a large number of firms of relatively equal size (perfect competition) and reaches its maximum value of 10,000 when a market is dominated by a single firm (monopoly).[29] The HHI increases when the number of firms in a particular market decreases, and the HHI increases as the disparity in size among firms within a particular market increases. As a rule of thumb, an index value in excess of 2,500 is generally regarded as reflecting a market that is highly concentrated.

When the search-engine piece of Alphabet (Google Chrome) is evaluated as a standalone business for purposes of calculating a HHI value, it registers as being within a highly concentrated market. When the advertising piece of Alphabet (Google AdWords) is evaluated as a standalone business, it registers as being within a less concentrated market.[30]

Those firms that want to keep themselves at a distance from regulatory scrutiny may engage in efforts to portray themselves as entities with diversified revenue streams, of which none has a predominant market share.

The powers of governmental regulatory bodies are considerable, and can be applied in ways that can be seen to be appropriate or abusive, as the following two case studies help to illustrate.

***

Case study: Google and the European Commission

There is a sentiment that the European Commission's Competition Commissioner (under the auspices of the European Community), is taking up the role of being the world's regulator of technology companies.[31] It is certainly the case that the largest-ever fines related to antitrust accusations against tech companies have been issued by the European Commission, and there are indications that there may be more to come.[32] In 2017 Google was fined €2.42 billion related to claimed abuses of search-engine dominance, and in 2018 Google was fined €4.34 billion for claims of anticompetitive practices related to search issues connected with Android (Google's mobile operating system).

Let's first consider the 2017 case of search-engine dominance. Google was essentially accused of prominently surfacing its own suggestions when a user searched for a product or service. The competing results of comparison websites were allegedly given less prominence, often appearing past an initial page of listings.[33]

Second, there is the 2018 case involving Android. In contrast with iPhones where Apple elected to have a closed operating system, iOS, Android phones use an operating system, also called Android, which Google chose to make available as an open-source option.[34] Anyone developing an app in iOS can only make that app available from Apple's App Store. By contrast, an app developed with Android can be made available from Google Play or from outside of Google Play.[35]

Google makes its Android operating system available for free, but allegedly placed a special conditions on its commercial use that applied to certain cell-phone providers like Samsung and LG.[36] The European Commission alleged that Google required phone manufacturers to use a particular version of Android, prohibited the installation of alternative builds of Android, and insisted on the preinstallation of various Google apps and services, such as Search and the Chrome browser. The European Commission felt that these requirements were anticompetitive, and Google has the option to appeal.

As to why it is that European regulators have been more aggressive than US regulators with respect to fines and restrictions for companies such as Google and Facebook, there are a few viewpoints on this. While it could of course be entirely attributable to the European regulators wishing to toe the line in terms of enforcing rules, perhaps there are some political overtones as well; one theory suggests that Europe wants to assert itself on commercial matters it deems to be of particular significance. An earlier such instance involved GE, at the time when Jack Welch was CEO.

In "The Anatomy of the GE-Honeywell Disaster," *Time Magazine*, July 8, 2001, Michael Elliott details the story of Welch's gambit to prevent the Pratt & Whitney division of United Technologies Corporation from acquiring Honeywell International. Apparently, within less than an hour of learning of the proposed acquisition on a visit to the New York Stock Exchange in October 2000, Welch was on the phone to line up his board to make a counteroffer. Within two days, Welch believed GE had maneuvered itself into the dominant position for an acquisition, and even postponed his retirement for the integration. Mario Monti, the European Union's Commissioner for Competition, had other ideas.

In brief, the very things that Welch saw as being so attractive about the deal were precisely what Monti viewed as its anticompetitive elements; namely, that combining Honeywell's cockpit controls with GE's engines and aircraft financing division would prohibitively constrain competition. In the end, GE was not successful with the acquisition, and Elliott observed nearly 20 years ago that, "The biggest lesson of all from the GE case is this one: soon, something like it will happen again." Elliott went on to say the following:

> Monti and his counterparts around the world aren't taking on these cases because they want to stick it to the ugly Americans. They are doing so because in a globalized world, the country where a company has headquarters matters much less than where it does business.[37]

True then, and true today.

True for Bricks, and true for Clicks.

Case study: The merger of AT&T and Time Warner

On October 22, 2016, AT&T and Time Warner announced their intention to merge. Although the size of the proposed merger was large in terms of market capitalization, initial reaction to the news was generally that the merger made sense.[38] On February 27, 2017 the Federal Communications Commission (FCC) indicated that the agency was not likely to need to look at the merger from a regulatory standpoint. Prior to confirmation, the new head of the US Department of Justice (DoJ) Antitrust Division indicated in an interview that he did not believe the merger would be blocked. However, on November 20, 2017 the DoJ announced its intention to pursue an antitrust case to prevent the merger.

A trial to hear the case lasted six weeks, and on June 12, 2018, Judge Leon released his verdict with a 172-page statement.[39] Judge Leon ruled that the merger ought to be allowed to proceed, and made it clear that he did not wish for the DoJ to pursue a stay.[40] A "stay" is an act that seeks to temporarily halt a judicial proceeding or outcome by order of a court.

The argument made by AT&T and Time Warner was that although they would become a large company, the nature of the merger was more vertical than horizontal and as such was not really an anticompetitive action.[41] With Time Warner being more involved with creating entertainment content and AT&T more involved with providing channels for distributing content, they viewed their merger as being vertical in nature. The DoJ, on the other hand, foresaw an ability for a merged firm to have a considerable market share within the entertainment industry generally, and with powers to set prices for goods and services without substantial checks against their doing so.

Although the DoJ did not pursue a stay, in accordance with Judge Leon's wishes, on August 6, 2018, the DoJ did appeal Judge Leon's ruling.[42]

The rationale for why Judge Leon urged the DoJ not to pursue a stay relates to the burden that is placed on several stakeholders due to the uncertainty of a decision being placed under review. Not only are the respective companies in limbo with respect to planning for any subsequent phases of an integration, but equity shareholders are also forced to either wait out an ultimate determination or choose to unwind their positions altogether.

On December 6, 2018, oral arguments were heard pertaining to the appeal, and in February of 2019, the DoJ lost its appeal to seek a blocking of the AT&T and Time Warner deal.

In the matter of Google in Europe, it has been said that the firm has been unfairly caught up in the net of Europe's interest in fiercely protecting consumer privacy, and that part of a broader message this sends to larger internet companies is that they should be very careful how they tread more generally on all matters relating to consumer-generated data and decision-making, whether these are related to search activity only, or to online commerce-related activities. In the instance of the AT&T–Time Warner merger, there has been speculation that the executive branch of federal government may perhaps have had issues related to CNN (a Time Warner holding) and that this maybe played a role in the government's pursuing a case against the merger.[43] One would hope that in all of these instances, cases were pursued on the basis of their merits and not of political considerations.

In sum, it can be challenging to determine what business a company is in, and the answer may not be what the company itself claims it to be. The relevance here is that if a meaningful way to value a company is to look at it in terms of how it is faring relative to its peer group, then it's essential to define what that peer group is. If it is more relevant to look at where revenues are derived from (Google AdWords versus Google Search), then that needs to be evaluated. If there is a symbiotic relationship between the two – the venue (or medium) and the cash flow source (CFS) – then that must be considered as well.

A venture's being labeled as "technology" or "tech" (or "disruptor," "disintermediator," or other), ought not to imply a status somehow deserving of an extra-special (i.e., beneficial) category for valuation purposes. It is a company. It either generates cash flow or it doesn't, and if it doesn't, then it's paramount to set a reasonable timeframe for when it will, and to plan an exit if objectives are not being achieved.

Microfinance, microinsurance, and microproperty

Microfinance refers to small investments that can make a huge difference. The prefix "micro" in the context of financial services is a reference to offerings associated with developing countries. The three "micro" offerings we consider are microfinance, microinsurance, and microproperty. Perhaps ironically, many developing economies have been early adopters of technology on a widespread basis relative to some developed countries. For example, many developing countries were quick to adopt cellphones owing to the ease of making a relatively low-cost investment (the device and a monthly plan) in exchange for instant communication with the world (or at least with anyone else who had a phone). In the area of finance in particular, and leveraging the ubiquity of mobile devices, mobile pay solutions have greatly facilitated the growth of e-commerce in developing markets. In essence, mobile banking services (whether offered by banks or alternatives) have effectively served to bring financial services into every corner of a country, inclusive of loans and the administration of accounts payable and receivable, with even greater opportunities in store for the sector.

Cellphones have proved to be an extremely influential venue for digital finance in developing countries. For example, bKash in Bangladesh reaches a substantial portion of the country's adult population, and offers convenient and relatively inexpensive ways to make payments and transfer money. The firm bKash and other venues like it across the developing world also provide for a safe place to store funds.

These payment venues provide other benefits as well: for example, they provide a means to access additional financial services such as interest-bearing savings, credit, insurance, and transactions in investment products. Cellphones also generate data that providers can use to create new offerings and to improve the customer experience.

The pace at which developing countries are adopting a variety of financial products is rather impressive. These include: one-month M-Shwari consumer loans offered by Commercial Bank of Africa (CBA); M-Pesa in Kenya, a cellphone-based money transfer, financing and microfinancing service; and the life insurance products that are marketed to Tigo (Ghana) cellphone prepaid customers. One million M-Shwari loans were issued within about a month of the product's launch, pushing CBA from a modestly sized corporate lender to one of the largest retail entities in Kenyan banking. Tigo's Family Care life insurance product doubled the size of the insurance market in Ghana in its first year.

One definition of microinsurance offered up by the International Association of Insurance Supervisors is as follows:

> While the term "inclusive insurance" is aimed at excluded or underserved markets the term "microinsurance" has been defined as insurance that is accessed by low-income populations, provided by a variety of different entities, but run in accordance with generally accepted practices (which include the Insurance Core Principles).[44]

In an article entitled "The Benefits of Microinsurance," Brian Z. Brown seeks to make the case for microinsurance products to be designed differently from traditional insurance products, and in so doing cites Katie Biese of the MicroInsurance Centre, who advocates for "SUAVE" in the design of microinsurance products.[45] Specifically, this stands for:

- **S**imple: Insurance products that are structured and explained in simple terms, with few or no exclusions and with benefits being of a clearly defined amount
- **U**nderstood: With many microinsurance consumers being first-time buyers, a clear rationale for reasons to have insurance can be more effective
- **A**ccessible: Customers need to be reached and sold products via channels with greater financial means that can appeal to lower-income entities: these might include cooperatives, input suppliers, microfinance groups, or even mobile devices
- **V**aluable: Products need to make economic sense in terms of the protections being provided in relation to the risks being mitigated
- **E**fficient: While low cost is certainly important, so too are manageable deductibles and a provider's ability to pay out on claims quickly when an adverse event arises.

With respect to types of microinsurance that can exist, these include property, crops, livestock, and regional disaster. With a case-study example involving Ghana, Brown cites an October 2011 flood that affected a marketplace near Accra, which is one of Ghana's most populated urban areas. A specialized microinsurance intermediary by the name of MicroEnsure had previously partnered with a local insurer and microfinance bank to offer coverage for local businesses related to damage from flood, fire, and earthquakes. The tailored product, called Obra Pa (meaning "Good life in the future") became a mandatory purchase for customers taking out particular microfinance loans. Benefits include payment of the business's outstanding loan and a fixed cash benefit, and while the insurance did not cover all losses faced as a result of the flooding, insureds were able to recover more quickly and without having to resort as quickly to the sale of assets or tapping into savings, or incurring additional loans. In the end, 92% of insureds said it was a good idea to purchase the coverage, and would recommend it to others.[46]

Another program is the G7 Climate Risk Insurance Initiative, launched in 2015 to improve insurance access for 400 million of the most vulnerable people in developing countries by 2020.[47] There is also Blue Marble Microinsurance, which is a consortium of nine companies publicly committed to providing commercially viable insurance protection to the underserved, such as its crop insurance ventures in Zimbabwe and Colombia.[48]

A number of studies show interesting relationships between growth and entrepreneurship in developing countries. For example, there is the finding that as cities in developing countries grow larger, employment in new start-ups increases more than proportionately relative to more established businesses. There is also support for the theory that the presence of many small suppliers is strongly associated with employment growth in start-ups, with this being explained by smaller establishments providing a greater diversity of specialized suppliers for local firms.[49]

Against this backdrop, the role of urbanization generally can play an extremely vital and meaningful role with developing countries, also in terms of where and how real estate investments are made.[50] Even a relatively straightforward evolution of having formal property titles be made available in squatter settlements could aid with home ownership and the ability to use a house as collateral for a loan.[51] In brief, it would seem that a reasonable case can be made for how less restrictive land market practices and a greater distribution of land rents could be seen as a move toward efficiency and the facilitation of urban growth.[52]

To be sure, there are particular challenges for microproperty in many emerging countries today, such as the weakness of the judicial systems needed to support the many legal aspects of real estate transactions, as well as a predominance of lower-income populations that cannot readily afford to be involved in real estate investments.[53] Nonetheless, there are niches available for entry into these markets, and for the moment they tend to be predominated by digital offerings. For example, basic blockchain technologies are being developed to help strengthen the process of creating contracts and to reduce fraud, and apps are emerging to help real estate investors find opportunities. In brief, the building out of a basic technology infrastructure with Click solutions seems to be going faster than advancements on the Bricks side of the business, and this space is certainly worth watching, as certain individual countries look to be making more rapid progress than others. Perhaps the very consideration that microproperty presently lags behind microfinance and microinsurance in its evolution may mean that it is better primed for superior future growth.

Whether FinTech or microfinance, for-profit or nonprofit, one thing all these entities have in common is the desire to be successful so as to remain viable on an ongoing basis.[54] There are clear differences between the relevant demographics for FinTech and microfinance, but they share fundamental commitments to offer a value-added good or service that enhances quality of life. In the case of for-profit companies, a core objective is to make money that can be kept for ongoing investment in people, products, and market share, while for nonprofits a core objective is to make money so that it can be given away.

Notes

1 See "Betting on billions: How rands and advertisers can unlock the power of mobile gamers," (n.d.), *NewZoo*. https://newzoo.com/insights/trend-reports/betting-on-billions-how-brands-and-advertisers-can-unlock-the-power-of-mobile-gamers/.
2 In actuality, a quick search online for "Zombie Apocalypse insurance" reveals that there are apparently a couple of options available (though a little dubious in appearance), and it's somewhat unclear how safe an insured might be when leaving their

shelter to retrieve and deposit a claim check (as apparently a feature of an apocalypse is that internet services are down, hence prohibiting electronic fund transfers).

3 The role of luck, or good timing, or whatever other terms might be desired, can be key for the insurance industry. Weather can be a very important factor in the profitability of many types of insurance coverage, and the nature of a particular hurricane, hail, or flood season could mean the difference between significant profitability and perhaps even bankruptcy. There have been many examples of narrowly missed disasters from strong storms that bypassed a coastline or densely populated areas in the last several hours of the potential threat.

4 Matteo Carbone and Adrian Jones, "Bigger and redder: A look at Q1 '18 https://www.carriermanagement.com/features/2018/06/15/180464.htm; Carbone and Jones (2018, March 12), "Five dispatches from InsurTech survival island," *LinkedIn*, https://www.linkedin.com/pulse/five-dispatches-from-insurtech-survival-island-matteo-carbone-/; Carbone and Jones (2017, July 20), "Insurtech is the way to keep the insurance sector relevant," *LinkedIn*, https://www.linkedin.com/pulse/insurtech-way-keep-insurance-sector-relevant-matteo-carbone-/.

5 CREtech (2017), *Real Estate Tech Annual Report 2017: Global analysis of investment in real estate tech/proptech*. CREtech. See https://www.cretech.com/reports/.

6 Indeed, as of this writing, there look to be discussions in the future between Airbnb and insurance carriers for this type of combined offering.

7 Stacey English and Susannah Hammond (2018, June 26), "Cost of compliance 2018: Regulatory change and continuing uncertainty," *Reuters*, June 26, 2018.

8 Although not as far-reaching in scope of application, the LEI initiative (Legal Entity Identifier) is very important, as it seeks to uniquely identify each distinct legal entity around the globe that engages in a financial transaction. By associating each individual entity's name (e.g., ABC finance company) with a unique 20-character identifier, the risk of confusing transaction counterparties is appreciably reduced.

9 As one example of an alternative definition, in the December 2015 issue of the *Harvard Business Review*, in their article "What is disruptive innovation?," Clayton M. Christensen, Michael E. Raynor, and Rory McDonald state the following: "'Disruption' describes a process whereby a smaller company with fewer resources is able to successfully challenge established incumbent businesses."

10 "Disintermediation" relates more to the idea of directly connecting the beginning- and endpoints of a single process, as with a user going online to place an order for the purchase of an equity versus going through a broker at an investment bank who will in turn place the order. "Aggregation" involves the notion of a website performing a service of pulling together multiple options, as with a user going to one website for multiple insurance quotes rather than visiting many sites.

11 Readers may certainly have their own thoughts as to helpful delineations that can be made across these designations.

12 When using metrics such as market cap in the context of making distinctions among categories of disruptor, innovator, and aggregator/disintermediator, certainly care needs to be taken to allow for nuances (as well as larger distinctions) of competitive environment, size of potential market, and so forth.

13 Mehrdad Baghai, Stephen Coley, and David White (1999), *The Alchemy of Growth: Practical Insights for Building the Enduring Enterprise* (New York: McKinsey and Company). Another crossover example could be Amazon, as it could fairly be classified as an aggregator (of retail products) and disruptor (of the online shopping experience).

14 Dane Stangler and Sam Arbesman (2012, June), *What Does Fortune 500 Turnover Mean?*, Ewing Marion Kauffman Foundation.

15 Scott D. Anthony, S. Patrick Viguerie, and Andrew Waldeck (2016), *Corporate Longevity: Turbulence Ahead for Large Organizations*, Innosight Executive Briefing Spring 2016 (Lexington, MA: Innosight).

16 My very first paid job, which I took prior to turning 10 years old, was delivering the free paper, *Shoppers*, in Mansfield, Massachusetts. *Shoppers* was available for free, and the task of distributing it was generally regarded as a stepping stone to obtaining the "real" job of delivering paid subscription papers. *Shoppers* was made up of about 90% advertising, with the other 10% consisting of local news stories. In my view the business model of *Shoppers* is akin to the present-day business model of Facebook, Google, Instagram and others: Free plus add-on. In the case of *Shoppers*, the paper was the "free" element, and the "add-on" to pay for the paper was the advertisements. Comparable products exist today, such as magazines in the real estate industry in which articles on local history or happenings are accompanied by ads for home purchases and rentals.

17 Since firms are run by people, with no two persons being identical, it stands to reason that no two companies would be identical. Scientists have also recently announced that even identical twins do not share the exact same DNA (2018, March 11), "The claim: Identical twins have identical DNA," Anahad O'Connor, *New York Times*, p. F5.

18 An interesting website in this regard is Flippa.com, which is an online marketplace for buying and selling internet businesses.

19 A very helpful guide for understanding the various risk considerations of established companies is provided by Standard & Poor's Rating Service, https://www.spratings.com/scenario-builder-portlet/pdfs/CorporateMethodology.pdf.

20 "The Berkus Method: Valuing an early stage investment," posted March 25, 2012; https://berkonomics.com/. The Berkus Method was first revealed in *Winning Angels* (2001) by Harvard's David Amis and Howard Stevenson, and has been refined in various ways since that time.

21 See BillPayne.com.

22 For helpful context and definitions of these and other accounting references, please refer to the glossary. For the present context, EV is enterprise value, and EBITDA is earnings before interest, taxes, depreciation and amortization, which is regarded as a good measure of a company's operating profitability.

23 EBITDA stands for earnings before interest, taxes, depreciation and amortization, and is regarded as a good measure of a company's operating profitability.

24 Benjamin Graham is the author of excellent books on value investing, including *The Intelligent Investor* (2006) and *Security Analysis* (cowritten with David L. Dodd, 2008). Warren Buffett is a student of Graham's, and has successfully applied value investing to his own business Berkshire Hathaway.

25 The Replacement or All-in method suggests that at minimum a company is worth whatever may have been put into it by the founders in terms of foregone income (sweat equity). For example, an executive who otherwise may have earned a salary of $X per annum but instead devoted time to building a company would have the foregone salary counted toward the company's value. The Rule of Thirds method states that anyone willing to invest in the pre-revenue stage of a company ought to be deserving of having a one-third stake, regardless of the industry or evolution of future dilution. And the Cayenne Consulting "High tech start-up valuation estimator" consists of a series of questions that can be answered online, with a valuation generated at the end of the process.

26 There has been some latitude with divining precisely when Google began. The Google.com domain was registered on September 15, 1997, and Google filed for incorporation on September 4, 1998. Prior to either of those dates, Google founders Larry Page and Sergey Brin had done considerable work with developing key ideas that would become important aspects of the new company. More information on this and Google's turn to profitability is contained in this SEC filing relating to Google's IPO in 2004: https://www.sec.gov/Archives/edgar/data/1288776/000119312504143377/d424b4.htm#toc59330_11.

27 For example, peaks in ratios of IPOs with negative EPS occurred in 2007 (preceding the housing bubble and credit crisis), and 2000 (preceding the dotcom crash).

28 The website CSImarket.com is an excellent resource for market share statistics.

29 See Chapter 5 for more of an exposition on the characteristics of perfect competition, monopoly, and other market structures.

30 In the context of online digital ad spending, Google's US market share is estimated to be around 37% (eMarketer, March 2018), while Google's share of all marketing spend in the United States (digital and non-digital) is estimated to be about 15% (MAGNA Forecasts, 2018–2019). Meantime, Google's estimated share of the search market in the United States is near 90% (see StatCounter.com).

31 On April 4, 2018, the *Wall Street Journal* published an article entitled "The woman who is reining in America's technology giants," with the subtitle, "European Union antitrust chief Margrethe Vestager has become the *de facto* global regulator for US companies such as Google and Apple."

32 Contributing to the drama of the levying and size of the EU fines was the context of a previous antitrust case involving Microsoft versus the US Department of Justice (DoJ) in 2000. In that case, there was an original finding as well as an appeal, and with the final settlement no fines were imposed. At the heart of the dispute was an accusation by the DoJ that Microsoft abused a monopoly power with Intel-based personal computers in its treatment of operating system and web browser sales. A good overview of the case is available online in *The Microsoft antitrust case* by Nicholas Economides (2001); see http://neconomides.stern.nyu.edu/networks/Microsoft_An titrust.final.pdf.

Other large fines issued against tech companies by regulators in countries outside of the United States include Facebook's €110 million penalty in 2014 for providing misleading information related to its acquisition of WhatsApp, and the United Kingdom fining Facebook £500,000 over the matter of Cambridge Analytica. Hints of other antitrust filings that may be in the offing include a potential case against Google's AdSense. AdSense is a Google service that provides a way for website owners to earn money by permitting the placement of ads in webpages. The EU is investigating how the structuring of AdSense may hamper online-search advertising of Google rivals.

33 The resolution to the matter has involved Google setting up an auction system whereby Google competitors bid for space alongside Google Shopping; Google had to prove that it was making a profit by means of the auction, in order to provide evidence that competitors were successful in getting more coveted webpage exposure.

34 Some aspects of Apple's iOS are open-source, but the preponderance of its operating system are closed-source; it would be quite a challenge to make a new operating system from it. By contrast, Google's open-source Android operating system is built on code from the "Android Open Source Project." Google acquired Android Inc., the original developers of the Android operating system, in 2005. While it is the case that Android is more open than iOS, there are ways that pieces of Android can be designed to be closed.

35 Sideloading (installing an iPhone app not available through the App Store) can be done, though it involves jailbreaking (removing software restrictions imposed by Apple), and can result in a voiding of phone warranties and protections.

36 According to a Gartner study published in 2018 (press release, May 29, 2018), the Android operating system accounts for about 80% of cellphone market share.

37 Michael Elliott (2001, July 8), "The anatomy of the GE-Honeywell disaster," *Time Magazine*.

38 As of early 2019, the merger of AT&T and Time Warner places it as the fourth-largest in the United States, with the largest in the United States being the acquisition by America Online of Time Warner in 2000 for $164.75 billion. The largest global

merger was Vodafone and Mannesmann at $180.95 billion in 2000. Interestingly, AT&T was involved with three of the top 10 mergers in the United States to date.

39 Despite its length, the opinion makes for interesting and sometimes humorous reading. In one instance, for example, the judge likens a government witness's model in support of the merger as a "Rube-Goldberg contraption." In other places Judge Leon quotes testimony at length from government witnesses who were simply not very convincing. Finally, Leon also shares very interesting thoughts on the role of digital finance in the marketplace, and how this contributed to his thought process. Specifically, as early as page 2 of the opinion, Leon states that "Facebook's and Google's dominant digital advertising platforms have surpassed television advertising in revenue."

40 The full opinion may be found at https://ecf.dcd.uscourts.gov/cgi-bin/show_public_doc?2017cv2511-146; regarding the stay, Judge Leon stated, "To use a stay to accomplish *indirectly* what could not be done directly – especially when it could cause certain irreparable harm to the defendants – simply would be unjust" (pp. 171 and 172; italics are as printed in the opinion).

41 If an oil-drilling company were to acquire an oil-distribution company, this would be considered a vertical merger. An oil-drilling company acquiring another oil-drilling company would be an example of a horizontal merger.

42 Interestingly, on July 31, 2018, the DoJ posted a notice on its HHI webpage stating "update," but without indicating what had changed. Using the website archive.org, it is sometimes possible to see what a webpage looked like on a previous date, and the difference looks to be related to a change in hyperlink. In the page version that existed prior to July 2018 (updated on July 29, 2015), the hyperlink refers to section 5.2 of the "Horizontal Merger Guidelines" (of August 19, 2010) entitled "Market Shares", while the hyperlink provided on July 31, 2018, refers to Section 5.3 entitled "Market Concentration"; perhaps prelude to DoJ's July 2019 announcements. See https://www.justice.gov/atr/herfindahl-hirschman-index.

43 For example, see https://www.washingtonpost.com/news/the-fix/wp/2018/06/12/aiming-at-att-and-time-warner-trump-shot-from-the-hip-and-missed/?noredirect=on&utm_term=.d60c7d4ab6f4.

44 Source: IAIS. Issues paper on conduct of business in inclusive insurance, November 2015, p. 5.

45 Brian Z. Brown, "President's message: The benefits of microinsurance," *Actuarial Review*, September/October 2018, and http://www.microinsurancecentre.org/.

46 B. Magnoni, T. Chandani, and E. Zimmerman (2012), "Milk brief 10 – Doing the math with property insurance in Ghana," Appleton, WI: MicroInsurance Centre.

47 https://www.insuresilience.org/about.

48 www.bluemarblemicro.com/ventures.

49 Helpful papers with interesting insights related to entrepreneurship in developing countries include:
   O. Figueiredo, P. Guimaraes, and D. Woodward (2002), "Home-field advantage: Location decisions of Portuguese entrepreneurs," *Journal of Urban Economics, 52*(2), 341–61;
   E. Ghani, W. R. Kerr, and S. O'Connell (2011). "Spatial determinants of entrepreneurship in India." Cambridge, MA: Harvard University.

50 The challenge can be significant, as with the case of Nigeria, where titled properties account for less than 3% of properties available for transactions; see PTCLR (2018). "Land reform: Proposed registration will sanitise land administration," Vanguard Newspaper, June 6, 2018.

51 R. Di Tella, S. Galliani, and E. Schargrodsky (2007), "The formation of beliefs: Evidence from the allocation of land titles to squatters," *Quarterly Journal of Economics, 122*(1), 209–41.

52 Gilles Duranton, "Growing through cities in developing countries," *The World Bank Research Observer*. Published by Oxford University Press on behalf of the International Bank for Reconstruction and Development, The World Bank, 2014.

53 Olufemi Adedamola Oyedele (2018), *Challenges of investing in real estate in developing nations*, Working Paper, 10.13140/RG.2.2.10904.85766, https://www.researchgate.net/publica tion/328942113_Challenges_of_Investing_in_Real_Estate_in_Developing_Nations.

54 It could certainly be argued that even among for-profit companies there can be appreciable differences in orientations of the risks they face and how they can be best positioned for those. For example, in the insurance industry it is very much expected that there will be losses, and that these will come from claims paid on policies that become subject to an adverse event. Similarly, in banking it is also expected that there will be losses, and these can come from loans that experience a default, or poor returns on investment from capital markets transactions. In brief, due to the very nature of these businesses, there is the expectation of having losses and a key corporate objective is to mitigate risks as best as possible, and to have more profitable days than unprofitable ones. Conversely, for firms involved with selling tangible products, the products themselves are not inherently risky (at least not in the same way as an insurance policy, loan, or stock), though all firms are certainly subject to macro risks related to strength of the economy, shifting consumer tastes, and other exigencies.

Bibliography

Adrian, T., & Ashcraft, A. B. (2016). Shadow banking: A review of the literature. In Garett Jones (Ed.), *Banking crises: Perspectives from the new Palgrave Dictionary of economics* (pp. 282–315). London: Palgrave Macmillan.

Agarwal, S., Lucca, D., Seru, A., & Trebbi, F. (2014). Inconsistent regulators: Evidence from banking. *Quarterly Journal of Economics*, *129*, 889–938.

Allayannis, G., & Cartwright, K. (2017). Cutting through the fog: finding a future with Fintech. Darden Case No. UVA-F-1767. SSRN: https://ssrn.com/abstract=2974594.

Alt, R., & Puschmann, T. (2012). The rise of customer-oriented banking - electronic markets are paving the way for change in the financial industry. *Electronic Markets*, *22*(4), 203–215.

Amis, D., & Stevenson, H. (2001). *Winning angels*. Upper Saddle River, NJ: FT Press.

Anthony, S.D., Viguerie, S.P., and Waldeck, A. (2016). *Corporate longevity: Turbulence ahead for large organizations*. Innosight Executive Briefing Spring 2016. Lexington, MA: Innosight.

Arner, D.W., Barberis, J., & Buckley, R.P. (2015). The evolution of Fintech: A new post-crisis paradigm. *Georgetown Journal of International Law*, *47*(4), 1271–1320.

Arner, D.W., Barberis, J., & Buckley, R.P. (2016). FinTech, RegTech, and the reconceptualization of financial regulation. *Northwestern Journal of International Law & Business*, *37*, 371–414.

Autio, E., S. Nambisan, L. D. W. Thomas, L.D.W., and M. Wright. (2017). Digital affordances, spatial affordances, and the genesis of entrepreneurial ecosystems. *Strategic Entrepreneurship Journal*, *12*(1), 72–95.

Ba, S., & Pavlou, P. A. (2002). Evidence of the effect of trust building technology in electronic markets: Price premiums and buyer behavior. *MIS Quarterly*, *26*(3), 243–268.

Baghai, M, Coley, S., & White, D. (1999). *The alchemy of growth: Practical insights for building the enduring enterprise* (New York: McKinsey and Company).

Bailey, J.P., & Bakos, Y. (1997). An exploratory study of the emerging role of electronic intermediaries. *International Journal of Electronic Commerce*, *1*(3), 7–20.

Bakos, Y. (1998). The emerging role of electronic marketplaces on the internet. *Communications of the ACM*, *41*(8), 35–42.

Bamberger, K.A. (2009). Technologies of compliance: Risk and regulation in a digital age. *Texas Law Review*, *88*, 669–739.

Barrett, M., Davidson, E., Prabhu, J., & Vargo, S. (2015). Service innovation in the digital age: Key contribution and future directions. *Management Information Systems Quarterly*, *39*(1), 135–154.

Berkus, D. (2012, March 25). The Berkus Method: Valuing an early stage investment. *Berkonomics*. https://berkonomics.com/.

Betting on billions: How brands and advertisers can unlock the power of mobile gamers. (n.d.) *NewZoo*. Retrieved from https://newzoo.com/insights/trend-reports/betting-on-billions-how-brands-and-advertisers-can-unlock-the-power-of-mobile-gamers/.

Birks, D. F., Fernandez, W., Levina, N., & Nasirin, S. (2013). Grounded theory method in information systems research: Its nature, diversity and opportunities. *European Journal of Information Systems*, *22*, 1–8.

Bitner, M. J., Brown, S. W., & Meuter, M. L. (2000). Technology infusion in service encounters. *Journal of the Academy of Marketing Science*, *28*(1), 138–149.

Bord, V. M., & Santos, J.A.C. (2012). The rise of the originate-to-distribute model and the role of banks in financial intermediation. *Economic Policy Review 21*.

Breidbach, C., & Ranjan, S. (2017). How do Fintech service platforms facilitate value co-creation? An Analysis of Twitter data. In Proceedings of the 38th International Conference on Information Systems (ICIS), December 10–13, 2017, Seoul, South Korea.

Brown, B.Z. (2018). President's message: The benefits of microinsurance. *Actuarial Review*, September/October 2018. http://www.microinsurancecentre.org/.

Butler, T. (2017). Towards a standards-based technology architecture for RegTech. *Journal of Financial Transformation*, *45*, 49–59.

Carbone, M., & Jones, A. (2018, June 15). Bigger and redder: A look at Q1 '18. *Carrier Management*. Retrieved from https://www.carriermanagement.com/features/2018/06/15/180464.htm.

Carbone, M., & Jones, A. and Jones (2018, March 12). Five dispatches from InsurTech Survival Island. *LinkedIn*. Retrieved from https://www.linkedin.com/pulse/five-dispatches-from-insurtech-survival-island-matteo-carbone/.

Carbone, M., & Jones, A. (2017, July 20). Insurtech is the way to keep the insurance sector relevant. *LinkedIn*. https://www.linkedin.com/pulse/insurtech-way-keep-insurance-sector-relevant-matteo-carbone/.

Chircu, A. M., & Kauffman, R. J. (1999). Strategies for internet middlemen in the intermediation/disintermediation/reintermediation cycle. *Electronic Markets*, *9*(1–2), 109–117.

Christensen, C. M., & Overdorf, M. (2000). Meeting the challenge of disruptive change. *Harvard Business Review*, *78*(2), 66–77.

Christensen, C. M., Raynor, M. E., & McDonald, R. (2015, December). What is disruptive innovation? *Harvard Business Review* (December 2015), 44–53.

Chuang, L.-M., Liu, C.-C., & Kao, H.-K. (2016). The adoption of Fintech service. *International Journal of Management and Administrative Sciences*, *3*, 1–15.

CrEtech (2017). *Real Estate Tech Annual Report 2017: Global analysis of investment in real estate tech/proptech*. CRETech. Retrieved from https://www.cretech.com/reports/.

Cummins, J. D., & Doherty, N. A. (2006). The economics of insurance intermediaries. *Journal of Risk and Insurance*, *73*(3), 359–396.

Di Tella, R., Galliani, S., & E. Schargrodsky, E. (2007). The formation of beliefs: Evidence from the allocation of land titles to squatters. *Quarterly Journal of Economics*, *122*(1), 209–41.

Doelin, J. van der, & Sante, M. van. (2018). PropTech: What is it and how to address the new wave of real estate startups? ING Economics Department. Retrieved from https://think.ing.com/uploads/reports/ING_EBZ_PropTech-Technology_in_the_real_estate_sector-June_2018_tcm162-148619.pdf.

Duranton, G. (2014). Growing through cities in developing countries. *The World Bank Research Observer*. Oxford: Oxford University Press/The International Bank for Reconstruction and Development, The World Bank.

Dyer, J. H., & Singh, H. (1998). The relational view: Cooperative strategy and sources of interorganizational competitive advantage. *Academy of Management Review*, 23(4), 660–679.

Economides, N. (2001). *The Microsoft antitrust case*. (Research Paper). Stanford, CA: Stanford University. Retrieved from http://neconomides.stern.nyu.edu/networks/Microsoft_Anti trust.final.pdf.

Eickhoff, M., Muntermann, J., & Weinrich, T. (2017). What do FinTechs actually do? A taxonomy of FinTech business models. In *Proceedings of the 38th International Conference on Information Systems*. December 10–13, 2017. Seoul, South Korea: ICIS.

Elliott, M. (2001, July 8). The anatomy of the GE-Honeywell disaster. *Time Magazine*.

English, S., & S. Hammond (2018, June 26). Cost of compliance 2018: Regulatory change and continuing uncertainty. *Reuters*, June 26, 2018.

EY Global Insurance. (2013). Insurance in a digital world: The time is now. Retrieved from https://www.ey.com/Publication/vwLUAssets/EY_Insurance_in_a_digital_world:_The_time_is_now/$FILE/EY-Digital-Survey-1-October.pdf.

Fichman, R. G., Dos Santos, B. L., & Zheng, Z. (2014). Digital innovation as a fundamental and powerful concept in the information systems curriculum. *MIS Quarterly*, 38(2), 329–A15.

Figueiredo, O., Guimaraes, P., & Woodward, D. (2002). Home-field advantage: Location decisions of Portuguese entrepreneurs. *Journal of Urban Economics*, 52(2), 341–61.

Fitzgerald, M., Kruschwitz, N., Bonnet, D., & Welch, M. (2014). Embracing digital technology: A new strategic imperative. *MIT Sloan Management Review*, 55(2), 1–12.

Fjeldstad, Ø. D., & Ketels, C. H. M. (2006). Competitive advantage and the value network configuration. *Long Range Planning*, 39(2), 109–131.

Garven, J. R. (2002). On the implications of the internet for insurance markets and institutions. *Risk Management and Insurance Review*, 5(2), 105–116.

Ghani, E., Kerr, W.R., & O'Connell, S. (2011). *Spatial determinants of entrepreneurship in India*. Cambridge, MA: Harvard University.

Graham, B. (2006). *The intelligent investor: The definitive book on value investing. A book of practical counsel*. New York: HarperCollins.

Graham, B., & Dodd, D. L. (2008). *Security analysis*. New York: McGraw-Hill.

Gimpel, H., Rau, D., & Roeglinger, M. (2017). Understanding FinTech start-ups – a taxonomy of consumer-oriented service offerings. *Electronic Markets* (2017), 1–20. Retrieved from https://www.researchgate.net/publication/320932728_Understanding_FinTech_start-ups_-_a_taxonomy_of_consumer-oriented_service_offerings.

Hacklin, F., Raurich, V. & Marxt, C. (2004). How incremental innovation becomes disruptive: The case of technology convergence. *IEEE International Engineering Management Conference* (Vol. 1, pp. 32–36). Singapore: Institute of Electrical and Electronics Engineers.

Haldane, A. G. (2012). Towards a common financial language: Securities Industry and Financial Markets Association (SIFMA). At the "Building a Global Legal Entity Identifier Framework" Symposium, New York. http://www.bis.org/review/r120315g.pdf.

JWG. (2017). RegDelta: Part of our MiFID II solution. Retrieved from https://jwg-it.eu/insight/mifid-programme-planner/.

Lecamus, V. (2017, July 11). PropTech: What is it and how to address the new wave of real estate startups? *Medium*. Retrieved from https://medium.com/@vincentlecamus/

proptech-what-is-it-andhow-to-address-the-new-wave-of-real-estate-startups-ae 9bb52fb128.

Koch, T., & Windsperger, J. (2017). Seeing through the network: Competitive advantage in the digital economy. *Journal of Organization Design*, 6(1), 6.

Magnoni, B., Chandani, & E. Zimmerman, E. (2012). *Milk brief 10 – Doing the math with property insurance in Ghana.* Appleton, WI: MicroInsurance Centre.

Mayer, R. N. (2008). Online insurance. In J. J. Xiao (Ed.), *Handbook of consumer finance research* (pp. 125–135). New York: Springer.

McDowell, H. (2017). The trade news. Retrieved from https://www.thetradenews.com/ Sell-side/Banks-spent-close-to-$100-billion-on-compliance-last-year/.

McKnight, D. H., Choudhury, V., & Kacmar, C. (2002). Developing and validating trust measures for e-commerce: An integrative typology. *Information Systems Research*, 13(3), 334–359.

McNulty, L. (2017). Top regulator: City firms must bear responsibility for RegTech risks. *Financial News.* https://www.fnlondon.com/articles/city-firms-must-bear-responsibil ity-for-regtech-risk-20170516.

Memminger, M., Baxter, M., & Lin, E. (2016). Banking RegTechs to the rescue? *Bain.* http://www.bain.com/publications/articles/banking-regtechs-to-the-rescue.aspx.

O'Connor, A. (2018, March 11). The claim: Identical twins have identical DNA. *New York Times*, p. F5.

Oyedele, O. A. (2018). *Challenges of investing in real estate in developing nations.* (Working Paper 10.13140/RG.2.2.10904.85766). Retrieved from https://www.researchgate.net/publica tion/328942113_Challenges_of_Investing_in_Real_Estate_in_Developing_Nations.

Packin, N. G. (2018). RegTech, compliance and technology judgment rule. *Chicago-Kent Law Review*, 93, 193–220.

Palmer, J. (2017). *The data journey: Finding and fixing the bumps and holes in the road.* Data Standards for Granular Data Conference, European Central Bank.

Philippon, T. (2015). Has the US finance industry become less efficient? On the theory and measurement of financial intermediation. *American Economic Review*, 105, 1408–1438.

Philippon, T. (2016). *The FinTech opportunity.* (NBER Working Paper 22476).

Porter, M. E., & Millar, V. E. (1985). How information gives you competitive advantage. *Harvard Business Review*, 63(4), 149–160.

PricewaterhouseCoopers. (2016). Top insurance industry issues in 2016 – InsurTech. *PricewaterhouseCoopers.* Retrieved from http://www.pwc.com/us/en/insurance/publica tions/top-insurance-industry-issues-insurtech.html

Puschmann, T. (2017). Fintech. *Business & Information Systems Engineering*, 59(1), 69–76.

Rai, A., & Tang, X. (2013). Research commentary – information technology-enabled business models: A conceptual framework and a coevolution perspective for future research. *Information Systems Research*, 25(1), 1–14.

PTCLR. (2018, June 6). Land reform: Proposed registration will sanitise land administration. *Vanguard Newspaper.*

Sarkar, M., Butler, B., & Steinfield, C. (1998). Cybermediaries in electronic marketspace: Toward theory building. *Journal of Business Research*, 41(3), 215–221.

Schreieck, M., & Wiesche, M. (2017). How established companies leverage IT platforms for value co-creation–insights from banking. ECIS 2017 Proceedings (p. 1726).

Stabell, C. B., & Fjeldstad, Ø. D. (1998). Configuring value for competitive advantage: On chains, shops, and networks. *Strategic Management Journal*, 19(5), 413–437.

Stangler, D., & Arbesman, S. (2012, June). *What does Fortune 500 turnover mean?* Ewing Marion Kauffman Foundation.

The 20 most innovative companies in real estate (or PropTech). (2018, Feb. 6). *Go Weekly.* https://medium.com/go-weekly-blog/the-20-most-innovative-companies-in-realestate-or-proptech-2e0242b80e32.

The woman who is reining in America's technology giants: European Union antitrust chief Margrethe Vestager has become the *de facto* global regulator for US companies such as Google and Apple (2018, April 4). *Wall Street Journal.*

Tilson, D., Lyytinen, K., & Sørensen, C. (2010). Research commentary — digital infrastructures. *Information Systems Research, 21*(4), 748–759.

Tyler, T. (2017). RegTech and FinTech's impact on the regulated sector. *Aid Compliance.* http://www.aidcompliance.com/regtech-fintechs-impact-regulated-sector/.

Walport, M. (2015). *FinTech futures: The UK as a world leader in financial technologies.* London: UK Government Office for Science.

Weill, P., & Vitale, M. (2002). What IT infrastructure capabilities are needed to implement e-business models? *MIS Quarterly Executive, 1*(1), 17.

Yoo, Y., Richard, J., Boland, J., Lyytinen, K., & Majchrzak, A. (2012). Organizing for innovation in the digitized world. *Organization Science, 23*(5), 1398–1408.

Zavolokina, L., Dolata, M., & Schwabe, G. (2016). FinTech – What's in a name? *Proceedings of the 37th International Conference on Information Systems.* December 11–14, 2016. Dublin, Ireland: ICIS.

3

BIG DATA

A corollary to the increasing magnitude of digitization in commerce is the proliferation of datapoints that are created on a daily basis. While there are likely many datapoints that can help contribute to unique insights, there can also be a great deal of noise. To identify the value-add within especially large sets of data, special skills, tools, and creative thinking can be tremendously helpful. Thankfully, there are a variety of courses and models available online to assist, and many of these are free (or freemium) and open-source. The data may be numerical (structured), or include text, images, or audio (unstructured). Platforms that can be helpful with organizing this information into meaningful insights consist of statistical packages, graphics software, and clustering algorithms.

"Big data" is one of those terms that can mean different things to different people. To suggest a working definition for our purposes here, let's say that big data is the opportunity to explore a variety of many different types of information that may yield new perspectives.

Terms and concepts commonly referenced in the context of big data include the following:[1]

> Advanced analytics: With the benefit of capturing relationships (as with correlations) among key data elements, whether real-time, daily, or other, predictive analytic elements can be brought into play. Perhaps as related to the sales funnel, or even financial planning and revenue expectations, advanced analytics can assist with forecasts and help identify areas doing well and those in which additional oversight may be useful.

Artificial intelligence: This describes any device that can perceive aspects of its environment and take actions aligned with those perceptions to accomplish a particular objective.

Blockchain: A blockchain is essentially a group of records (blocks) linked together digitally with the use of cryptography, and with each block containing a cryptographic hash of the previous block along with a timestamp and any transaction data. A key design element of blockchain is its resistance to tampering, and as such it is seen as offering a desirable platform for all manner of financial contracts and processes. SBI Sumishin Net Bank has successfully applied blockchain in a trial run with the application of Mijin (a platform to create blockchains) in relation to complex accounting systems. With the real-world simulation, over 2 million virtual bank accounts were evaluated for their ability to process close to 100,000 transactions per hour, with a reduced risk of failure and fraud.[2]

Cloud: The cloud not only represents a place where digital applications can ultimately live on a full-time basis, but it is a powerful platform for vetting new ideas, with enhanced collaboration opportunities.

Cognitive computing: On-site personal inspections made by individuals can be an expensive proposition for insurance companies when a claim is made, especially when the claim may involve hazardous conditions. Today there are drones with cameras that can be fitted with special lenses to detect weak water-damaged roofs, or even chemical leaks. In some instances the technology can even generate an estimated dollar amount of damages on the basis of is the information it processes. As a result, the need for fixes can be detected sooner, and damage can be mended faster, and with less expense. Cognitive or sensory abilities include sight, taste, smell, hearing, and touch.

In-memory computing: For entities offering internet purchases for which demand can be especially intense at specific times (e.g., providers of popular concert tickets, or monthly commuter passes for trains and buses), in-memory computing can permit a far greater number of concurrent users and with faster processing speeds. With the ability to compress data (with reduced storage requirements) and store it in main memory, in-memory computing permits faster calculations. The benefit of increased speeds in the context of larger data sets is transformational.

Machine learning: Machine-learning technology is concerned with generating outcomes (e.g., predictions), and the process permits learning along the way with an ability to continuously adapt. Machine learning can be supervised, with software designed to look for particular things, and unsupervised, whereby software is designed with an openness to new discoveries without explicit guidance as to what it should be seeking.

Robotics: Banks have been using robotic technologies for some time, such as ATMs (Automated Teller Machines), which help to reduce staff costs and potential errors, as well as providing customers with 24/7 access to services otherwise limited to business hours. For any task requiring physical exertion, robotics can potentially offer a contribution, minimizing human error caused by fatigue, repetition, illness, or complexity of task. Tasks can be also be completed at less cost, and performed in places where humans cannot go (such as to seal off an area with a poisonous gas leak), or where a robot can stay longer (repairing an oil well a mile beneath the ocean's surface).[3]

Visualization: While the accessibility and computability of data have advanced considerably, so too have new ways to present that data. With a picture being worth a thousand words, powerful tools can help to bring new understandings.[4] And while data is commonly thought of as being numerical (or structured), data can be unstructured as well (text, images, sounds, etc.). Company dashboards are increasingly popular, especially when real-time insights are available. Dashboards can generate tables and charts for a variety of financial metrics and Key Performance Indicators (KPIs), and can show how progress is being made on a particular day (or over a longer period of time) as well as in relation to a previous day (or previous period of time). Dashboards can be particularly helpful when they can flag a particular point of a critical path likely to impede progress. For example, with regards to the sales funnel, if a day's incoming submissions are not of a proportion to help achieve that day's targeted quotes, then an alert could be generated to push more aggressively on submission strategies. With a click on a particular metric of interest, users may be able to drill down into specific data relating to where bottlenecks are greatest, or where efficiencies are strongest.

Figure 3.1 presents three common methods for generating and collecting digital financial data.

Certainly one highly-touted aspect of big data is that it can help with creating algorithms that have great predictive capability. A challenge with this, however, is that data typically represents observations or recordings of things that have already happened. Accordingly, as long as the future looks really similar to the

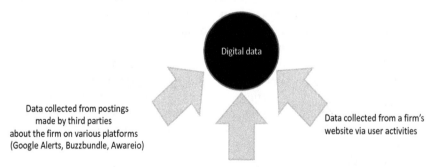

FIGURE 3.1   Three common methods for generating and collecting digital financial data

past, any data-intensive algorithm or model could be expected to do a decent job of generating meaningful forecasts and insights. However, such a model might hold up well for a period of time, but then be deemed inadequate with a new set of drivers that have emerged. In statistics this phenomenon is sometimes referred to as "overfitting"; that is, pinning down a model's parameters so tightly that it may give off grossly misleading signals when a new trend emerges. Figure 3.2 helps to illustrate this.

While the various aspects of analyzing and using big data can be done by the firm with the data, some firms have had interesting results with crowdsourced endeavors. For example, Lending Club made publicly available the historical performance of its portfolio along with comments provided by people who had been granted loans from the online company. One particular study examined relationships between the words used to describe borrowing needs and subsequent loan performance. Words and phrases that supported well-defined and short-term needs (e.g., "my daughter is getting married") tended to be associated with reduced credit risk, while words connoting desperation were observed with markedly higher default rates even after controlling for credit scores and other commonly reported borrower attributes. It was found that people who were newly unemployed and borrowing to do something about it (e.g., taking classes to obtain new skills), were more likely to stay current on obligations relative to the baseline cohort. Finally, it was learned that people who write at a higher level, as measured by the Flesch-Kincaid scale, defaulted at a lower rate than those with weaker writing skills.[5]

In the investments world, analysts have long sought value-adding insights from a variety of data sets, including sizes or number of sun spots, average rainfall, phases of the moon, and even consumer sentiment as expressed via social-media platforms. There are also many trading strategies that are entirely

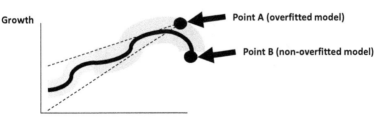

Overfitted models may fail to capture turning points

Growth — Point A (overfitted model)

Point B (non-overfitted model)

Cycles of a core business, or economic sector

A challenge that can exist with a model that is overfitting the data is that it may narrow in on a specific point for an expected outcome (as at Point A) as predicated upon the incorporation of past data, but fail to capture a turning point (as at Point B) which might be captured by a model that is not overfitting the data

FIGURE 3.2   Overfitted versus non-overfitted models

predicated upon prices of assets. For example, analysts will try to discern patterns in historical prices of stocks or precious metals or other assets that
openly trade on an exchange. These analysts will then attempt to execute
trading strategies based upon the patterns they see. Generally speaking, this
approach to trading is referred to as technical analysis.

Figure 3.3 presents a technical analysis of Tesla's equity prices (symbol TSLA)
that includes two moving averages; one on a 20-day historical basis, and another
on a 120-day historical basis.[6] As shown, the respective averages can help to
serve as momentum indicators of sorts, but cannot be considered to be reliable.
At the circle indicated by the letter A, the 20-day average indicates positive
momentum by piercing through the 120-day average from underneath, while at
letter B there is a suggestion of the momentum slowing via the 20-day average
moving back below the 120-day average from above.

In the insurance world, claims data are an important source of insights. By
studying details of what gives rise to an insurance company needing to pay out
on adverse events, policies can be better tailored to target particular types of
risks and to ensure that consumers pay only for the specific coverages they want.

In brief, there are data streams of one sort or another with just about every
industry, and what is required is to identify the sources and uses of information
that will best help drive desired outcomes.

These outcomes may be related to strategies for minimizing expenses, maximizing revenues, or both. In some instances particular metrics are devised, and
are often labeled Key Performance Indicators (KPIs). KPIs can exist with broad
applications (e.g., knowledge of a company's revenue-to-employee ratio is valuable, regardless of the industry), and some exist with narrow applications.

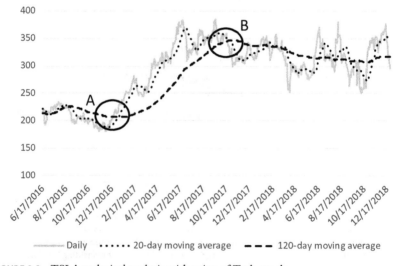

FIGURE 3.3 TSLA technical analysis with price of Tesla stock

One of the more infamous company-specific KPIs is the McDonald's French fry ratio. The expression "Would you like fries with that?" has become a metaphor for businesses wanting to push cross-sales of products. For business analysts at McDonald's, using the French fry ratio (and variations of it) provides insight as to combinations of products being purchased and the success of various locations with encouraging customers to perhaps buy something more than what they may have originally intended. For a shoe store it may be the cross-sell of polish or a pair of laces. For a clothing store it may be a perfume or a belt. With online shopping, it may be a sampling of items on the page just before check-out which displays what other users also recently purchased.

For digital business, Google Analytics offers a variety of metrics captured with every user's click on a website. A sampling of these metrics includes the following:

Acquisition overview: This permits a monitoring of traffic sources engaging with a website; for example, are people finding your site by organic search (via a browser inquiry), or going to your site via direct hits (typing in your domain name), or linking to your site from another venue (e.g., a blog or a social-media platform) as a referral?

Sessions: The number of sessions (visits) of users to a website, whether it is their first session or a repeat visit, bounce rate (rate at which users leave after visiting just one page), and average session duration.

Social overview: Measures the impact of social media on a site, as by providing information about the networks where a site's content is being shared.

Conversions: A conversion is created when a visitor takes a specific action at a site. Actions can include everything from downloading a marketing brochure, to making a purchase.

Behavior flow: Permits a tracking of the webpages attracting the most hits, how many users exit at each stage, and the routes they take among various pages at a site.

Exit pages: The exit page is the last one viewed by a user, and is the last impression left with a visitor. A high exit rate for a particular page would suggest that it might be a good candidate for A/B testing with the aim of keeping users around for longer. A/B testing refers to the process of creating a new page (an A page) at a site to see how users respond to it in relation to the previous or currently used page (the B page). A/B testing can also simply involve the simultaneous comparison of two webpage designs to evaluate which is better, regardless of whether one has been used previously or not.

With the collection of these datapoints, tremendous insights can be obtained related to user interests. Knowing these interests can help with selling users more goods and services.

***

Though there can certainly be insights gained from large sets of data, sometimes there can be beauty in things that are small as well, and that includes small data.

A colleague of mine works with developing countries on finance topics, and recently shared this story about a cellphone service provider. The provider operated within a region of Africa, and wanted to evaluate when to extend payment terms to users falling behind on their bills. A study was commissioned to help determine when a cellphone customer would be a good credit risk. For users who simply could not make a monthly payment on time, the phone service provider wanted to determine if a method could be devised for choosing when an extension of credit would be a relatively safe decision.

Due to the developing world context, the service provider did not have access to a great deal of information about individual users and their personal creditworthiness. What the cellphone provider did have, however, was information related to a user's phone habits. For example, the cellphone provider was able to see if more of a user's calls were inbound or outbound (perhaps suggestive of the user having a large circle of family and friends), and if more calls were to or from urban areas versus rural (maybe supporting a user's access to more employment opportunities). In the end, with a handful of datapoints from a user's phone patterns, the cellphone provider was able to develop a decision rule for whether or not to extend credit with a success ratio in excess of 90%.

***

One area of finance where large volumes of data are at the center of things is shadow banking.[7] Shadow banking is a reference to activities typically considered the purview of traditional banks (public or private sector), such as printing money (central banks) or taking in deposits and making loans (private banks), yet with those activities being carried out by non-traditional banks. One way to think of shadow banking is that it encompasses any activities banks could do and may choose not to (e.g., providing overdraft services), or are restricted or discouraged from doing by regulatory authorities (e.g., providing loans to higher risk companies or persons), or are simply quasi-bank type activities (e.g., cryptocurrencies). Shadow banking has a rather long and extensive pedigree, dating back to at least the time when merchants first offered their customers the opportunity to purchase goods or services on credit.[8] Table 3.1 presents modern-day examples of traditional bank functions being performed by non-traditional banks, with citations of online entities engaged in these various activities. For each of the instances cited, a variety of data sets can potentially be involved.

As indicated in Table 3.1. for an entrepreneur looking to garner sufficient seed capital to create a prototype, sources of funds might be both personal (per SoFi) and professional (per Kabbage).

Whether or not shadow banking is regarded as being a positive phenomenon can be very much dependent upon your particular perspective.

For example, innovators and entrepreneurs might see opportunities to satisfy market demand in areas where traditional banks might choose to shy away. With

TABLE 3.1 Traditional bank functions being performed by other entities (shadow banking)

Overdraft alternatives

	Examples	Online entities
	Advances against paychecks	Earnin, DailyPay, PayActiv, FlexWage
	Advances against tax refunds	H&R Block, Jackson Hewitt, Liberty Tax Service

Deposit alternatives

	Examples	Online entities
Money market funds	Government debt, corporate debt	Synchrony
Money market securities	Commercial paper, bankers' acceptances	Cat Financial PowerInvestment

Loan alternatives

	Examples	Online entities
B2B – P2P credit	Purchases of accounts receivables	BlueVine
B2C credit	Auto dealer financing, Affinity credit cards	Ford Motor Credit Company, First Bankcard
C2C credit (Crowdsourcing)	Start-up financing	Kickstarter
Commercial mortgages	Business expansion, equipment, cash flow	Lending Tree
Personal lines of credit	Bank overdrafts, credit card installments, HELOC	Credible, Regions
Personal loans	Short-term borrowing, special situations, credit card advances	SoFi, LightStream
Personal mortgages	Personal and commercial properties	Quicken loans, Better mortgage
Repurchase agreements	Pairing of cash-surplus firms with liquidity-demand firms	Tradeweb
Securitization	Auto loans, credit cards, royalties, etc.	BearingPoint, Simon
Small business line of credit	General operations, other	Kabbage
Small business loan	General operations, other	CIT, Prosper, Lending Club
Student loans	Undergraduate and graduate programs, certifications	Sallie Mae, Earnest (refinancing)

In some instances a bank may have a degree of involvement on a supporting basis, and private equity firms may be involved with shadow banking, either working with online entities or alongside them

high-risk loans, traditional banks may be averse to providing capital for start-ups who anticipate a few years of losses prior to any revenue being realized. Conversely, these may be precisely the kinds of opportunities that online crowdfunding venues might most actively seek to attract.

For the regulatory community, shadow banking ventures might be perceived as embodying high levels of risk, particularly because certain activities might fall outside of governmental jurisdiction and oversight. Another cause for concern could be related to the potential domino effects of shadow banking dynamics. Consider the role of repurchase agreements in the financial crisis of 2008.

Repurchase agreement transactions (or repos) are generally quite large (typically in the millions of dollars), and as such tend to be concentrated among the largest of corporations and investing entities. Repos can be structured to be either term (with a set maturity date) or open (with a rolling feature, and no formal maturity date). Most term repos tend to be for a period of 90 days, though repos with a maturity of one year can exist, and sometimes terms can be for even longer than that. The majority of repo transactions are concluded within one day. A repo transaction occurs when Party A has securities (typically bonds of one type or another, though repos can also be carried out with equities) and desires cash, and Party B has cash and desires a return from putting that cash to work. Hence, Party A "loans" their securities to Party B at one price, and Party A simultaneously agrees to "return" those same securities to Party B at another (higher) price. Party A benefits from receiving Party B's cash (and uses the cash to manage liquidity, finance inventories, or speculate), and Party B benefits from earning a return on the difference in prices applicable to the transaction.

So … is a repo an "investment" situation, or a "loan" arrangement? From a tax standpoint, repos are treated as a collateralized (backed by securities) loan, though it is certainly easy to see how a repo could be regarded as a purchase-and-sale transaction (not a borrow-and-lend scenario).[9] Table 3.2 presents a comparison of traditional banking demand deposits with shadow banking repo transactions.

A reason for the focus on repos here is that many market historians attribute the large volume of repos in 2008 with being an important factor in deepening the Great Recession of December 2007 to June 2009. Just as the "run on the banks" is regarded by many economists as having exacerbated the Great Depression, many economists saw the "run on repo" as making for a more difficult financial environment with the Great Recession; instead of a rush by investors to remove cash from the banking system (via deposit withdrawals), there was a rush by investors to remove cash from repo operations (via withdrawing from transactions).[10] Figure 3.4 shows the build-up in loans including repo transactions leading up to the Great Recession, and the precipitous decline of these as the recession took hold.

To be sure, there are many reasons why the Great Recession emerged and unfolded in the way it did, and it can certainly be argued that the drying up of market liquidity related to disappearing repos was perhaps more a symptom of prevailing fundamental dynamics relating to financial ills (just as the run on banks in the Great Depression is seen by many historians as arguably more a reaction to tumultuous times rather than a cause of the economic collapse).[11]

At minimum, it can most certainly be agreed all-around that neither the run on the banks nor the run on repo did anything to help push the US economy in a more positive direction, and in the moment likely made matters far worse.

TABLE 3.2 Demand deposits versus repos

Demand deposits	*Repos*
Reserves are a minimum level of demand deposits, imposed on banks by regulation, where shortfalls can be borrowed from the central bank	Haircuts are a level of margin imposed by the buyer of collateral in a Repo transaction. For example, if a security is worth $10 million and there is a haircut of 2%, then the amount of cash provided in the transaction is $9.8 million
Deposits are guaranteed by the government at set levels	Cash in a repo transaction is backed by the security(s) put up as collateral
Deposit rates are flexible and can be raised to attract cash when reserves are low or when expected returns on certain banking activities are high	Repo rates are flexible and can be raised to attract cash when liquidity is low or when expected returns on certain activities requring cash are high
The loans arranged by traditional banks from demand deposits are at least initially held on the bank's balance sheet, though can later be securitized into a bond and sold into the marketplace (and removed from the balance sheet)	International Financial Reporting Standards (IFRS) require that securities used for repo are classified as "collateral" rather than "investments" on the asset side of the balance sheet, and are classified as a "collateralized borrowing" on the liability side

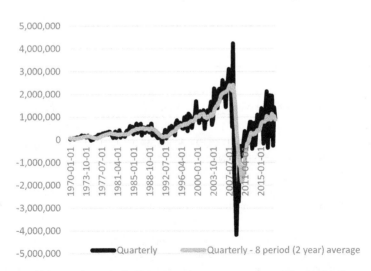

FIGURE 3.4 Business loans including repurchase agreements, millions of dollars

Table 3.3 presents a comparison of factors that characterize a run on the banks versus a run on repo.

If repos were a large and significant part of shadow banking in the lead-up to the Great Recession, what are the large and growing aspects of shadow banking today? This question can be answered with the following observations:

- In the five-year period between 2002 and 2007, the world's non-bank financial assets increased from $30 trillion to $60 trillion, or 124% of global GDP. Presently these assets comprise $160 trillion, or 148% of global GDP.[12]
- In 2007 non-bank financial assets accounted for nearly one quarter of the world's financial assets, and today they comprise nearly half (48%).[13]
- As an alternative to approaching a bank for a loan, a company can go to the marketplace and borrow via a bond offering. Relative to equities, bonds are not terribly liquid assets.[14] With the growth of bond-ETF products (Electronically Traded Funds) to over $800 billion in 2018, bond managers may one day have to contend with investors wanting to suddenly dump bonds in favor of another asset class (perhaps even cash) which could precipitate fire sales of these already hard-to-unwind securities.[15]
- The size of the United States high-yield bond market and leveraged loan market are both close to double what they were in 2007.[16]
- In 2007, 29% of outstanding corporate loans were covenant-lite (i.e., weak with investor protections), and in 2018 the figure is greater than 75%.[17]

TABLE 3.3 Run on banks versus run on repo

Run on the banks	*Run on repo*
Within the traditional banking system	Within the securitized banking system
Withdrawl of cash deposits	Withdrawl of repo agreements
In the absence of ready cash, banking entities look to sell assets, often quickly and at fire-sale prices	In the absence of ready-cash, finance entities look to sell assets quickly and at fire-sale prices
As money flows less freely within the banking system and is hoarded, liquidity is reduced	As money flows less freely within the financial system, liquidity is reduced
Reduced liquidity adds frictions to the marketplace, heightens credit risk, and complicates decision-making in the private and public sectors	Reduced liquidity adds frictions to the marketplace, heightens credit risk, and complicates decision-making in the private and public sectors

The "securitized banking system" is not within the "traditional banking system" (thus placing the former within a shadow banking classification) by virtue of repo loans originating with securities firms rather than banks

The above bullet points are certainly not exhaustive in terms of shadow banking risks to watch, and trends will ebb and flow with business cycles. The statistics cited here will change (some for better, others for worse), and that is perhaps the point … these are moving targets, and observing what's growing, shrinking, and emerging can help us be better prepared for what may happen.

Table 3.4 provides a summary of why shadow banking matters.

In the public sector and the historical domain of central banks, currency substitutes are emerging. In some instances it is on a small scale as with Amazon coins and miles programs, while in other cases cryptocurrencies such as Bitcoin and Litecoins are emerging as global mediums of exchange.[18]

***

At one time (though in some circles this is perhaps still true today) a popular business adage among CEOs was "Half the money I spend on advertising is wasted; the problem is I don't know which half."[19] With the plethora of marketing tools available today for tracking every advertising dollar, especially in the context of the internet, it ought to be fairly straightforward to determine what's working and what's not, and how to go about correcting what seems to be broken. Perhaps a better adage for the information age of today is something like "Half the data I process isn't value-add; the problem is I don't know which half." In brief, it can be a real challenge to discern which particular metrics offer

TABLE 3.4 Why shadow banking matters

Why shadow banking matters
• Though this is not always the case, oftentimes the firms that become involved with shadow banking activities are seeking to take on the risks that traditional banks do not wish to bear (or cannot bear or are limited with bearing, owing to regulatory or other considerations)
• Many shadow banking activities fall outside of the scope of regulatory bodies for active oversight, or are only marginally monitored by authorities
• Many shadow banking activities do not have government guarantees or safety nets in the form of insurance, or access to central bank resources that could be helpful in a crisis (such as special borrowing facilities)
• There can be multiplier effects when shadow banking activities or entities encounter problems. For example, if the shadow activity involved providing lines of credit, then many users might suddenly find themselves in a bad situation with the credit lines withdrawn. In turn, business relationships of those users might also find themselves in tough positions if lines of credit were going to be used to pay suppliers or to finance key links in the business chain.
• The internet has helped to reduce the amount of initial capital and time required to set up shadow banking operations, facilitating the proliferation of these entities

up greater promise of identifying meaningful strategies for revenue maximization or expense reduction, and which are simply noise. Special relationships or correlations that seem to exist across data sets for one period of time may not hold up in another, and may simply cease to exist as a data stream altogether at some point for any number of reasons such as collection issues, the reassignment of an analyst or programmer, or other. In brief, more successful marketing efforts may be those that seek to continuously tap into diversified and evolving sets of data, with a nimble and opportunistic approach to identifying correlations with success.

Increasingly, marketing and communications are being combined into a single department (sometimes referred to as marcom). For firms where these functions are housed in separate departments, marketing often focuses on customers, sales, and brand awareness, with communications (or public relations or external relations) focusing on everyone else, such as government entities or regulatory bodies, community groups, media, and financial or other external (as well as internal) stakeholders. Yet with the internet offering up a single venue (from internal company emails to external social-media posts), a single point of official corporate information flows is emerging for several firms, leading to greater efficiency of resources, consistency of messages, meaningfulness of metrics, and accountability of participants.

***

For firms that anticipate delving into a particularly large project, as with an artificial intelligence (AI) or comparable initiative, it would be advisable to source a project infrastructure that is scalable and elastic. That is, a platform that can grow in size as the project evolves, and that can adopt desirable new features that come along either internally or externally. A development platform should ideally scale on demand, particularly so that time and money do not have to be additionally expended at each new stage of the initiative. Figure 3.5 presents a perspective for reaching AI insights, starting from business intelligence (BI) tools and apps, up to a full-fledged custom AI program.

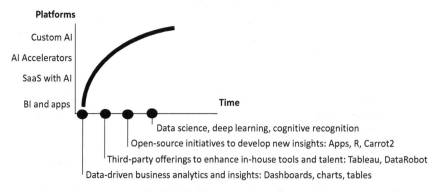

FIGURE 3.5 Stages of AI insights

It can also be helpful to know that there is a wide range of choices available for cloud computing. There is the public cloud, as well as opportunities with private clouds and virtual private clouds. Some firms avoid the cloud altogether and prefer an on-premises solution. It is also possible to allocate certain aspects of work to a private cloud, and then later bring that in-house, and vice versa. Accordingly, when sketching out possible platform solutions, it can be helpful to choose venues that make it easier to switch from one setup to another if needed.

Open-source software is popular with many development projects for its accessibility, speed, and user forums, in which a variety of helpful suggestions may be found. In some contexts, as with deep learning, open-source software may be the only viable option. For this reason, it could be prudent to identify vendors that build on a foundation of open-source software. Further, it may be advisable to use solutions that make use of standard hardware rather than new technology, and simplicity along with reasonable cost structures can be key as well.

It can also be helpful to think about the relevant participants in a large data project and what their roles will be. Table 3.5 provides a sampling of how one possible arrangement might look.

TABLE 3.5 Example of development project participants

Contributor	Role
Business Analyst	Works directly with stakeholders to define project requirements
Lead Data Scientist	Principal investigator, responsible for ensuring model accuracy and validity
Peer Data Scientists	Provide an independent review of the project with ability to offer suggestions for improvement
Machine Learning Specialists	Provide expertise in sub-specialties, as with image recognition or natural language processing
Compliance Specialists	Verify that project complies with both internal and external best practices and reporting requirements
Data Engineers	Develop production data pipelines and links to sources and uses of information
DevOps Specialists	Provide provisioning, support, and guidance for AI platform
Data Management Specialists	Manage source and target data platforms and assist with connectivity
Application Developers	Develop end-user applications and features
AI Engineers	Embed AI in end-user applications as desired
Systems Administrators	Support production infrastructure with improvements or fixes as needed
Security Specialists	Maintain compliance with security policies, internal and as externally required

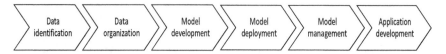

FIGURE 3.6   Example of an application development process

It can be helpful to realize at the outset that different participants may be looking for different outcomes. Businesspeople may want dashboards to track overall results in a visual format that's easy to design, data scientists may want the ability to code in Python or R, developers may need to integrate AI into production applications, and there may be certain preferences for applications (as with Google Docs, Tableau, or various Application Programming Interfaces (APIs).

It can take a considerable amount of time to develop a data model, with a number of factors involved related to considerations such as data collection, determining the model's role, deciding who needs to be involved, and more. Taking time at the outset to develop a plan and think through the critical path is a small investment of time and resources that could pay handsome dividends.

Finally, it can be valuable to seek out vendors who have 24/7 support so that you can get the help you need when you want it, and many vendors today also provide free ongoing training as new features are created.

***

Monetizing data

If you are thinking about monetizing your company data, the following considerations may help to guide you.

- What are your goals?
  Are you seeking to create a data business solely intended to generate an alternative revenue stream, or do you see it an opportunity to grow new or existing customer relationships? The response to this question could affect the approach taken to the business on a more general level, as well as specific procedures related to data policies and governance.

- What is the value of your data?
  The perceived value of your data may have a lot to do with the end user interested in it. Pricing could be on a subscription basis or per download, and in some instances you may not want to charge at all (for example where data access could be used to close a deal or entice a customer to renew a contract).

  If your data is unique in some way or is otherwise difficult to obtain, a premium price structure could be reasonable. An add-on to price could also be appropriate if you can offer a particular ease of downloading data, or if fewer restrictions are placed on how the data may be used.

  Even if you are contemplating no fees for datapoints, it may be advisable to charge a setup fee; that is, a nominal charge to cover the time and expense for someone on your staff to establish an initial data link and ensure that it is working properly.

And finally, if data is going to be made freely available, there may be advantages to having the charges enumerated in a pricing agreement, though these should be accompanied with the statement that fees are waived under a particular arrangement. The rationale for this is as follows:

a. It provides a gentle reminder to the user that they are indeed receiving something of value.

b. If at some point in the future there emerges a reason for why charging might be appropriate (e.g., the customer moves to another firm but still desires the data, or enhanced data features become available), then a template is in place to accommodate this. And when charging is introduced, it does not necessarily have to be at 100% of list prices; a flat discount can apply, as well as a stepladder approach to increases over time.

- Can you anonymize your data?
  If your data originates with you, then you might be in a position to sell it in whatever form you wish. If your data does not originate with you (and even if it does), you may want to anonymize it in some way.

  For example, if you are in the business of selling auto insurance policies, there may be third-party interest in knowing how many policies you sell each month in various parts of the country. Maybe economists would value this information for its potential to improve their forecasts related to regional economic activity and growth. Rather than report exactly how many policies you sold, you might prefer to create an index that reflects when more or fewer policies are issued.

- Are you in a position to handle the logistics of data sales?
  Would you need an additional resource to support a data business, with responsibilities including contract negotiations, customer inquiries, collating and loading data sets, and more?

- Do you care about downstream considerations?
  Once your data is provided to someone you know, do you care if they sell it, or if they give it away? Do you want to take the stance that you are always the owner of your data, and that you are simply lending (or leasing) its value as a resource? If your data is sold to someone, do you mind if they resell it with a substantial markup in price?

  Do you have any concerns as to how your data may be used by others, aside from monetary considerations? For example, if a user takes the data and creates a new product based upon the data characteristics, is that okay with you?

- Do you want to retain ownership of your data?
  If the answer is yes, then safeguards need to be explicit. Further, there should be a clear understanding within your firm as to who owns the data (i.e., who bears ultimate responsibility and accountability for it), and how revenues are to be allocated.

- How will data be accessed?

In addition to defining how users may apply your data, which ought to be clearly outlined within licensing agreements and elsewhere, there is the matter of how users will get your data, whether this is via a webpage or direct delivery or proactively pulling the data from a database. Related to deliveries are considerations of timeliness and frequency of data updates. For example, is data is made available in real time or with a delay? If there is a service level agreement (SLA) which sets out minimal delivery objectives to be met, these need to be defined as precisely as possible.

Another important consideration is whether the end user might need to bear any unique expense related to the accessing of data. If a special setup is required on their side, there may be a reluctance to be a user even if the data is free. An easy-to-use platform in the cloud, or a simple API, could be viable solutions.

- Can the data be provided with a value-add?
  One way your particular data might be perceived as having greater value is if it is delivered in an enhanced way. For example, perhaps your data is provided not only in raw form (the numbers), but with numbers shown in a variety of graphic contexts as well. Another possibility might be to provide a couple of URLs for open-source data that complements your data set in some way, or to insert some commentary as to what is new or different about the data in the most recent reporting period. Finally, perhaps you can let users know that you are open to variations on what you provide, and hence grow your offering on the basis of what users express as strong needs.
- What can be done to ensure data integrity?
  It is of paramount importance to have proper internal controls and safeguards to ensure that data is timely, accurate, and complete. It may only take one bad experience for a user to decide that another data source is more desirable
- Third-party delivery venues
  Rather than taking on the responsibility of maintaining a delivery platform, it is possible to have your data delivered by third-party data stores. If this route is taken, it is imperative to negotiate terms that protect your interests and that create a meaningful experience for your user relationships. One advantage to using a third-party service is that it can mean getting your data to market faster, and exposing your data offering to a much wider audience. There are typically fees associated with third-party delivery services, however, though these are often negotiable.

In brief, any time a contract or agreement comes into play it can be a difficult document to amend, so getting it right the first time can justify a meaningful investment of time and attention. When successful, the sale of data can make for a nice revenue stream with something readily at hand.

***

If asked to think of a seminal moment in data science in the context of hardware, many of us might think of when the first chip became commercially available, or when the first computer was publicly sold, but for a few of us it was when the first telegraph came into operation. Rather than condensing alpha-numeric data in the essence of zeroes and ones in a context referred to as computer code, it was in the context of dots and dashes and referred to as Morse code, and it truly revolutionized information flows in dramatic ways. Not the least of which was with respect to how news was collated and disseminated.

Prior to the telegraph, it would not be uncommon for 10 newspapers to each send their own reporter to cover an important event. When the telegraph came along, it became feasible for only one or two reporters to be present who could then share their stories with others. In fact, there was an initial concern among journalists when the telegraph first came out that their jobs would become scarce, but in fact just the opposite occurred. With this new platform for the proliferation of information, the number of newspapers grew quite dramatically, and along with that newspapers became much more partisan in the views they were expressing so as to appeal to particular niches of readers, and to differentiate the kinds of writing they were providing. The telegraph, in a sense, served to democratize the basic facts of a given story, but what readers wanted next was a particular take on what those facts meant. Editorial pages received greater prominence, and opinion generally emerged as an important element of what readers really wanted to have. And, of course, as the technology improved, there was an evolution of hard-wired telegraph lines into wireless and mobile, whereby ships in distress hundreds of miles from shore could send out an SOS for help, which could be picked up by anyone else with another mobile device, known as a receiver.

In a way, big data is a relative concept, though it generally conveys the idea of plentiful information. Touchpoints in history when information flows seemed to burst forth in almost indigestible ways would include the advents of the printing press, the telegraph, the telephone, and the internet.

***

Examples of digital data offerings in the insurance industry include:

- YouSurance: principles of epigenetics (study of heritable phenotype changes that do not involve alterations) are used to replace traditional life insurance underwriting practices, and analysis of saliva is used to provide longevity predictions.
- Ingo Money: insurance companies (as well as third-party administrators) can quickly and securely disburse digital funds to over 4 billion consumer debit, credit, prepaid, or online wallet accounts.
- Sureify: insurers are enabled to digitally engage with customers via web, mobile, and a variety of personal health and device data sources.

- Atidot: permits carriers to evaluate customer data in real time via technology that easily accommodates big data; it has applications for predictive analytics, and is customized for life insurance.
- Carpe Data: leverages social media, online content, and other forms of alternative data in order to gain insights into risk characteristics across the insurance life cycle.
- Benekiva: facilitates claims automation, beneficiary management, and asset retention via a cloud-based, blockchain-backed AI platform.
- Ask Kodiak: provides brokers selling commercial insurance with a way to search for eligible carrier markets, while providing carriers with a digital marketing platform that reports out analytics on what agents and brokers are seeking.

And for financial analysis, one example of a powerful digital advancement is something called XBRL. The acronym XBRL stands for eXtensible Business Reporting Language, and it is commonly used in broader contexts to refer to the ability to file, search, and analyze millions of data elements related to public company filings with the Securities and Exchange Commission (SEC).

***

The framework of XBRL is a powerful tool as it provides users with a fully searchable database of line-item detail of all manner of SEC filings. Detailed segment breakouts, schedules, and roll forwards are available for searching, analyzing, and comparing over time and across multiple firms, and in a near-instantaneous fashion. Analysts and others can examine multiple documents side by side, search on geographic segment revenue across multiple jurisdictions (companies reporting revenue in both the United States and China, for example), and explore the granularity of a company's footnote and then search on that across multiple companies to seek similarities or anomalies. But although US public companies submit filings that are about 80% comprised of pre-existing XBRL data tags (corresponding to "gross revenue," "net income," "interest expense," and more) sourced from a taxonomy (data dictionary) with about 20,000 entries, there is an average use of near 20% of so-called "extensions" or "custom tags."[20] This can be a concern when the custom descriptors are not well defined, or when different companies use different tags to describe the same thing and thus frustrate analysts' attempts to identify common traits across financial metrics.

Meantime, data providers are stepping up by offering advanced tools that can be used to pull even more information from companies' public filings that goes well beyond numbers from income statements and balance sheets.[21] For example, non-GAAP information can also be tagged, as with KPIs including product warranty accruals or number of active users, or Management Discussion and Analysis (MD&A) commentary, SEC comment letters, or environmental, social, and governance data. A side-by-side redlining analysis of a previous MD&A section with the current one, for example, could provide interesting insights.

***

On a recent visit to Trinity College Dublin, I had the opportunity to visit the Long Room, which is filled with over 200,000 books.[22] The books are shelved not according to title or author but by size, with larger and heavier books on bottom rows and smaller, lighter books on the upper stacks. Practically speaking, the risk of a large book falling from an upper shelf and becoming damaged (or landing on the head of an unsuspecting patron) is mitigated with the simple solution of situating bigger texts closer to the ground. There is also the reduced risk of someone perhaps losing their balance while holding an especially large text in one hand and navigating a tall ladder with the other.

How quaint.

And yet, 300 years from today when students of history learn that we presently store our larger electronic files in clouds for retrieval as needed, rather than keeping them on laptops or mobile devices on which smaller file sizes are more manageable, that too may seem quaint.

While data have benefitted from thoughtful storage and management practices for hundreds of years, some of the fundamental challenges have remained remarkably consistent through the ages, although many creative solutions have been developed along the way.

Another vignette deserving of our attention involves a precocious start-up that opportunistically leveraged a game-changing technology to transform the retail industry: it enabled customers to order goods from the convenience of home, and with home delivery as well. This is the story of a company called Sears, and the year was 1893.[23] Leveraging the telegraph as a way of placing large orders with distant companies and instantly communicating with vast warehouses, Sears and Roebuck succeeded with bringing stores directly to consumers.[24] Sears and Roebuck revenues grew remarkably fast in the 10 years between 1895 and 1905, from just under $1 million to about $38 million.[25]

Notes

1 There are many variations on the terms and concepts presented, such as natural language processing, natural language generation (engaging with people in natural language, voice, and text), deep learning (machine learning with artificial neural networks), and the robo-advisors and chatbots used on consumer-facing websites to assist with a variety of inquiries and tasks (reconciliations, case management, trade processing, and fund administration) as well as with risk management (fraud detection), geospatial analytics, and more.

Gartner produces a "Hype cycle for emerging technologies" that is both informative and entertaining, and is worth a look from time to time to see how various trends are ebbing and flowing in relation to one another. See Gartner.com.

2 "SBI Sumishin Net Bank succeeds in using blockchain for their mission-critical systems: Using 'mijin' by Tech Bureau Corp" (2016), http://forums.mijin.io/en/599.html.

3 Iron Ox states that they use a human led, robotics-first approach to farming, and with great efficiencies for land and water usage.

4 Sometimes, however, and even for very experienced users of data and graphics, there can be misleading information among the "thousand words" of a picture. For example, on December 19, 2018 the US Federal Reserve released a "dot plot" of the type it has issued since 2012 to provide a graphical representation of where members of the rate-setting Federal Open Market Committee believe the mid-point of interest rate ranges ought to be at the end of the next three years (plus "longer run"). Along the vertical axis was the implied fed funds rate, and along the horizontal axis was time in years. The dot plot indicated expectations for two rate hikes in 2019, and the Dow Jones Industrial Average declined by more than 500 points, reaching a 52-week low. What the dot plot failed to reveal, however, was how strongly (or, in this case, how weakly) the Fed actually felt about those two rate-hike indications. Specifically, confidence in those forecasts was weakening in a significant way, as was revealed in the written minutes of the two-day meetings (December 18 and 19) which came out later. The Dow and other indices finished trading that day off of their lows.

5 Tony Hughes (2018, November 9), "Credit risk assessment: The benefits of text-based analysis," *Global Association of Risk Professionals*, https://www.garp.org/#!/risk-intelligence/all/all/a1Z1W000004BP1EUAW.

6 A variety of technical analysis calculations can be performed, and many of these can be easily invoked using Yahoo Finance or Google Finance. At Yahoo Finance, for example, users can apply moving averages, Bollinger Bands, Alligators, Oscillators, Donchian channels, and a variety of other exotic-sounding mathematical manipulations.

7 "Shadow banking" was first referenced as a term by PIMCO (Pacific Investment Management Company) executive director Paul McCulley at a Federal Reserve meeting in 2007.

8 While there may be earlier examples, in the early 1800s there were tailors in London who extended credit to certain clients, and some of those tailors even compared customer experiences among themselves.

9 "Tax issues for repo buyers and sellers," *Lexology*, November 2, 2015, https://www.lexology.com/library/detail.aspx?g=b0cd0f45-d27a-4c51-9978-3840f4bdd394.

10 For additional reading related to the "run on repo," see: Adam Copeland, Antoine Martin, and Michael Walker (2014), "Repo runs: Evidence from the tri-party repo market," *Journal of Finance, 69*(6), 2343–2380; Gary Gorton and Andrew Metrick (2010), "Regulating the shadow banking system," *Brookings Papers on Economic Activity* (Fall), 261–312; Gary Gorton and Andrew Metrick (2012), "Securitized banking and the run on repo," *Journal of Financial Economics, 104*(3), 425–451; Gary B. Gorton and Andrew Metrick (2012, October), *Who Ran on Repo?* (NBER Working Paper No. 18455) (Cambridge, MA: National Bureau of Economic Research), see https://www.nber.org/papers/w18455.pdf; Peter Hördahl and Michael King (2008, December), "Developments in repo markets during the financial turmoil," *Bank for International Settlements Quarterly Review*, pp. 37–53; Arvind Krishnamurthy, Stefan Nagel, and Dmitry Orlov (2014), "Sizing up repo," *Journal of Finance, 69*(6), 2381–2417; Zoltan Pozar and Manmohan Singh (2011), *The non-bank nexus and the shadow banking system* (IMF Working Paper WP/11/289).

11 For additional reading related to the "run on the banks" in the Great Depression, see:

W. A. Barnett and M. Chauvet (2011), "How better monetary statistics could have signaled the financial crisis," *Journal of Econometrics, 161*, 6–23; B. Bernanke (1995), "The macroeconomics of the great depression: A comparative approach," *Journal of Money, Credit and Banking, 27* (1), 1–28; K. Brunner and A.H. Meltzer (1968), "What did we learn from the monetary experience of the United States in the Great Depression?", *Canadian Journal of Economics 1* (2), 334–348; O. Damette and A. Parent (2018), "Did liquidity shortage episodes induce a shift in the Fed's

monetary policy over the Great Depression?" *Macroeconomic Dynamics, 22,* Special
Issue 7 (Recent Insights into Financial, Housing, and Monetary Markets) October 2018, 1727–1749.

12 Financial Stability Board.

13 Ibid.

14 When Coca-Cola issues more stock, it simply adds to its existing outstanding supply
of shares, which trade under the symbol KO on the New York Stock exchange.
When Coca-Cola issues bonds, however, it typically creates a new bond each time,
and this is generally the case for most corporations. As a result, there tends not to be
deep liquidity for individual corporate bonds.

15 Electronically Traded Funds are portfolios of financial securities (stocks, bonds, other)
that trade like a single security on an exchange.

16 BoA Merrill Lynch Global Research, S&P Leveraged Commentary & Data.

17 Moody's, "Loan Covenant Quality Indicator ends 2017 with weakest ever yearly
score," April 19, 2018, and LeveragedLoan.com, "Covenant-lite Leveraged Loans:
After Default, Whither Recoveries?," July 23, 2018.

 Covenants are the terms and conditions that borrowers must adhere to in conjunction with loans that have been given, and "covenant-lite" is a reference to weaker
terms and conditions being imposed. With a record issuance of loans and leveraged
loans, and with non-banks becoming increasingly active in these loans (see Miriam
Gottfried and Rachel Louise Ensign (2018, August 12), "The new business banker:
A private-equity firm. Firms are lending more where traditional banks won't – and
sometimes competing with them, too," *Wall Street Journal*), it is a phenomenon worth
monitoring. So too are nuances of borrowing dynamics that may suddenly emerge,
such as the increasing practice of "collateral stripping," whereby borrowers seek to
move collateral out of reach of creditors.

18 Among the safeguards enjoyed by traditional banks, and by the users of traditional
banks, are the provision of deposit insurance, bank access to the short-term credit
discount window of the Federal Reserve, and bank access to the Federal Reserve
check-clearing and inter-bank system.

 In a speech on November 8, 2013 entitled "The crisis as a classic financial panic" at
the Fourteenth Jacques Polak Annual Research Conference, Washington, DC, Ben
Bernanke stated in reference to challenges of the Great Recession that, "The Fed lent
not only to banks, but, seeking to stem the panic in wholesale funding markets, it also
extended its lender-of-last-resort facilities to support nonbank institutions, such as
investment banks and money market funds, and key financial markets, such as those
for commercial paper and asset-backed securities." See https://www.federalreserve.
gov/newsevents/speech/bernanke20131108a.htm.

19 Attributed to John Wanamaker, 1838–1922, regarded as a pioneer in marketing.

20 SEC, Division of Economic and Risk Analysis, and in the context of US GAAP
taxonomy.

21 In some instances data providers focus on normalizing and cleansing numerical data
within filings to help ensure integrity of reported values.

22 Built between 1712 and 1732, the architecture of the library apparently served as
inspiration for the Star Wars film *Attack of the Clones.*

23 Richard Sears had successfully experimented with mail-order businesses prior to this
with specialty products such as watches and jewelry, but it was in 1893 that Sears teamed
with Alvah Roebuck and they decided to greatly expand their catalogue offerings.

24 Among the ways in which this was transformational was that in late 1800s and early
1900s, many African Americans were finding themselves discriminated against in commerce. Mail-order deliveries greatly facilitated an availability of goods, along with the
extension of credit, that some physical stores simply would not help to provide: see
 https://en.wikipedia.org/wiki/Sears, and Derek Thompson (2017, September 25),
"The history of Sears predicts nearly everything Amazon is doing," *The Atlantic,*

https://www.theatlantic.com/business/archive/2017/09/sears-predicts-amazon/
540888/.
25 Alfred D. Chandler Jr. (1977), *The Visible Hand: The Managerial Revolution in American
Business* (Boston, MA: Belknap Press).

Bibliography

Acharjya, D.P., & Kauser Ahmed, P. (2016). A survey on big data analytics: Challenges,
open research issues and tools. *International Journal Advanced Computer Science Application*,
7 (2016), pp. 511–518.

Barnett, W. A., & Chauvet, M. (2011). How better monetary statistics could have signaled
the financial crisis. *Journal of Econometrics*, *161*, 6–23.

Benjelloun, F.-Z., Ait Lahcen, A., & Belfkih, S. (2015). An overview of big data opportunities, applications and tools. *Intelligent Systems and Computer Vision (ISCV)*, 2015 (pp. 1–6).
New York: IEEE.

Bernanke, B. (2013, November 8). The crisis as a classic financial panic. Speech given at
the 14th Jacques Polak Annual Research Conference, Washington, DC. Retrieved
from https://www.federalreserve.gov/newsevents/speech/bernanke20131108a.htm.

Bernanke, B. (1995). The macroeconomics of the great depression: A comparative
approach. *Journal of Money*, Credit and Banking, 27(1), 1–28.

Brunner, K., & Meltzer, A. H. (1968). What did we learn from the monetary experience of
the United States in the Great Depression? Canadian Journal of Economics 1(2), 334–348.

Chandler, A.D., Jr. (1977). The visible hand: The managerial revolution in American business
(Boston, MA: Belknap Press).

Chen, C.L.P., & Zhang, C.-Y. (2014). Data-intensive applications, challenges, techniques
and technologies: A survey on big data. *Information Science*, *275* (2014), pp. 314–347.

Chen, M., Mao, S., & Liu, Y. (2014). Big data: A survey. *Mobile Networks Applications*, *19*,
171–209.

Copeland, A., Martin, A., & Walker, M. (2014). Repo runs: Evidence from the tri-party
repo market. *Journal of Finance*, *69*(6), 2343–2380.

Coronel, C., & Morris, S. (2016). *Database systems: Design, implementation, & management*.
Boston, MA: Cengage Learning.

Covenant-lite leveraged loans: After default, whither recoveries? (2018, July 23). *Levera-
gedLoan.com*.

Damette, O., & A. Parent, A. (2018). Did liquidity shortage episodes induce a shift in the
Fed's monetary policy over the Great Depression? *Macroeconomic Dynamics*, *22*, Special
Issue 7 (Recent Insights into Financial, Housing, and Monetary Markets) October 2018,
1727–1749.

De Carvalho, O.M., Roloff, E., & Navaux, P.O. (2013). A survey of the state-of-the-art in
event processing. Paper presented at the 11th Workshop on Parallel and Distributed
Processing (WSPPD).

Di Martino, B., Aversa, R., Cretella, G., & Esposito, A. (2014). Big data (lost) in the cloud.
International Journal Big Data Intelligence, *1* (2014), pp. 3–17.

Dinsmore, T. (2016). Streaming analytics. In *Disruptive analytics* (pp. 117–144). New York:
Springer.

Emani C.K., Cullot, N., & Nicolle, C. (2015). Understandable big data: A survey. *Computer
Science Review*, *17* (2015), 70–81.

Fang, H., Zhang, Z., Wang, C.J., Daneshmand, M., Wang, C., & Wang, H. (2015).
A survey of big data research. *IEEE Network*, *29* (2015), 6–9.

Furht, B., & Villanustre, F. (2016). Introduction to big data. In *Big data technologies and applications* (pp. 3–11). Cham: Springer International Publishing.

Gandomi, A., & Haider, M. (2015). Beyond the hype: Big data concepts, methods, and analytics. *International Journal Information Management, 35*(2015), 137–144.

Gorton, G., & Metrick, A. (2010). Regulating the shadow banking system. *Brookings Papers on Economic Activity* (Fall), 261–312.

Gorton, G., & Metrick, A. (2012). Securitized banking and the run on repo. *Journal of Financial Economics, 104*(3), 425–451.

Gorton, G.B., & Metrick, A. (2012, October). *Who ran on repo?* (NBER Working Paper No. 18455). Cambridge, MA: National Bureau of Economic Research. Retrieved from https://www.nber.org/papers/w18455.pdf.

Gottfried, M., and Ensign, R.L. (2018, August 12). The new business banker: A private-equity firm. Firms are lending more where traditional banks won't – and sometimes competing with them, too. *Wall Street Journal.*

Hördahl, P., & King, M. (2008, December). Developments in repo markets during the financial turmoil. *Bank for International Settlements Quarterly Review*, pp. 37–53.

Hughes, T. (2018, November 9). Credit risk assessment: The benefits of text-based analysis. *Global Association of Risk Professionals*. Retrieved from https://www.garp.org/#!/risk-intelligence/all/all/a1Z1W000004BP1EUAW.

Khan, N., Yaqoob, I., Hashem, I.A., Inayat, Z., Ali, W.K., Alam, M., Shiraz, M., Gani, A. (2014). Big data: Survey, technologies, opportunities, and challenges. *Science World Journal.*

Krishnamurthy, A., Nagel, S., and Orlov, D. (2014). Sizing up repo. *Journal of Finance, 69* (6), 2381–2417.

Krishnan, K. (2013). *Data warehousing in the age of big data* (1st edition). San Francisco: Morgan Kaufmann.

Kune, R., Konugurthi, P.K., Agarwal, A., Chillarige, R.R., & Buyya, R. (2016). The anatomy of big data computing. *Software: Practical Experience, 46* (1) (Special Issue: Cloud and big data computing), 79–105.

Lee, I. (2017). Big data: Dimensions, evolution, impacts, and challenges. *Business Horizons 60*(3), 293–303.

Loan Covenant Quality Indicator ends 2017 with weakest ever yearly score. (2018, April 19). *Moody's.*

Loganathan A., Sinha, A., Muthuramakrishnan, V., & Natarajan, S. (2014). A systematic approach to big data. *International Journal Computer Science Information Technology, 4*(9), 869–878.

Lovalekar, S. (2014). Big data: An emerging trend in future. *International Journal Computer Science Information Technology, 5*, 538–541.

Luo, C., Li, T., Chen, H., & Fujita, H. (2016). Efficient updating of probabilistic approximations with incremental objects. *Knowledge-Based Systems, 109*(2016), 71–83.

Lyko, K., Nitzschke, M., & Ngonga Ngomo, A.-C. (2016). Big data acquisition. In J.M. Cavanillas, E. Curry, & W. Wahlster (Eds.), *New horizons for a data-driven economy* (pp. 39–61). Cham: Springer.

Manoochehri, M. (2013). *Data just right: Introduction to large-scale data and analytics.* Upper Saddle River, NJ: Addison-Wesley.

Mazumder, S. (2016). Big data tools and platforms. In S. Yu & S. Guo (Eds.), *Big data concepts, theories, and applications* (pp. 29–128). Cham: Springer.

McAfee, A. & Brynjolfsson, E. (2012). Big data: The management revolution. *Harvard Business Review, 90* (2012), 60–68.

Najafabadi, M.M., Villanustre, F., Khoshgoftaar, T. M., Seliya, N., Wald, R., & Muharemagic, E. (2015). Deep learning applications and challenges in big data analytics. *Journal Big Data, 2*(1), 1.

Pozar, Z., & Singh, M. (2011). *The non-bank nexus and the shadow banking system.* (IMF Working Paper WP/11/289).

Prasad, B.R., & Agarwal, S. (2016). Comparative study of big data computing and storage tools: A review. *International Journal Database Theory Applications, 9* (2016), 45–66.

Qiu, J., Wu, Q., Ding, G., Xu, Y., & Feng, S. (2016). A survey of machine learning for big data processing. *EURASIP Journal Advanced Signal Processing* (2016), 1–16.

Radha, K. & Rao, B.T. (2016). A study on big data techniques and applications. *International Journal Advanced Application Science, 5* (2016), 101–108.

Raghav, R.S., Pothula, S., Vengattaraman, T., & Ponnurangam, D. (2016). A survey of data visualization tools for analyzing large volume of data in big data platform. *International Conference on Communication and Electronics Systems (ICCES)*, IEEE (2016), pp. 1–6.

Rajaraman, V. (2016). Big data analytics. *Resonance, 21*(2016), 695–716.

Salleh, K.A., & Janczewski, L. (2016). Technological, organizational and environmental security and privacy issues of big data: A literature review. *Procedia Computer Science, 100* (2016), pp. 19–28.

Sangeetha, J., & Prakash, V.S.J. (2017). A survey on big data mining techniques. *International Journal Computer Science Information Security, 15* (2017), 482.

SBI Sumishin Net Bank succeeds in using blockchain for their mission-critical systems: Using "mijin" by Tech Bureau Corp. (2016, October 10). *Mijin.*

Schmarzo, B. (2013). *Big data: Understanding how data powers big business.* Hoboken, NJ: John Wiley & Sons.

Sears. (n.d.). In *Wikipedia.* Retrieved June 17, 2019, from https://en.wikipedia.org/wiki/Sears.

Shireesha, R. (2016). *A study of tools, techniques, and trends for big data analytics. IJACTA, 4 (2016)*, 152–158.

Skourletopoulos, G. (2017). Big data and cloud computing: A survey of the state-of-the-art and research challenges. In C. Mavromoustakis, G. Mastorakis, & C. Dobre (Eds.), *Advances in mobile cloud computing and big data in the 5G era* (pp. 23–41). Cham: Springer.

Tax issues for repo buyers and sellers. (2015, November 2). *Lexology.* Retrieved from https://www.lexology.com/library/detail.aspx?g=b0cd0f45-d27a-4c51-9978-3840f4bdd394.

Thompson, D. (2017, September 25). The history of Sears predicts nearly everything Amazon is doing. *The Atlantic.* Retrieved from https://www.theatlantic.com/business/archive/192017/09/sears-predicts-amazon/540888/.

Tsai, C.W. (2016). Big data analytics. In B. Furht & F. Villanustre (Eds.), *Big data technologies and applications* (pp. 13–52). Cham: Springer.

Wang, L. (2016). Machine learning in big data. *International Journal Advanced Applications Science, 4* (2016), 117–123.

Wu, X. Zhu, X., W., G.-Q., & Ding, W. (2014). Data mining with big data. *IEEE Transfer Knowledge Data Engineering, 26* (2014), 97–107.

PART II

Digital finance and traditional finance

4

THEORETICAL FOUNDATIONS AND MODERN APPLICATIONS

In the swirl of modern advancements there can be the understandable inclination to regard innovations as being without precedent, and by extension, to see the experiences leading up to those developments and those resulting from them as something entirely new. In some instances this might be the case, but oftentimes it is not. When the telegraph emerged, along with Morse code, a new language consisting of dots and dashes, information flows transformed supply chain management, consumer access and market share, and the dissemination of news and opinion. The telegraph even evolved from cable to wireless. Decades later, aided by another new language predicated on zeroes and ones, all manner of electronic devices are transforming the way business is done and how information is shared. From whence we came, we shall return. And with respect to formal theories related to practical financial applications, many of these have been recognized with a Nobel Prize in Economics, and others have significantly helped to advance the understanding and application of business practices in a variety of ways. Theory and historical precedence help provide context, understanding, and a cornerstone for future growth, as well as gentle reminders that some "new" ideas might have a rather long historical pedigree.

In *The Wealth of Nations*, Adam Smith refers to the fundamental role of information in a variety of political and economic contexts, but none are as succinct as the vignette related to the particular search practices of eighteenth-century seafaring entrepreneurs seeking to maximize their hit ratios in relation to a single key performance indicator (KPI); the presence of gold. It is also in *The Wealth of Nations* that Smith, who has long been regarded as the father of economics, first references the notion of "perfect information" and the enormous value of information generally, which over centuries has come to be identified with the fundamental tenets of free markets and competition.[1]

The following factors can be said to be key elements related to information dynamics:

- Speed
- Completeness
- Symmetry
- Accuracy

It is possible for each of the above to prevail all at once, but this is rare.

In the 1700s, the speed of information from colonial America to Great Britain was limited to the swiftness of the fastest schooner, and the news reports typically reflected the particular viewpoints of the author who had penned the document. In the late 1800s, the speed of information from New York to London was reduced from weeks to hours with the invention of the telegraph and laying of the transatlantic cable, and an increased diversity of views became available to readers. And in the late 1900s the speed of information was reduced again, from hours to fractions of a second, with the arrival of the internet and a proliferation in the number of channels available for sharing viewpoints.[2] Figure 4.1 offers a view of the stages of digital financial metrics, from creation to dissemination.

Perhaps we can think of the telegraph and internet as venues, with each serving multiple audiences. For example, telegraph audiences included people working in transportation, news, government business, and more. Messages could be

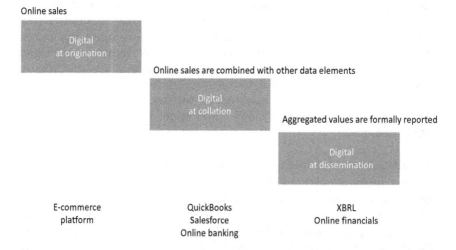

FIGURE 4.1   Stages of digital financial metrics: From creation to dissemination

sent over publicly shared telegraph wires (or wireless frequencies), or specially created private connections, and could be sent encrypted or non-encrypted. Internet channels support all manner of communications (emails, blogs, instant messaging, VOIP, video conferencing, webpages, text, images, video, audio, etc.) which can be encrypted or non-encrypted, sent via servers that are protected or unprotected, and on public or private venues.

Through the ages there have been a variety of mediums used for speedy communications, inclusive of fire and smoke, carrier pigeons, hot air balloons, and many others.

In a 1954 conference speech, Canadian professor Marshall McLuhan first made public the phrase "the medium is the message." In his 1964 book *Understanding Media: The Extensions of Man*, McLuhan said the following:

> The medium is the message because it is the medium that shapes and controls the scale and form of human association and action. The content or uses of such media are as diverse as they are ineffectual in shaping the form of human association. Indeed, it is only too typical that the "content" of any medium blinds us to the character of the medium.[3]

Whether the medium is cable, television, radio, print, or digital, McLuhan would assert that its form embeds itself in the message to influence how others perceive that message.

With decades now having passed since McLuhan's first pronouncements, it is perhaps worth revisiting the medium–content dynamic in a digital context. For example, in McLuhan's day, radio, television, and newspapers were rather distinct forms, with consumers unable to access one via the other (e.g., a newspaper could not be accessed via television). Today, the content of radio stations, television and cable stations, and newspapers can all be accessed digitally online. Moreover, the more popular sources of news for consumers today also include digital venues, such as Yahoo News, Google News, and the *Huffington Post*, ranking in the top three of preferred consumer sources.[4] With the proliferation of all these venues via what is arguably a single and rather large medium, "digital," and in a context whereby there is the sentiment among some that all manner of information seems to just blend into one large firehose of dissemination, perhaps the role of the "medium" is diminishing in deference to proliferating and obfuscating "content."[5] That "the medium is the message" is still seen as prescient and poignant today, speaks to the light it continues to shine on fundamental tenets of communication and the media, and both the opportunities and risks of those tenets.

The importance of information permeates modern theories of economics and finance, and has been further enshrined as Nobel Prizes have been awarded for the advancement of ideas to which information flows are fundamental. For example, the 2013 Nobel Prize in Economics was awarded to three individuals (Eugene Fama, Robert Shiller, and Lars Peter Hansen) for their respective ideas related to information dynamics. Table 4.1 presents a perspective of theory and effects.

TABLE 4.1 Theory and effects

THEORY	*Underlying elements*	*EFFECTS*	*Underlying elements*
MPT	Price-based: Risk (standard deviation of prices) versus return (price averages), with multi-asset portfolios benefitting from diversification effects achieved via varying correlations of prices	Small-cap effect	Price-based: Market capitalization is calculated as price times number of outstanding shares
CAPM	Price-and rate-based: Prices of specific securities are used in relation to prices of reference index values (to calculate betas), which are then used with reference to a risk free rate and an expected market rate of return	Value effect	Financial metrics and price-based: Per the Benjamin Graham approach, to qualify as a value investment (and hence benefit from a value effect) particular parameters must satisify specific conditions, with these parameters including a consideration of debt, book value, and earnings, plus price and dividend yield (and others)
		Low-volatility effect	Price-based: Relative standard deviations of prices across securities
		Momentum effect	Price-based: Trend of prices, where trend may be evaluated in a few different ways (unadjusted, moving averages, other)
		Knowledge effect	Metrics-based: Corporate knowledge investments, generally encapsulated under the rubric of "research and development"

What may be particularly striking to some in the above table is the degree to which prices factor into underlying dynamics of various market theories and effects. Very early on we are taught that a definition of something ought not to include reference to what we are defining (e.g., that it is better to define "run" as faster than a walk, rather than as "the act of running"), and yet so many ideas called upon to explain price dynamics invoke a consideration of prices. An exception to this is the knowledge effect. For a helpful overview of what may be regarded as R&D from a tax perspective, see https://www.swansonreed.com/examples-qualifying-non-qualifying-rd-activities/

Eugene Fama is associated with the Efficient Market Hypothesis (EMH), which states that with efficient markets "the current price [of an investment] should reflect all available information … so prices should change only based on unexpected new information." The EMH is further broken down into three forms; weak, semi-strong, and strong.

The weak form of EMH states that future stock prices cannot be predicted with reference to past stock prices. There is an adage in investing which states "The trend is your friend," though some investors are quick to add the qualifier that this is only the case "until the end when it bends." To be sure there are bull markets in which the trend is predominantly upward, and bear markets for which the trend is decidedly downward. A great challenge for trend-followers, however, is knowing precisely when bends will occur, and being able to correctly anticipate enough of them to perform better by actively trading anticipated turning points in the market versus simply buying an index fund linked to the S&P 500, or some other index.[6]

In a paper entitled "Technical analysis around the world," its authors set out to test over 5,000 technical analysis rules. Technical analysis essentially relies upon historical price data to drive current trading decisions. The authors conclude that technical trading rules do not result in returns that are statistically superior to what could have been expected from random data variation, although "There is some evidence that technical analysis works better in emerging markets, which is consistent with the literature that documents that these markets are less efficient, but this is not a strong result." Hardly a ringing endorsement, and other research draws similar conclusions.[7]

The semi-strong form of EMH posits that any published information is ineffective with predicting future prices, because such public information would already be reflected in a stock's price. There are some investors who engage in fundamental analysis, so-called because it involves the review of a stock issuer's profile including current financials, earnings history, debt burden, market share, intellectual property, and so forth. As these are all things included in a firm's public filings (as with quarterly 10-K and annual 10-Q reports), the semi-strong form of EMH states that by virtue of these being made public they have no value-add with respect to forecasting future value; anything that is already known today is priced into a stock's price today.

Fund managers who invest in market indices (S&P 500 or others) are generally called "passive" investors, while fund managers who actively engage in individual stock selection are called "active" investors. To be sure, there are successful cases of active investors who have been able to outperform investment benchmarks on a consistent year-in and year-out basis. Investors of years past such as Peter Lynch, Benjamin Graham, T. Rowe Price, Jr., John Neff, and Sir John Templeton certainly come to mind, for example. But there are also many studies that show how tough it is to be smarter than the marketplace, and the huge success of low-expense index-only firms like Vanguard suggests that there is value in passive strategies. The debate of "passive" versus "active" will likely continue for some time, though Morningstar has created a useful way of framing the debate with an index measurement approach.[8]

Finally, the strong form of EMH states that everything that is knowable, including unpublished information, is also already reflected in current prices. Even if you were to have insider information and could legally trade with it, you would not be able to gain any special price advantage relative to someone who did not have that insider information. Since trading on insider information is simply wrong, and with public disclosure being such a priority of regulators, it would seem that misuse of insider information should not be so prevalent. Generally speaking, the strong form of EMH would suggest that abrupt price moves in the absence of new information should not be common, but they are. This can be considered a vulnerability of EMH in the context of actual experiences, and other EMH weaknesses have been cited as well.[9]

Up until the emergence of the information economy in the late 1960s,[10] economists typically thought of barriers to entering into a particular business as consisting primarily of capital-based considerations. That is, large capital requirements would dictate which firms were more likely candidates to be considered as oligopolists or monopolists. Someone who woke up one morning and decided to be a player in the production of steel, automobiles, or ships, would have a considerable challenge ahead in terms of raising the capital necessary to build or acquire the necessary facilities and labor. In an information economy, barriers to entry have more to do with labor. And data.

Google started as a research project in 1996 by Larry Page and Sergey Brin when they were graduate students at Stanford University. As such, Page and Brin were able to leverage university resources, including when they sought to file a patent.[11] Brin was additionally supported by a National Science Foundation Graduate Fellowship, and when at Stanford both Brin and Page were working on the Stanford Digital Library Project (SDLP), which had the goal of "… enabling technologies for a single, integrated and universal digital library." The SDLP was in turn the beneficiary of funding from a variety of federal agencies. When the search engine came online, it was on Stanford's website, with the domain google.stanford.edu.[12]

Google came to life with what would seem to have been minimal monetary outlays for Page and Brin. Other noteworthy internet businesses that began in college dorms include Microsoft, Facebook, Dell, Dropbox, Kinkos, Reddit, Snapchat, Yahoo, WordPress, and others.[13] The very provenance of these businesses certainly supports the notion that information-centered businesses can, at least initially, get started with more labor than machinery.

Twenty years ago someone in business without an office outside of their home might be perceived as lacking credibility. Today credibility might be questioned due to the lack of a website. The financial services business that I launched in 2005 and subsequently sold to a client would never have gotten off the ground if I had not been able to leverage the power of the internet. I was also amazed, and continue to be so today, at the volume and size of business that was transacted without a personal handshake.

Curiously, although the internet has changed many things for business, a few things have remained remarkably consistent. First, the number of days required to legally set up a business for an operation has gone relatively unchanged since 1996.[14] Secondly, the percentage of firms to achieve sales of $100 million or more has remained pretty much the same since 1980, at 0.04% (that's four one-hundredths of 1%).[15] To be sure, there are now more unicorn companies (firms valued at $1 billion or more) emerging within narrower spans of time relative to any other period in history (adjusting for time value of money), and while their experience accounts for an extremely small subset of start-ups (in the third decimal place of a percentage, or thousandths of 1%), they are deserving of our consideration as an interesting phenomenon.

While the sheer number of unicorns that have appeared within such a span of time is certainly impressive, an equally daunting and related phenomenon is how fast firms have become unicorns in the past decade. Contributing factors, aside from the fact that they are clearly tapping into huge unmet needs, include the following:

- Low cost of capital.
- Availability of capital for technology/internet-related projects.
- Low regulatory environment.
- The global platform of the internet, which allows a good idea to have an accelerated take-off.
- Though hard to quantify, there is also the factor of a perception of "winner takes all," attributable to aggressive branding, scale, and network effects, and all of which have been greatly facilitated by the existence of the internet. Announcements of enormous war chests can also be intimidating to potential entrants.
- The relatively low number of founders required to get an enterprise started.

An element in common of each of these factors is their respective association with some aspect of a lowering of a potential barrier to entry. In the industrial age, the notion of associating higher market shares with lower barriers to entry was a contradiction in terms. Today it is this dichotomy that often helps unicorns to be successful, and the internet is the autobahn on which ideas seemingly travel without speed limits.

Figure 4.2 presents a more recent evolution of unicorns.

***

Another approach to the idea of big data is to take a closer look at "big." In the business world "big" is sometimes linked with conglomerates, oligopolies, or even monopolies, and with the idea that these structures convey power in the marketplace. Indeed, with the explicit goal of seeking to have a check against that power, the US Department of Justice references the Herfindahl–Hirschman Index (HHI) as a means of evaluating whether proposed mergers or acquisitions

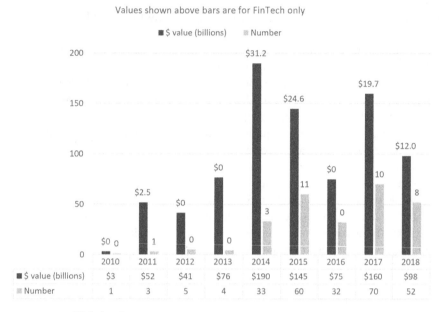

Values shown above bars are for FinTech only

■ $ value (billions)   ■ Number

	2010	2011	2012	2013	2014	2015	2016	2017	2018
■ $ value (billions)	$3	$52	$41	$76	$190	$145	$75	$160	$98
■ Number	1	3	5	4	33	60	32	70	52

FIGURE 4.2 Global unicorn start-ups

might result in a company having too much market share (see also Chapter 2 for more on the HHI).

At one time a monopoly was thought of in terms of its unique control over its own information (a utility knowing its own costs and setting its own prices), while today monopolies can also be thought of in terms of their unique control over the information of others.

In consideration of the power of knowledge, perhaps an HHI of data would be an appropriate metric for companies as well. Some types of data could be excluded; for example, health services companies necessarily need to collect personal medical information, and the uses of that data are set forth in HIPPA legislation and elsewhere. But massive amounts of data today do not meet the standards of medical or financial security, although they can nonetheless be extremely valuable to the companies collecting it and using it for their own purposes, or selling it to others.

Over a 24-hour period in July 2019 the Federal Trade Commission announced a $5B fine against Facebook related to privacy allegations, and the Department of Justice announced an antitrust investigation of Google, Apple, Facebook, and Amazon for monopolistic activities. Prior to 2019 the highest privacy fine was levied against Google for $148 million, and curiously in 2018 the European Commission set a fine of $5B against Google for an alleged antitrust matter (more on this in Chapter 2). Perhaps a revelation to come from the

DoJ's investigation is that privacy matters have been upgraded to a level of severity previously accorded to antitrust matters.

***

There is a long-standing interest in wanting to better understand determinants of equity performance. In 1990, Harry Markowitz and William Sharpe were recognized with a Nobel Prize in Economics for their contributions to this topic.[16] For Markowitz, his Modern Portfolio Theory (MPT) proposes that an investment's risk and return characteristics should not be viewed in isolation, but in a broader context of how the investment choice is situated in relation to a portfolio's overall risk–return profile.[17] William Sharpe's Capital Asset Pricing Model (CAPM) suggests that the equity market itself taken as a whole is the best metric for helping to explain any one particular equity's performance.[18]

Weaving itself into the theories of Markowitz and Sharpe is the EMH.

With EMH positing that investors are rational and that asset prices reflect full information, the rate of return on an investment is driven by the systematic risk (market risk) of the asset. This is reflected in the CAPM, where an equity's expected return is defined as being a risk-free rate plus a return factor that reflects the systematic risk associated with the equity. As such, the CAPM is consistent with MPT, since the latter asserts that an investor is compensated for market risk which cannot be eliminated by diversification, and is not compensated for idiosyncratic risk which can be eliminated with diversification.[19]

As an alternative to the EMH, which is sometimes seen as a complement to it, there is also said to be a behavioral view of what can influence equity prices. In brief, this school of thought asserts the notion that investors are capable of making, and do indeed often make, systematic errors with their investment decisions. As human beings, investors have particular biases they might act upon which can contribute to errors being made. An exercise I use at the start of every term when I teach finance at Columbia University is to ask students what they would pay for a pen that I hold up for them to see. I ask them to mark that price on a piece of paper, and I then ask them a second question: What price do you think someone else would pay for the same pen? In the years that I've done this, there has yet to be an instance where the average of the second price is lower than the average of the first price.[20] This optimistic bias as to what someone else might pay is a behavioral consideration. So too is an investor's under- or overreacting to news related to a company's growth prospects. The culmination of systematic risk related to a knowledge company in particular (i.e., the systematic risk that can be expected for any stock plus the systematic errors created by other investors owing to exigencies of knowledge-intensive firms) suggests that investors would need compensation for these accumulated risks; hence, abnormal returns for this class of companies.

Intuitively, there is a compelling narrative here with the notion of an investor requiring extra expected compensation for taking on additional risk, where that risk is in the form of an opaqueness related to a firm's knowledge investments. This intuition is supported by economic theory as well.[21]

***

While the writings of Markowitz and Sharpe help tremendously with establishing a theoretical context for us to think about matters related to digital finance, and in particular what helps to explain movements in stock prices, other influences have been cited by academics and practitioners over the years. These additional influences include:

- the small-cap effect,
- value effect,
- low-volatility effect, and
- momentum effect.[22]

And to these we add the knowledge effect, which is defined as being a pricing anomaly whereby persistent excess returns are experienced by highly innovative companies.

The knowledge effect is something Lev and Gu write about in *The End of Accounting*, though initial ideas on this topic were originally presented in a series of studies by Lev in the 1990s. Lev studied 20 years' worth of financial data and identified relationships between a firm's level of knowledge capital and its stock price performance. With additional research, Lev presented the hypothesis of a market inefficiency linked to missing information related to a company's knowledge investments. Lev's analysis suggests that the missing information contributes to investors consistently undervaluing highly innovative companies that generate above-average returns. To be clear, it's not so much the idea that relevant information is really missing, but that it is being unnecessarily obscured.[23]

Simply stated, knowledge is generally produced by a firm when it invests in research and development (R&D), educates its employees, and engages in marketing and advertising. The shortcoming that these investments tend not to come into full view of investors is largely attributable to accounting practices stemming from the 1970s. The anomaly has contributed to investors making a systematic error when evaluating the fundamentals of companies that are particularly engaged in knowledge development. As a result, this systematic error has surfaced with a persistent risk premium, or excess return, among companies with appreciable knowledge investments.

For more modern times, the start of the knowledge capital phenomenon is often traced back to 1971, when Intel released the first commercially available integrated semiconductor.[24] Since then, the technology can be said to have been an integral aspect of advancements in healthcare, DNA sequencing, smartphones and other mobile devices, robotics, advanced automation, digital distribution technologies, and more.

Meanwhile, soon after the 1971 commercialization of the semiconductor, US accounting regulations were adopted in 1974 to mandate that companies expense knowledge spending, and that they not be required to provide details of their knowledge activities.[25] As cited at the time by the Financial Accounting Standards Board (FASB), that particular information is "not sufficiently object-ive, is confidential in nature, or is beyond the scope of financial accounting."[26] Accordingly, R&D investments, marketing, brand development, employee train-ing, and more are today all required to be expensed.

An alternative to the expensing of knowledge would be to capitalize it; that is, not charge it against current period revenues, but record it as an asset on the balance sheet as an investment.[27]

There is certainly an intuitive appeal to the idea that an investment is some-thing that creates long-term value for a company, and hence should be capital-ized and recorded as an asset, whether tangible or intangible.[28] By forcing companies to expense knowledge investments, the FASB acted to deprive investors of information that could be helpful for evaluating innovative activities.[29]

Criticisms of SFAS No. 2 emerged soon after it was put into effect, as with a 1975 paper by Bierman and Dukes asserting that expensing R&D would con-tribute to "faulty measurement of income and changes in income through time."[30] Even the FASB stated that it "… did not undertake a major research effort for the project. The FASB staff interviewed a limited number of selected financial analysts and commercial banks and reviewed a substantial number of published financial statements."[31]

Meantime, recent work further supports findings of above-average equity returns for R&D-intensive companies. In seeking to understand this, Lev, Gu, and others generally see two possible explanations:

1. Above-average returns appear to be driven by a "systematic mispricing of shares" that stems from investor lack of information in terms of companies' knowledge investments. With the market slow to recognize future benefits of R&D, though being fully aware of the potential negative impact of large expenses (per R&D) on net profits, stock prices discount the perceived weight of expense outlays. In time, as R&D investments become publicly recognized, stock prices rise, often with analysts playing successive games of catch-up to keep pace with advancements. These bursts of favorable returns are what become manifest as "abnormal" returns.

   This explanation would be consistent with the behavior theory described earlier, whereby investors can under- and then overreact to imperfect flows of information.

2. Above-average returns are driven by the extra risk that investors bear with R&D-intensive equities, which stems from lack of full disclosure related to the expense treatment of knowledge investments.

   This explanation would also seem to be consistent with EMT, in which abnormal returns are the expected compensation for investors taking on extra risk in the absence of expensing details.

Lev in particular finds that named knowledge leaders have higher "future market share, future sales growth and future return on assets" relative to knowledge followers, and he additionally finds that both equity price volatility and earnings variability are lower with the former.[32]

***

In physics there is something we call the first law of thermodynamics, and it states that energy is something that cannot be created or destroyed. It can move around quite a bit, however, and perhaps seem to disappear in one place only to re-emerge somewhere else. For many, big data is about using data in creative ways to better understand where energy and opportunity may be retreating and where it may move next.

In the insurance world, for example, many people were complacent with just accepting the notion that there would be less revenue in the property and casualty sector due to the disappearance of retail outlets as a result of growth in internet sales. But the decline in insuring properties was simply replaced by growth in insurance revenues linked to covering risks involved with shipping.

And then there is the future of driverless cars. Many in the insurance world are lamenting an inevitable decline of revenues related to insuring drivers, but a shift will transpire whereby the risks posed by physical drivers will be replaced by those posed by lines of computer code and its associated hardware.

When the energy of one sector looks as though it is on the decline, look for where it might resurface; whether from human drivers to computer code, or shopping at a physical store to online, or anything else.

Follow the energy!

***

P*Q

While there are a variety of ways to make revenue generation into a complex subject, a rather simple and straightforward way to frame it all is within a context of P times Q (Price times Quantity, or P*Q).

If we take the prices of all the goods or services generated by a company and multiply those by the respective number of units sold, we have gross revenue. For some firms gross revenue may be equivalent to gross sales. Figure 4.3 presents steps in a hypothetical journey of sales data.

Can digital financial metrics comprise 100% of a firm's financial reporting data stream?

Data creation	Data collation	Data reporting
Online sales generate digital revenue numbers at point of sale	Revenues of individual sales are rolled up into an aggregate value	Results are collated for management to review

FIGURE 4.3   Steps in a hypothetical journey of sales data

Once revenues or sales are obtained, they can be adjusted in the following ways:

- Subtract cost of goods sold (COGS) to obtain gross profit.
- Deduct operating expenses to obtain operating income.
- Deduct non-operating income or expenses to obtain net income.

And also be viewed as a ratio to variables such as:

- Returns or refunds.
- Number of employees.
- Visitors (to Brick locations, or Click venues).
- Marketing expenditures, and more …

Figure 4.4 presents a more detailed perspective of P and Q and what they represent.

"P" might represent a single price, or a vector of several prices

Click price(s) might or might not differ from Brick price(s)

Price(s) can be fixed, or adjustable in relation to a variety of considerations (total purchases, loyalty points, special offers, etc.)

"Q" might represent a single product or service, or a vector of several products or services

Products and services available online may not be the same as at stores

Combinations of products and services online may not be the same as at stores

Supply chain management is important

When combined with other data, P and Q can be used to generate other insights such as KPIs related to customer experience, effectiveness of marketing, customer acquisition costs, and more.

FIGURE 4.4   Parsing P*Q

If the venue for P*Q is a website, then there can typically be much more data collected beyond simply recording transactions. Simply by virtue of a user using an online venue, even free online tools (Google Analytics, Bitly, Piwik) can report on such things as time spent on a webpage, pages visited prior to checkout, number of clicks per page, and so on.

As anyone who has studied economics can tell you (along with many others who have not), price is determined at the intersection of supply and demand. A good or service is provided when there is a seller willing to sell at a particular price, and a buyer willing to pay that price. Sometimes sellers and buyers might have a range of prices in mind at which they would be willing to transact, but with transactions ultimately occurring at particular price points. For any firm, decisions of what price to charge resides with the person(s) and process(es) designated for that role. However, whether prices are approved by someone on a quarterly basis or are continuously subject to change per an algorithm that captures all manner of customer and product data, prices are at the epicenter of a company's being. In brief, it is P*Q that determine revenues, and it is revenues less expenses that determines profitability.

Figure 4.5 presents a perspective on cash flows for various contexts of finance.

Let us now take a look at some pricing strategies across Bricks and Clicks.

Naturally, some industries may have greater flexibility than others with setting prices. For example, digital travel sites are generally in a position of having to pass along whatever airfares happen to be offered by the airlines, and it is hard to mark up prices because users are going to the site precisely to seek great deals.[33] With other sites, however, such as those with exclusive offerings of unique or luxury products or services, there can be some latitude with marking up prices, as well as flexibility with reducing prices on some goods to offset higher-priced items, hence using a diversified portfolio approach with the sales strategy.[34] Table 4.2 presents disruptors, innovators, and aggregators/disintermediaries in the context of P*Q, and Figure 4.6 delves into a perspective of P*Q in the context of Uber as a disruptor.

Raising flows: Banks, IPOs, friends and family, online venues

Managing flows: Asset managers, accountants

Protecting flows: Risk managers, insurance companies

Analyzing flows: Auditors, ecurities analysts

FIGURE 4.5 Follow the cash flows: Various contexts of finance

TABLE 4.2 Disruptors, innovators, and aggregators/disintermediators, and P*Q

High P and Q impact	Moderate P or Q impact	Little to no P or Q impact
Disruptors	Innovators	Aggregators/Disintermediators
Airbnb: Regarding P, Airbnb has opened up a wide spanse of pricing options for persons who seek lodging, appreciably weakening the price-setting power of hotels where limited supply was a dominant factor. As regards Q, the breadth of consumer choice has been dramatically expanded, and not just in terms of physical lodging characteristics but also in terms of services (or lack of them, often resulting in lower P). Airbnb has also been able to successfully apply its model on a global basis.	Ameritrade: As an intermediary between the stock market (exchanges) and investors, Ameritrade doesn't have much flexibility with P; prices of stocks are determined by the marketplace. Further, the core products (stocks) sold via Ameritrade's website are also non-differentiable (a share of stock in IBM purchased via Ameritrade is going to be the same share of IBM stock purchased from any other brokerage). The ability for users to transact online without human involvement, however, permits Ameritrade to lower its commissions with the benefit of a lower P relative to other firms.	TripAdvisor: As a venue that collates prices and services (P and Q), the value-add is more in the sourcing of multiple user options presented on a single platform.

Situational: Varying P for periods when demand is especially strong

Experiential: Varying P for a shared ride versus a single ride, or a ride in a standard car versus a luxury vehicle

Transparency: P is known to the user at the start of the ride

On the supply side of Q, Uber tapped into an entirely new segment of available drivers

On the demand side of Q, Uber transformed the operational elements of on-demand car transportation including ordering, availability, tracking, and payments

Global: The Uber P*Q model can be replicated across markets around the world

Uber qualifies as a disruptor with its material influence on dynamics affecting both P and Q on a variety of levels

FIGURE 4.6 P*Q in the context of Uber as a disruptor

A key differentiation between Bricks and Clicks can be the process whereby payment is exchanged for goods or services; that is, payments for P*Q.

With Bricks, goods are typically provided immediately and in a near-simultaneous exchange for a customer's payment. Payment can be in the form of cash, check, a debit/credit card, or increasingly in the form of an electronic payment via a mobile device.

For Clicks, digital goods are typically provided immediately and in a near-simultaneous exchange for a customer's payment, and with payment being per some electronic method only (i.e., no physical exchange of cash, paper checks, or plastic cards). By digital goods we mean downloadable software, images, music, documentation, or confirmations, among other possibilities. It might be a song from iTunes, the purchase or sale of an equity or bond, the purchase of auto insurance, or any other transaction that can be fully executed online. To describe it in a slightly different way: if it can be sent via an email as an attachment or otherwise, then it is digital.

Of course, it is also possible to purchase physical goods online, and in these instances there is typically a lag between the moment an order is placed and when payment is provided, and when the goods ultimately arrive. It is increasingly the case that delivery is made within 24 hours of when a purchase is made, and with continuous efforts to shorten the time span.

But that's not the end of the story.

With Bricks, it is entirely possible that an in-store purchase will be returned. Even when a customer can see, sample, touch, and perhaps even experience an item in person, returns are made from time to time. Indeed, it is estimated that about 9% of Brick purchases are returned.[35] With Clicks, not surprisingly, the frequency with which returns are made is of a magnitude greater than with Bricks, and is estimated at 30%.[36] Further, 92% of online consumers indicate they would buy again from a retailer if the returns process were easy; 79% of consumers want free shipping; and 67% of online shoppers check the returns policy page prior to making a purchase.[37]

Figure 4.7 shows a simple P*Q finance model for consumer retail.

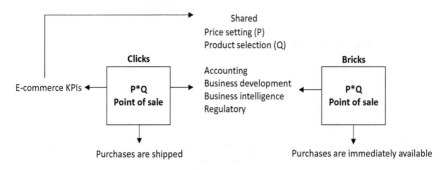

FIGURE 4.7 A simple P*Q finance model for consumer retail

As for cancelation experiences involving services, these appear to follow the same pattern as physical products; cancelations seem to occur in greater frequency with Clicks relative to Bricks. That is, businesses offering in-person services (e.g., by-appointment beauty salons or barber shops, or auto repairs and maintenance) experience no-shows with a lower frequency than online businesses offering services by internet (e.g., tax advising consultations, webinars, hotel and travel reservations, and so on). Perhaps the intuition here is that breaking an appointment with someone who will ultimately be faced (a barber or plumber) is more difficult than breaking one with someone who seems more anonymous (an online hotel representative), or quite possibly it's even more basic that that; maybe, on balance, in-person appointments are generally considered to be more important (doctors, mechanics) than those arranged as online meetings. Perhaps there is sometimes a monetary consideration, whereby a deposit is forfeited for a no-show. In this regard it is of interest to note that in 2018 the state of California put into effect a law to make it easier for consumers to cancel subscription services online. Specifically, the law provides that consumers who accept an automatic renewal or continuous service online (for web hosting, music or streaming content, cyber protection, newspaper delivery via physical or electronic venues, or similar) must also be able to cancel that service online (e.g., without having to make a phone call).[38]

In some instances it may be possible to initiate steps that may help to reduce cancelation experiences. For example, it has been found that if hoteliers reach out to consumers after they make a reservation well in advance of the date of their stay, this can help increase the percentage of those consumers who actually end up keeping their reservation.[39]

The greater frequency of returns to online providers of goods can perhaps be explained with the following considerations:

- In many instances, the return process is marketed as being an incentive for purchasing from a particular online provider (e.g., return shipping is free).
- Because a shopper is not able to see, sample, touch, or experience an item in person, a variety of colors, styles, and sizes might be ordered, with the intent of returning the items that are subsequently deemed as undesirable.
- There is an anonymity factor: a return does not require an in-person visit, explanation, or confrontation.

So at least as far as return patterns for goods go, very different experiences can exist within Bricks and Clicks. In brief, with Clicks, a customer's payment marks the beginning of a series of subsequent events, rather than the completion of a transaction as in the case of Bricks. With Clicks, after a customer payment is made, the goods need to be sourced, shipped, and delivered undamaged. Then, owing to the greater likelihood of returns relative to Bricks, Clicks are involved with shipping risks associated with unwanted items, and must then issue any applicable refunds or credits. And finally, it has been shown to generally be the case that items are returned sooner to Bricks relative to Clicks, and this imposes lag considerations for the latter.[40]

These various considerations require Clicks to think more about internal controls and accounting policies than their Brick counterparts, and technological solutions are emerging as powerful tools. As Clicks are based online and able to collect enormous amounts of data related to user preferences and purchasing patterns, this information can be analyzed to seek clues related to strategies for maximizing customer service experiences while minimizing costly returns.

Another challenge for Clicks in this regard relates to establishing effective revenue recognition practices. For example, Clicks already know that they will receive a significant number of returns, which will mean a lower revenue relative to original sales, and then there are the expenses incurred with return shipping. Figure 4.8 offers a perspective of how much estimation can go into the reported revenues of a firm, when uncertainties related to considerations such as returns can mean making some educated guesses.

There is also the matter of inventory management. With Bricks, a clerk's casual walk to the storage room can provide them with a good idea of what is on hand to augment the items on showroom shelves. But with Clicks, multiple warehouses thousands of miles apart might be feeding miscellaneous products onto web pages and ultimately into virtual shopping carts, while it is physically impossible to get a personal glance at what is in stock at a given moment in time. Plus, as there is a greater frequency of returns for online purchases, Clicks need to know when popular items are coming back so they can be passed along to another buyer.

Integrated systems, tested policies, and real-time insights are crucial, and success requires not only the necessary pieces, but a vision and commitment to bringing them together into an effective cohesive whole.

***

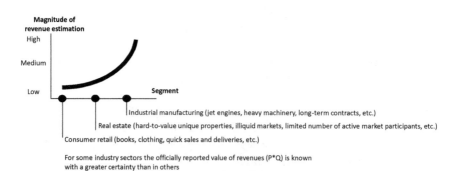

FIGURE 4.8   Magnitude of estimation with officially reported revenues

The Law of One Price is a commonly cited cornerstone of economics. It holds that the price of identical products ought to be the same regardless of where they are sold in a free market (after adjusting for any currency conversions) when there are no trade restrictions. On the other hand, the term "price dispersion" is a reference to how price differences can exist for identical products across sellers and markets (after any currency adjustments) in the absence of trade restrictions. In brief, the Law of One Price is more of a theoretical construct than a practical consideration, but it can be of great help as a context for better understanding price dynamics and the key role of P among Bricks and Clicks.

Bricks are of course free to set prices for goods at whatever level they please, though with the consideration that a price that is too high could result in no sales at all and a price that is too low may not cover the COGS and operational expenses. Beyond that, however, sellers may find it advantageous to charge asymmetric prices across goods so as to capture a differentiation among buyers who want to purchase everything in one location (one-stop shopping) relative to buyers who are willing to purchase different goods at various locations. For goods that are exclusively sold at Bricks, sellers might hope that buyers will find it inconvenient to go from store to store in search of a bargain. The internet is getting in the way of this, however, as buyers can easily check out Brick prices online, or even make their desired purchase at a Click instead of a Brick.[41] In brief, for goods that are fairly homogeneous in nature, the internet is serving to advocate more for the Law of One Price rather than foster price dispersion, with the following implications:

- Sellers of homogeneous goods who are unable to achieve a low cost base on a par with competitors will find it difficult to succeed.
- Ways to emphasize product uniqueness (e.g., how it the product is not truly homogeneous) may prove to be a helpful strategy.
- Introducing other dimensions of product sales (e.g., high levels of customer service, convenience, or relationship building) could be beneficial.

Amazon can be thought of as a place where the Law of One Price is very much a live case study playing out for all to see. For a variety of homogeneous goods, Amazon is making it easy for consumers to find competitive pricing and easy delivery. After a time, however, when perhaps other providers have left the marketplace owing to Amazon's dominance, Amazon might be able to find product segments where it can raise prices, even with homogeneous items. Perhaps as a hedge of sorts for a "race to the bottom" context, whereby firms compete to see who can go the lowest in price yet still stay in business, Amazon is experimenting with a variety of product-positioning strategies such as Amazon Boutique, which seeks to offer consumers less homogeneous/more unique choices in products.[42]

Figure 4.9 helps to illustrate the evolving dynamic of price dispersion in the context of Bricks and Clicks, and Figure 4.10 presents XTechs in relation to Bricks in the context of P*Q.

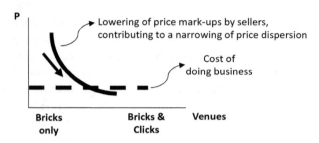

FIGURE 4.9   Evolution of price dispersion and price discovery, Bricks to Clicks

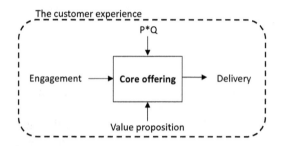

FIGURE 4.10   XTechs in relation to Bricks in the context of P*Q

***

While it can be exciting to think that so much of what is happening today in digital finance is all shiny and new and on the cusp of new frontiers (and much of it is), there is also great value in considering the theoretical underpinnings of these advancements, as many of their core attributes date back decades, if not centuries. As such, there is a wealth of experience and insight we can draw upon to learn from, and build upon.

Notes

1 *The Wealth of Nations*, Adam Smith (Pilgrim Classics, 2015), p. 271.
2 Without trying to twist this particular analysis into a pretzel of multidirectional twists and turns that all end up describing the same thing, perhaps we can think of the telegraph and internet as venues, with each serving multiple channels. For example, telegraph channels conveyed messaging related to transportation, news of all sorts, government communications, data, and other communications. Messages could be sent over publicly shared telegraph wires (or wireless frequencies), or specially created private connections,

and could be sent encrypted or non-encrypted. Internet channels support all manner of communications (emails, blogs, instant messaging, VOIP, video conferencing, web pages, text, images, video, audio, etc.), and can be encrypted or non-encrypted, sent via servers that are protected or unprotected, and appear on public or private venues.

Through the ages there have been a variety of mediums used for speedy communications, including fire and smoke, carrier pigeons, hot-air balloons, and more.

3   Marshall McLuhan (1964), *Understanding Media: The Extensions of Man* (Cambridge, MA: First MIT Press), p. 9.

4   "Top 15 most popular news websites" (continuously updated), *EBiz MBA Guide*, http://www.ebizmba.com/articles/news-websites (last accessed June 2019).

5   A thought-provoking article on this topic is "Whatever happened to the news?" (n.d.) by Daniel Hallin, *Center for Media Literacy*, http://www.medialit.org/read ing-room/whatever-happened-news.

6   John Bogle, the founder of The Vanguard Group, is said to have created the first index fund (matching an investment fund's performance to a market index such as the S&P 500). Index funds are generally characterized by fees that are lower than those for actively managed (non-index) funds.

7   See A.W. Lo, H. Mamaysky, and J. Wang (2000), "Foundations of technical analysis: Computational algorithms, statistical inference, and empirical implementation," *The Journal of Finance*, 55(4), 1705–1765, and C.H. Park & S.H. Irwin (2007), "What do we know about the profitability of technical analysis?" *Journal of Economic Surveys* 21, 4, 786–826.

8   Information on Morningstar's Active/Passive Barometer work may be found at https://www.morningstar.com/lp/active-passive-barometer.

9   A fairly balanced overview of the EMH may be found at Trevir Nath (2015, October 15), "Investing basics: What is the efficient market hypothesis, and what are its shortcomings?" *Nasdaq*. https://www.nasdaq.com/article/investing-basics-what-is-the-efficient-market-hypothesis-and-what-are-its-shortcomings-cm530860.

10   There are, to be sure, a variety of thoughts on when and how to mark the formal close of the Industrial age and the advent of the Information age. From the standpoint of the economy, one commonly cited demarcation references the work of M.U. Porat. Porat is said to have stunned a room of OECD bureaucrats with the announcement in 1975 that during the late 1960s the portion of US labor income linked with the information sector of the economy had already crossed over the 50% threshold; more people were earning income from information-related jobs than from industry. See M.U. Porat (1977), *The information economy, vol. 1* (Washington, D.C.: Office of Telecommunications, US Department of Commerce. For an engaging account of Porat's work and a brief history of the Information economy, see Benoît Godin, (2008), "The information economy: The history of a concept through its measurement, 1949–2005," *History and Technology*, 24(3).

11   In exchange, Stanford University was provided an early equity stake in Google.

12   See "Google of Larry Page and Sergey Brin" (n.d.), *History-Computer.com*, http://his tory-computer.com/Internet/Conquering/Google.html, and David A. Vise and Mark Malseed (2018), *The Google story: Inside the hottest business, media and technology success of our time* (New York: Random House), https://books.google.com/books/about/The_Google_Story.html?id=zyTCAlFPjgYC&source=kp_cover.

Interestingly, Google's own published history (see https://www.google.com/about/company/history/) makes little mention of resources or support other than to cite how an early search engine was run on Stanford servers.

Stanford's website provides PDFs of annual reports back to 1998, and states "Copies of past printed annual reports are available by calling 650-725-8396" (see at http://annualreport.stanford.edu/2015/). Callers requesting annual reports for 1996 and 1997

(Page's first web crawler was launched in March 1996), might be informed that they
need to stop by Stanford's offices to read the documents in person.

13 See Elizabeth Hoyt (2015, September 24), "20 of the coolest college start-ups ever,"
    Fast Web. http://www.fastweb.com/student-life/articles/the-20-of-the-coolest-
    college-start-ups-ever.

14 See http://data.worldbank.org/indicator/IC.REG.DURS.

15 See Paul Kedrosky (2013, May), *The constant: Companies that matter* (Kansas City, MO:
    Ewing Marion Kauffman Foundation), https://www.kauffman.org/~/media/kauffma
    n_org/research%20reports%20and%20covers/2013/05/companiesthatmatter.pdf.

16 To be sure, there are important foundational investment theories that predate Marko-
    witz and Sharpe, and these include the following:

    • John M. Keynes and Irving Fisher: Investments are made until the present value
      of expected future revenues are equal to the opportunity cost of capital;
    • Neoclassical theory, accelerator principle, and Tobin's Q: These assume an optimiza-
      tion behavior by the investor, whereby the neoclassical Tobin theories explicitly
      assume profit maximization and the accelerator principle assumes this implicitly.

    For a helpful overview of these investment theories, see Johan E. Eklund (2013),
    Theories of investment: A theoretical review with empirical applications, Working Paper
    (Sweden: Swedish Entrepreneurship Forum).

17 Markowitz presents these ideas in an essay entitled "Portfolio selection," published in
    1952 in the *Journal of Finance*, as well as in his book *Portfolio selection: Efficient diversifi-
    cation of investments* (New Haven, CT: Yale University Press), printed in 1959.

18 Sharpe presents these ideas in "Capital asset prices: A theory of market equilibrium
    under conditions of risk," *The Journal of Finance*, 19(3), 425–442, published in 1964.

19 Systematic risk is the risk inherent in the aggregate market that cannot be moderated
    via diversification, while unsystematic or idiosyncratic risk is specific to a firm or
    industry and can be moderated with diversification.

20 The second price also tends to have a lower standard deviation than the first price.

21 The perfection of information is an important notion in game theory, for example
    when considering sequential and simultaneous games. A simultaneous game is one in
    which each player chooses their action without knowledge of the action(s) chosen by
    others. Sequential games are those in which players take turns, such as by alternating
    moves. To the extent that such scenarios can help replicate actual business environ-
    ments, game theory constructs can help to evaluate the way firms might actually
    respond to one another in various situations, for example by means of marketing or
    pricing strategies.

22 • Small-cap effect: The small-cap effect (or small-capitalization effect, or small-
      firm effect) is observed when smaller firms outperform larger companies.
    • Value effect: An observed tendency of so-called value stocks to outperform the
      market in the long term relative to non-value stocks, and whereby value stocks
      are defined with reference to a particular stock-selection methodology (such as
      Benjamin Graham's criteria, explained in *Security analysis,* (2008, with David
      Dodd, New York: McGraw-Hill) and in other works he has authored.
    • Low-volatility effect: The low-volatility anomaly is the observation that port-
      folios of low-volatility stocks may have higher risk-adjusted returns relative to
      portfolios with high-volatility stocks.
    • Momentum effect: A tendency for rising equity prices to rise further, and falling
      prices to fall further.

23 Baruch Lev and Feng Gu (2016), *The end of accounting and the path forward for investors
    and managers* (Hoboken, NJ: John Wiley).

24 Which is to say that premodern knowledge advancements could perhaps be attribut-
    able to the printing press, or to the telegraph, which each in their own way

contributed appreciably to the dissemination of knowledge which theretofore had not enjoyed the same opportunities for dissemination.

25 Details are encapsulated in "Statement of financial accounting standards no. 2," October 1974; a direct write-off of R&D expenses is required.

26 See "Statement of financial accounting standards no. 2," October 1974.

27 Among recent discussions related to the definition and treatment of intangibles, there has been the OECD's initiative, "Guidance for tax administrations on the application of the approach to hard-to-value intangibles", June 2018 (seeking to broaden the definition of intangibles), as well as IAS 38 "Intangible assets" issued by the IFRS (which seeks to clarify the definitions of recognition, measurement, and disclosure). In brief, intangibles is a topic of global interest. For more on IAS 38, which is amended every so often (most recently in 2014) see https://www.iasplus.com/en/standards/ias/ias38.

28 An intangible asset is generally regarded as consisting of a company's reputation, brand, and intellectual property, inclusive of knowledge and know-how. Intangible assets are viewed as having no physical existence, yet constitute the long-term resources of a company. Value is derived from intellectual or legal rights as well as from value added to other assets. Two categories of intangible assets include limited-life intangible assets (e.g., patents, copyrights, and goodwill), and unlimited-life intangible assets (e.g., trademarks). Another way to think of intangible assets is that they cannot be destroyed (though a brand value can ebb and flow with a company's fortunes), and can be helpful as blueprints to rebuild tangible assets that have been destroyed. Owing to their not being physical objects with intrinsic value, intangible assets generally are not used as collateral for loans or bonds.

In a study published in 2017, Ocean Tomo found that a very large proportion of the S&P 500's market value was comprised of intangible assets as opposed to tangible assets. The proportion for Europe was less than the United States, and the proportion for selective Asian indices was less than the European experience. See Ocean Tomo (n.d.), "Intangible asset market value study," https://www.oceantomo.com/intangible-asset-market-value-study/.

29 It can be said that companies have an opportunity to disclose details of their knowledge activities in the Management Discussion and Analysis (MD&A) portion of public filings, though companies perceive a level of disclosure protection under FASB. The MD&A section of the annual report is where management can present in text what it chooses to amplify beyond what is presented in numbers (i.e., financial results), and where both qualitative and quantitative evaluations can be shared.

30 H. Bierman and R.E. Dukes (1975, April), "A critique of the FASB exposure draft on accounting for research and development costs," *Journal of Accountancy.*

31 See "Statement of financial accounting standards no. 2," October 1974.

32 If R&D-intensive equities are indeed characterized by both above-average returns and lower volatility, this would seem to be at odds with tenets of MPT and CAPM, where higher returns are aligned with higher volatilities. As such, it would imply that perhaps behavioral theories and EMH are better suited to help explain R&D-intensive equity dynamics; specifically, that abnormal returns are attributable to a systematic mispricing of knowledge activities, and stem from a lack of transparency as to what the activities are.

33 In an article published in 2014 in the *American Economic Journal* (*American Economic Journal: Economic Policy, 6*(1), 272–307, "Airline pricing, price dispersion, and ticket characteristics on and off the internet," Anirban Sengupta and Steven N. Wiggins found a clear price advantage for consumers purchasing airline tickets online.

34 Amazon has attempted to create designer boutique alternatives to its standard offerings, as with wedding dresses.

35 See Khalid Saleh (n.d.), "E-commerce product return rate – Statistics and trends," *Invesp.* https://www.invespcro.com/blog/ecommerce-product-return-rate-statistics/.

36 Ibid.

37 Ibid.

38 See Abrar Al-Heeti (2018, July 3), "Companies must let customers cancel subscriptions online, California law says," *CNet*. https://www.cnet.com/news/companies-must-let-customers-cancel-subscriptions-online-california-law-says/.

39 See Tony Loeb (2016, November 14), "An analysis of where cancellations come from," *The blog of Experience Hotel*. http://blog.experience-hotel.com/an-analysis-of-where-cancellations-come-from/. Perhaps the intuition here is that many consumers will book multiple places to stay, and then develop a more favorable disposition towards those hoteliers who care enough to reach out prior to the stay date. Perhaps a corollary exists with the insurance industry, where oftentimes a consumer will reach out to many potential insurers for quotes and then review them; maybe it is the insurance company who follows up with a timely note or call who is most likely to receive the new business.

40 Perhaps the consideration here is that purchases from Bricks are linked to stores near the shopper's home or workplace, making it fairly easy to return items in a timely manner. Conversely, for a Click shopper to return an item, they might need to wait until the weekend to have the time to get to the post office or shipping station or deal with other shipping requirements (e.g., printing a label, or obtaining a new shipping box to replace an original that was lost or damaged, packing the item, and so on).

41 For more readings on the phenomenon of price dispersion in the internet age, see Greg Kaplan, Guido Menzio, Leena Rudanko, and Nicholas Trachter (2016, August), "Relative price dispersion: Evidence and theory," Working Papers 16–6, Federal Reserve Bank of Philadelphia, as well as G. Kaplan and G. Menzio (2015), "The morphology of price dispersion," *International Economic Review, 56*(4), 1165–1206.

42 As a riff on the notion of One Price, some third-party food delivery services require that restaurants charge consumers the same price for items listed on their standard menu (i.e., no mark-ups for delivered items versus dining-in items). To work around this, many restaurants have simply created a second menu called their "catering menu," with delivery orders fulfilled from this separate, though standard, menu.

Bibliography

Acemoğlu, D., Ozdaglar, A., & Tahbaz-Salehi, A. (2016). Networks, shocks, and systemic risk. In A. Galeotti (Ed.), *The Oxford handbook of the economics of networks*. Oxford: Oxford University Press.

Aeppel, T. (2012, 17 January). Man vs. machine, a jobless recovery. *Wall Street Journal*. http://www.deanza.edu/faculty/lillybyron/pdf/ch2_manvmachineajoblessrecovery_jan2012.pdf.

Babus, A., & Carletti, E. (2010). Financial connections and systemic risk. European Banking Center Discussion Paper No. 2010–23S. Tilburg University, the Netherlands: European Banking Center.

Battiston, S., Gallegati, M., Greenwald, B., & Stiglitz, J.E. (2012a). Liaisons dangereuses: Increasing connectivity, risk sharing, and systemic risk. *Journal of Economic Dynamics and Control, 36*(8), 1121–1141.

Bernanke, B. (2009, April 14). Four questions about the financial crisis. Remarks at Morehouse College, Atlanta, GA. https://www.federalreserve.gov/newsevents/speech/bernanke20090414a.htm.

Bierman, H., & R.E. Dukes (1975, April). A critique of the FASB exposure draft on accounting for research and development costs. *Journal of Accountancy*.

Blanchard, O. (2017). The needs for different classes of macroeconomic models. *Realtime Economic Issues Watch* [Blog post]. Washington, DC: Peterson Institute for International Economics.

Caldarelli, G., May, R., Roukny, T., & Stiglitz, J. E. (2016). The price of complexity in financial networks. *Proceedings of the National Academy of Sciences of the United States*, 6 September, *113*(36), 10031–10036.

Camerer, C.F., Loewenstein, G., & Rabin, M. (2011). *Advances in behavioral economics*. Princeton, NJ: Princeton University Press.

Eklund, J.E. (2013). *Theories of investment: A theoretical review with empirical applications* (Working Paper). Sweden: Swedish Entrepreneurship Forum.

Fama, E.F. (2013). Does the Fed control interest rates? *Review of Asset Pricing Studies, 3*(2), 180–199.

Farhi, E., & Werning, I. (2016). A theory of macroprudential policies in the presence of nominal rigidities. *Econometrica, 84*(5), 1645–1704.

Gai, P., & Kapadia, S. (2010). Contagion in financial networks. *Proceedings of the Royal Society of London, 466*(2120), 2401–2423.

Gertler, M. (1989). Agency costs, net worth, and business fluctuations. *American Economic Review, 79*(1), 14–31.

Godin, B. (2008). The information economy: The history of a concept through its measurement, 1949–2005. *History and Technology, 24*(3).

Graham, B., & Dodd, D. (2008). *Security analysis*. New York: McGraw-Hill.

Haldane, A.G. (2009). Rethinking the financial network. Speech given at the Financial Student Association, Amsterdam, 28 April, available at http://www.bankofengland.co.uk/archive/Documents/historicpubs/speeches/2009/speech386.pdf.

Haldane, A.G., & May, R. M. (2011). Systemic risk in banking ecosystems. *Nature, 469*, 351–355.

Hallin, D. (n.d.). Whatever happened to the news? *Center for Media Literacy*. http://www.medialit.org/reading-room/whatever-happened-news.

Hendry, D.F., & Muellbauer, J. N. J. (2018). The future of macroeconomics: Macro theory and models at the Bank of England. *Oxford Review of Economic Policy, 34*(1–2), 287–328.

Hoyt, E. (2015, September 24). 20 of the coolest college start-ups ever. *Fast Web*. http://www.fastweb.com/student-life/articles/the-20-of-the-coolest-college-start-ups-ever.

Kaplan, G., & Menzio, G. (2015). The morphology of price dispersion. *International Economic Review, 56*(4), 1165–1206.

Kaplan, G., Menzio, G., Rudanko, L., & Trachter, N. (2016, August). *Relative price dispersion: Evidence and theory.* (Working Papers 16–6). Federal Reserve Bank of Philadelphia.

Kedrosky, P. (2013, May). *The constant: Companies that matter*. Kansas City, MO: Ewing Marion Kauffman Foundation. Retrieved from https://www.kauffman.org/~/media/kauffman_org/research%20reports%20and%20covers/2013/05/companiesthatmatter.pdf.

Lev, B., & Gu, F. (2016). *The end of accounting and the path forward for investors and managers*. Hoboken, NJ: John Wiley.

Lo, A.W., Mamaysky, H., & Wang, J. (2000). Foundations of technical analysis: Computational algorithms, statistical inference, and empirical implementation. *The Journal of Finance, 55*(4), 1705–1765.

Loeb, T. (2016, November 14). An analysis of where cancellations come from. *The blog of Experience Hotel*. http://blog.experience-hotel.com/an-analysis-of-where-cancellations-come-from/.

Markovitz, H. (1952). Portfolio selection. *The Journal of Finance, 7*(1), 77–91.

Markovitz, H. (1959). *Portfolio selection: Efficient diversification of investments*. New Haven, CT: Yale University Press.

McLuhan, M. (1964). *Understanding media: The extensions of man*. Cambridge, MA: First MIT Press.

Nath, T. (2015, October 15). Investing basics: What is the efficient market hypothesis, and what are its shortcomings?" *Nasdaq*. https://www.nasdaq.com/article/investing-basics-what-is-the-efficient-market-hypothesis-and-what-are-its-shortcomings-cm530860.

Ocean Tomo (n.d.). Intangible asset market value study. Retrieved from https://www.ocean tomo.com/intangible-asset-market-value-study/.

Page, L., &Brin, S. (n.d.). *History-Computer.com*. http://history-computer.com/Internet/Conquering/Google.html.

Park, C.H., & Irwin, S.H. (2007). What do we know about the profitability of technical analysis?, *Journal of Economic Surveys*, 21(4), 786–826.

Porat, M.U. (1977). *The information economy, vol. 1*. Washington, D.C.: Office of Telecommunications, US Department of Commerce.

Saleh, K. (n.d.), "E-commerce product return rate – Statistics and trends", *Invesp*. https://www.invespcro.com/blog/ecommerce-product-return-rate-statistics/.

Sengupta, A., & Wiggins, S.N. (2014). Airline pricing, price dispersion, and ticket characteristics on and off the internet. *American Economic Journal (American Economic Journal: Economic Policy)*, 6(1), 272–307.

Sharpe, W.F. (1964). Capital asset prices: A theory of market equilibrium under conditions of risk. *The Journal of Finance*, 19(3), 425–442.

Smith, A. (2015). *The wealth of nations*. Pilgrim Classics.

Top 15 most popular news websites. (Continuously updated). *EBiz MBA Guide*. http://www.ebizmba.com/articles/news-websites.

Vines, D., & Morris, N. (2015, June 9). Fixing the financial system: Adam Smith vs Jeremy Bentham. *INET Blog*. https://www.ineteconomics.org/perspectives/blog/fixing-the-financial-system-adam-smith-vs-jeremy-bentham.

Vise, D.A., & Malseed, M. (2018), *The Google story: Inside the hottest business, media and technology success of our time*. New York: Random House. https://books.google.com/books/about/The_Google_Story.html?id=zyTCAlFPjgYC&source=kp_cover.

5

FINANCIAL METRICS AND KPIs

For more than 100 years, firms have generated balance sheets and income statements, and have reported financial results in one way or another to tax authorities, investors, and regulatory agencies. Considerable research has recently emerged, however, to support the notion that the information content of financial metrics (earnings before interest, tax, depreciation, and amortization or EBITDA, cash flow, quick ratio, and so on) has weakened considerably in the past few decades. Specifically, the emergence and growth of a knowledge effect has rendered traditional accounting measures relatively ineffective in helping to understand the dynamics of corporate profitability. New metrics, such as industry-specific Key Performance Indicators (KPIs) can instead be referenced to shed light on what really matters to a firm's success.

Financial reporting

Prior to the coming of the internet, financial data in the business world was generally thought of as consisting of numbers found on a company's balance sheet or income statement. Assets, liabilities, retained earnings, and cash flow were typically seen as collectively comprising "financial data." Someone wanting to know the accounting profile of a company might simply ask, "What are its financials?"

Many market historians trace the first formal requirements for companies to report financials to the measures that emerged following the stock market crash of 1929.[1] In 1930 the New York Stock Exchange (NYSE) sought the input of the American Institute of Accountants (AIA) in an effort to improve the financial reporting of listed companies.[2] The principal author of the letter issued by the AIA in 1932 was G.O. May, who later wrote:

> The purpose of furnishing accounts to shareholders must be not only to afford them information in regard to the results being achieved by those to whom they have entrusted the management of the business, but to aid them in taking appropriate action to give effect to the conclusions which they reach regarding such accomplishments.[3]

The federal government then built upon the work of the NYSE in 1933 and 1934, with the passage of the Securities Act and the Securities Exchange Act.

Many firms were not entirely pleased with the new public reporting requirements, and had great concerns that if competitors could see their financial details it would be an open invitation to identify and exploit a firm's inner workings. It was argued that an asymmetry in disclosures was unfairly benefitting private companies relative to public firms, and these points continue to be made today.

Public companies must file the following reports with the US Securities and Exchange Commission (SEC):

- 10-K - an extensive annual report including year-end audited financial statements.
- 10-Q - quarterly reports.
- 8-K - a report for significant corporate events.
- Proxy statement - a report to shareholders.
- Other - registration statements, particularly documents filed by specific industries as with mutual funds, insurance companies, broker dealers and real estate investment companies.

In the 1970s the SEC worked with a third party to create and distribute microfiche versions of financial reports. The intent was to help reduce reliance on paper versions of filings, and public access to the microfiche was via designated SEC public reference rooms across the country. Although this move was a step forward from individuals having to write to each company requesting their financials via the US Postal Service (USPS), the microfiche solution was still burdensome and expensive. Persons were required to take notes by hand from microfiche files, or convert files into hard copies one page at a time in the reference rooms, or order copies from service bureaus. Timely access to financials was difficult.

Figure 5.1 illustrates a perspective on public accessibility to financials over time.

In 1984 the SEC allocated $30 million to start the EDGAR (Electronic Data Gathering Analysis and Retrieval) program, which was designed to make public access to financials more immediate and less expensive. The EDGAR system would permit electronic retrieval of an extensive database of filings, providing more ready access to helpful information. Soon a schedule was established to mandate that public corporations file their SEC documents electronically, and since 1996 all reporting companies have been required to file in this way. Today the public can have full access to company filings within minutes of

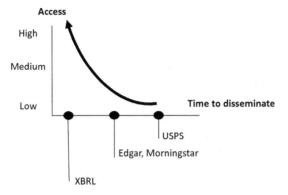

FIGURE 5.1   Public accessibility of financials over time

when a firm posts them online. Figure 5.2 helps to show the speed of public access to financials over time.

As mentioned in Chapter 3 on Big Data, data can be either structured (e.g., numerical data that can be placed into a spreadsheet) or unstructured (e.g., text, images, audio, and so on). In the context of financial data, financial metrics would naturally fall into the bucket of structured data. The numerical items reported in the tables of balance sheets and income statements (and related information) provide insightful perspectives. Textual information can also be helpful, and can be found within management commentary of financial filings and even within footnotes.[4] There is also metadata, which can be a helpful tool for financial analysts.[5] For example, some analysts have identified interesting correlations

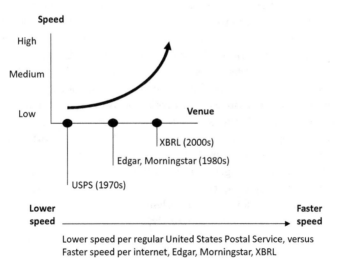

FIGURE 5.2   Speed of public access to financials over time

between the amount of text used in various sections of a financial report (e.g., "Forward-Looking information," and "Management Discussion and Analysis") and future price performance of the firm's equity.

Ten digital sources of information that can help with being informed about the competition include the following (and most are available for free):[6]

1. Cost of your industry's key Google AdWords.[7]
2. Relation of your company's name to others per Google Trends.
3. Relation of your company's offerings to others via Google Trends.
4. Breaking news about your industry, your competitors (and yourself) using Google Alerts.[8]
5. Market shares of key products per CSImarket.com.
6. Industry and firm write-ups provided by your sector's trade press, the financial press, and the rating agencies (e.g., Moody's and S&P).[9]
7. Social-media tracking services (e.g., Hootsuite, TweetReach, Klout).
8. Blogs that focus on your industry.
9. Activity related to your industry and firm on Twitter, Facebook, Instagram, Yelp, and others.
10. Social influencers who may speak about your industry or firm.

Some rather thoughtful and powerful commentary has been emerging to show that certain accounting metrics simply do not reflect meaningful insights with newer companies relative to older firms.

For example, in their book *The End of Accounting and the Path Forward for Investors and Managers* (2016), Baruch Lev and Feng Gu show that variations in financial metrics such as earnings and book value help to explain about 80–90% of stock price variations for those firms that launched their IPOs over the span of 1950 to 1959, while companies that launched their IPO since 2000 have only about 40–50% of their stock price variations explained by earnings and book value.[10] More on the work of Lev and Gu is provided in Chapter 4.

Lev's findings are supported by an article within the *Harvard Business Review* which summarizes the work of three professors, showing that earnings have less significance with younger companies relative to older companies because of differences in the way they invest. Specifically, "earnings explains only 2.4% of variation in stock returns for a 21st century company — which means that almost 98% of the variation in companies' annual stock returns are not explained by their annual earnings."[11]

Generally speaking, younger companies look to be less tangible capital intensive and more intangible capital intensive than older firms. A reason why this can present a challenge for financial analysts is that accounting rules handle tangible and intangible investments differently, with the latter not appearing on the balance sheet. Meantime, "intangible investments have surpassed property, plant, and equipment as the main avenue of capital creation for US companies."[12]

***

As we continue our exploration of insights that can be gained from company operations, we make a distinction between financial metrics and KPIs in the following way: a financial metric is derived from a firm's income statement or balance sheet (e.g., current ratio, or turnover ratio) while a KPI is separate from a balance sheet or income statement (e.g., number of active website users, or average time spent on key web pages).

Although there is value in keeping separate the notions of financial metrics and KPIs, they can certainly be mixed to create hybrid metrics, such as revenue generated by digital portals, or revenue in relation to discounts uniquely offered at a checkout page. There might even be insights about consumers who pay for Brick purchases with a mobile app as opposed to using cash or a credit card. But as much as the ability to collate unique data insights has grown appreciably, there can be situations where multiple categories can be appropriate, or can become blurred. For example, in the auto sector, are Tesla cars luxury vehicles that happen to be electric, or are they electric cars that happen to be luxury vehicles? Further, while transaction data tells you what people bought, it does not necessarily tell you what they want — and sales are not necessarily the same as demand.[13] Figure 5.3 presents a perspective of a typical sales funnel.

One characteristic of both financial metrics and KPIs is that they are calculated from historical valuations. Despite this, some financial metrics and KPIs can provide insight into what the future might bring, particularly if there looks to be a trend. For example, if debt and interest expense (financial metrics) have been steadily growing over the past eight quarters with a stable to declining trend in revenues, it could be a challenge to suddenly reverse course. However, an increase in expenses related to returned items (a KPI) may be fine if accompanied by rising sales, assuming the ratio of these is fairly unchanged over time. It can be insightful to know trend as well as point in time, and to connect dots

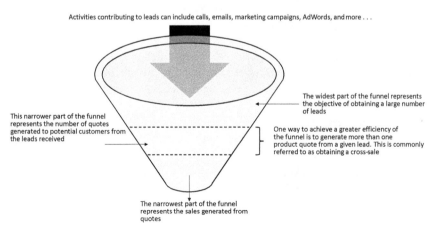

Activities contributing to leads can include calls, emails, marketing campaigns, AdWords, and more . . .

The widest part of the funnel represents the objective of obtaining a large number of leads

This narrower part of the funnel represents the number of quotes generated to potential customers from the leads received

One way to achieve a greater efficiency of the funnel is to generate more than one product quote from a given lead. This is commonly referred to as obtaining a cross-sale

The narrowest part of the funnel represents the sales generated from quotes

FIGURE 5.3   Perspective of a typical sales funnel

on key relationships for which it may well be expected (or at least explainable) that they move inversely to one another (returns and sales), or those for which it is more concerning when they do so (interest expense and revenue). To the extent that both financial metrics and KPIs can be used to help inform us what is going on, it is all the better to have a more complete perspective.

Meantime, creative approaches with KPI metrics are uncovering interesting correlations with revenue growth and stock prices. A recent *Harvard Business Review* article cites three areas worthy of exploration:[14]

- Digital magnitude: An aggregation of all digital measures that can be summed for a single company (web-page visits, page views, social-media views, visitors, and expressions of interest per number of likes or other). One company's digital magnitude can be compared with the digital magnitude of another, as one absolute value relative to another absolute value.
- Digital share: Digital magnitude of a company divided by the sum of digital magnitudes of all the companies in its peer group. One way in which this metric can be evaluated is by comparing it with traditional market share statistics; if digital share is larger than market share, this may portend an opportunity to increase market share.
- Digital momentum: A simple way to calculate a company's momentum in this regard is to collate monthly observations of cumulative daily momentum values, and evaluate whether they look to be increasing or decreasing. It might potentially be of interest to evaluate the presence of any seasonality, as with greater or lesser activity during particular times of the year.

Just as it is important for a company to think about how it grows its revenues and stock price, growing digital momentum may be an appropriate corporate strategy as well. This can include measuring success in relation to financial metrics (e.g., a ratio of revenue to digital share). Among other considerations, this places digital efforts squarely into the realm of active management for continuous alignment with corporate goals. Metrics are not just numbers reported in and of themselves and for their own sake, but can inform, instruct, and inspire. Figure 5.4 provides a perspective of the intensity of technology in relation to various finance activities.

One helpful context for applying financial metric/KPI insights is that of high touch/low touch. High touch refers to a greater degree of personal interaction (dining out) while low touch refers to a lesser degree of interaction (purchasing a ticket online). A helpful high-touch/low-touch measure can be revenues per number of employees, whereby a high ratio is reflective of relatively fewer employees being necessary to achieve a revenue target. A revenue-per-employee ratio can also can be a way of thinking about a business model as well. Prior to Starbucks, a cup of coffee in New York City could cost as little as $1 from a street-corner vendor. It would often be

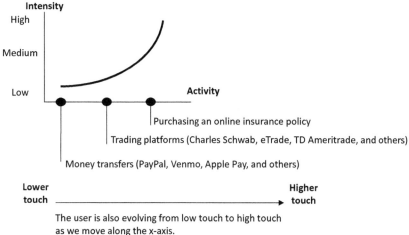

FIGURE 5.4 Intensity of technology in relation to finance activities

served out of a blue paper cup, ordered as a "coffee regular" (i.e., with milk and sugar) or just "black," and you were on your way. Then the Starbucks model came along, which meant that customers paid a multiple of street-corner prices, but also offered the experience of a hot drink prepared by a trained barista with a seemingly infinite variety of permutations, involving shots (caramel, vanilla), ratios (half caff, 2%), and free-form add-ons (quad, nonfat, one-pump, no-whip, mocha). Figure 5.5 presents a way to think about the notion of revenue per employee over time, and Figure 5.6 shows a way to think about expense per employee over time.

Starbucks took a comparatively low-touch cup-of-coffee business model and propelled the experience of serving a single cup of coffee into more of a high-touch mold. Conversely, Airbnb took a comparatively high-touch business model, that of providing people with a place to stay with unique amenities, and downgraded it to a lower-priced and fewer-frills experience.[15] Figure 5.7 offers a view of business models in relation to price and touch.

Table 5.1 provides a sampling of KPIs.

The metrics in Table 5.1 are devoid of isolated references to financial metrics (e.g., revenue, turnover ratios, or other), and the reason for this is that we want to highlight KPIs that are uniquely related to internet activities. There are two guiding principles applied in this regard. First, the KPIs cited in Table 5.1 do not appear on an income statement or balance sheet, and second, the KPIs are

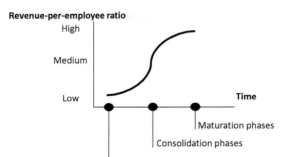

Ways that the revenue-per-employee ratio could improve over time would involve either the numerator (revenue) becoming larger, the denominator (employees) becoming lower, or both, and scenarios for these could include the following:

- Fewer tech persons required over time as the software evolves into more of a steady state (though oftentimes tech staffs grow to accommodate enhancements)
- Greater revenues as the product becomes more widely used and price mark-ups follow (though competitive pricing may help with gaining market share, or may be forced by offerings of new entrants)

FIGURE 5.5 Revenue per employee (RPE) over time

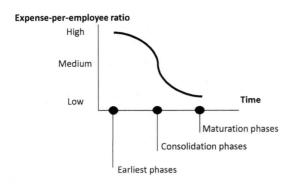

Ways that the expense-per-employee ratio could improve over time would involve either the numerator (expense) becoming smaller, the denominator (employees) becoming larger, or both, and scenarios for these could include the following:

- Employee training and supervising requirements decline over time along with employee expenses owing to a more experienced workforce
- Future employee additions do not require the greater level (and higher expense) of the special skills that were needed at the firm's time of launch

FIGURE 5.6 Expense per employee (EPE) over time

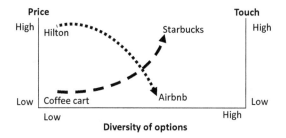

While the original business model of Starbucks was to turn a low-touch/low-price coffee sale (vendor) into a high-touch/high-price coffee sale, the business model of Airbnb was to take a high-touch/high-price stay (hotel) to a low-touch/low-price stay (a home)

FIGURE 5.7   Business models in relation to price and touch

easily calculable from readily available website analytics platforms (many of which are free).[16]

The KPIs in Table 5.1 represent just a sampling of measures that can be collated from internet activity, and firms may well create tailored metrics believed to be of particular relevance to their unique operations. It is also possible to use particular KPIs in combination with one another to create other KPIs. For example, taking the ratio of LTV (life-time value, or CLTV, customer life-time value) to CAC (customer acquisition cost) provides a measure of long-term revenue in relation to the cost of obtaining that revenue, and something better than a ratio of 1:1 would be desirable. Just how much greater a ratio could be reasonably expected would be a function of many considerations, including a firm's particular industry and whether it is a Brick, Click, or combination of the two. Figure 5.8 shows the value of financials versus KPIs in relation to Bricks and Clicks.

One way KPIs can be referenced in conjunction with financial metrics is by categorization of insight. For example, financial metrics are commonly cited with reference to the following four labels:

- Profitability
- Liquidity
- Efficiency
- Solvency.

Table 5.2 provides examples of KPIs and financial metrics for each of these categories.

There are also certainly many measures for comparison between Clicks and Bricks. For example, conversion rates of site visits to Clicks can be thought of as being similar to purchases from and store visits to Bricks, or time in a store with

TABLE 5.1 KPIs

Active issues: Number of queries in progress.

Affiliate performance rates: Measures which affiliate channels are most successful.

Average CTR: The percentage of users who click on a link.

Average order size: Also known as "average market basket," how much a customer typically spends on a single order.

Average position: Measures site's search engine optimization (SEO) and paid search performance. This demonstrates rank on search engine results. Many businesses have the goal of being number one (or at least top-tier) for targeted keywords.

Average resolution time: Amount of time it takes for a customer support issue to be resolved, starting when the customer first reaches out about the problem.

Average session duration: The average amount of time a person spends on site during a single visit.

Backlogs: Number of issues backed up and not addressed.

Banner or display advertising CTRs: Measures percentage of viewers who have clicked on the ad. This KPI will give insight into copy, imagery, and offer performance.

Blog traffic: Measures users going to blog site. It can be helpful to compare blog traffic to overall site traffic.

Bounce rate: How many users exit site after viewing only one page.

Chat sessions initiated: Number of chat sessions initiated online.

Churn rate: How quickly customers are leaving or canceling/failing to renew.

Clicks: Total number of clicks a link gets can be measured on webpages, social media, email, display ads, and more.

Concern classification: Evaluates customer support interactions in the context of severity of issues from perspective of user and the firm.

Conversion rate: Rate at which users are converting (or buying), and calculated by dividing the total number of visitors (to a site, page, category, or selection of pages) by the total number of conversions.

Cost per click (CPC): Amount paid to a browser ad service each time ad is clicked from a prominent position.

Cost performance index (CPI): The CPI for project management, like ROI, tells how much your resource investment is worth. CPI is calculated by dividing the earned value by the actual costs.

Cost variance: Just as it's helpful to compare real and predicted timing and hours, examine the total cost against the predicted cost. This will help to understand where to dial back and where to invest more.

Customer acquisition cost (CAC): Amount spendt on acquiring a new customer. This is measured by looking at marketing spend and how it breaks down per individual customer.

Customer lifetime value (CLV): Customer worth to business over the course of the relationship.

Customer retention rate (CRR): Percentage of paying customers who remain customers over a period of time.

Customer satisfaction (CSAT) score: Commonly measured by customer responses to a basic survey question: "How satisfied were you with your experience?" This can be measured with a numbered scale or choice of facial expressions or other.

Customer service chat count: Number of user chats on a webpage.

Customer service effectiveness (CSE): How productive individual staff persons are with handling inquiries quickly and without escalation.

Customer service email count: The number of emails received by customer support team.

Customer service phone call count: How frequently customer support team is reached via phone. May indicate need for a stronger online help system.

Cycle time: How long it takes for user to arrive at shopping cart from first webpage visit.

Day part monitoring: Times of day when site visitors appear and tracks peak traffic times at webpages of a site.

Email click-through rate (CTR): Percentage of those who actually clicked on a link after opening.

Email open rate: The percentage of subscribers who open email.

First response time: Average time it takes a customer to receive the first response to a query.

First time yield (FTY) and first time through (FTT): Measures efficiency of processes, as with need for a user to return unordered or damaged items. Divide the number of successful processes by the total number of processes.

Hit rate: Calculated by taking total number of sales of a single product and dividing it by the number of customers who have contacted customer service team about that product.

Mobile site traffic: Monitors the total number of users who use mobile devices to access pages.

Net promoter score (NPS): Measures customer relationships and loyalty via how likely customers are to recommend your brand to someone in their network.

New customer orders vs. returning customer orders: Compares new and repeat customers. Customer retention can potentially lead to even more business via references and greater orders over time.

New visitors vs. returning visitors: Reviewing how this metric evolves over time can help indicate effectiveness of new marketing and outreach campaigns.

Newsletter subscribers: Users who have opted into email marketing list.

Number and quality of product reviews: Provide valuable feedback. The quantity and content of product reviews are important KPIs to track for any ecommerce business.

Number of non-compliance events or incidents: Regulations, licenses, and policies businesses must follow.

Number of transactions: Total orders of a customer.

Pageviews per visit: Average number of pages a user views during each visit. If it's taking users too many clicks to find the products they're seeking then pages may need to be redesigned.

(*Continued*)

TABLE 5.1 Continued

Pay-per-click (PPC) traffic volume: Measures traffic to site via PPC campaigns.

Product affinity: Measures which products are purchased together. This measure can inform cross-promotion strategies.

Product relationship: Measures which products are viewed consecutively, and can be used to formulate effective cross-selling tactics.

Revenue per employee (RPE): Total revenue of the business divided by the total number of employees. This can be compared with other firms in your domain to benchmark headcount in relation to revenues.

Revenue per visitor (RPV): The average of how much a person spends during a single visit to site.

Service escalation rate: How many times a customer requests a service representative to redirect them to a supervisor or other senior employee.

Shopping cart abandonment rate: How many users are adding products to their shopping cart but not purchasing. If cart abandonment rate is high, there may be friction in the checkout process.

Site traffic: Total number of visits to site.

Site uptime: Measures when the site is down or lagging, for how long, and why.

Social followers and fans: Measures number of users who are on Facebook, Instagram, Twitter, Pinterest, Snapchat (or others), relative to the number who are fans. Many of those social media networks also have tools that e-commerce businesses can use to learn more about their social followers.

Social media engagement: Gauges how actively followers and fans are interacting with you on social media.

Subscriber growth rate: This tells how quickly subscriber list is growing.

Texting subscribers: Number of customers on text message contact list.

Time on site: How much time visitors are spending on website. Want to see more time spent on blog content and landing pages and less time spent through the checkout process.

Total available market relative to a retailer's share of market: Measures how much business is growing compared to others.

Traffic source: Tells where visitors are coming from or how they found site. Provides information about which channels are driving the most traffic, e.g. organic search, paid ads, or social media.

Unsubscribes: Measures drops from email list.

Yield: The number of products processed for sale within a certain period of time. Analyzing the variance on this from weekdays to weekends or holidays can lead to insights.

Bricks versus time on a web page with Clicks. Figure 5.9 presents financial metric categories and KPI corollaries.

Meantime, KPIs are increasingly finding their way into formal financial statements, as in the example of Facebook citing its number of active users in its 2015 10-K. Table 5.3 presents other KPI citations that have appeared in 10-Ks.

Finally, there are insightful measures a company can use that are not necessarily reflected in a balance sheet or income statement, or captured in a website. Here are some examples by industry:

With Clicks, traditional financial data in the way of accounting earnings are often not as insightful relative to traditional firms, and various KPIs may convey more meaning: for example, success related to acquiring new customers; launching new products and services; advancements in technology; innovative marketing initiatives; meaningful distribution alliances; growing numbers of users; increasing revenue per user; customer dropout rates; and increasing geographical diversity of users.

With the firm on more secure footing, traditional financial metrics can take on more meaning

As the business builds accounting earnings metrics turn positive, dependencies on KPIs lessen

In the earliest stages when accounting earnings are running negative, investors are more dependent on KPI-linked insights

With Bricks, investor expectations will tend to be focused more on traditional financial metrics, with a willingness to have senior management determine which KPIs are appropriate for success with accounting targets. As the new firm gains better understandings about important drivers to the business, the use of well-defined KPIs will naturally be expected to follow.

The word choice of "dependency" for the y-axis label of our two charts is deliberate in the sense of wanting to convey reliance rather than importance. Financial data and KPIs are both quite important, though what they can respectively contribute in the way of particular insights can vary over the lifecycle of a company. For the early stages of a digital firm when traditional financial data may not be as meaningful, KPIs may be more insightful.

In later stages KPIs are hand-in-glove with financial earnings targets

As the business builds and finds its way KPIs can evolve into more of a driver role

Investors are interested in traditional accounting insights from the very beginning

FIGURE 5.8   The value of financials versus KPIs, Bricks versus Clicks

TABLE 5.2 Financial metrics and KPIs

	Financial ratio	*KPI*
Profitability	Net profit margin: Net income/Net sales	Shopping cart abandonment rate: Uncompleted visit sales/Total visit sales
Liquidity	Current ratio: Current assets/Current liabilities	Churn rate: Canceled subscriptions/Total subscriptions
Efficiency	Asset turnover: Net annual sales/Average total assets	Repeat business: Repeat orders/Total orders
Solvency	Cash flow to debt: Operating cash flow/Total liabilities	Employee margin: Total revenue/Number of employees

Insurance: Percentage of renewed policies one year after original purchase, two years after, and so forth.

Media: Acquisition costs per subscriber, or churn (cancellation) rate.

Pharmaceuticals: Product pipelines, patents (pending and expiring).

Traditional financial metrics from balance sheets and income statements have played an important role for decades, and will continue to be an important aspect of understanding companies for a long time to come. Cash flow analysis, book value, and many other financial metrics provide important clues about a company. Another reality, however, is that the power of financial metrics to explain a company's stock price variation is diminishing, and other kinds of insights are required to obtain a more complete picture.

Financial metric categories and examples (Bricks or Clicks)		KPI corollaries (Clicks)	
Profitability	Net Profit Margin: $\dfrac{\text{Net Income}}{\text{Net Sales}}$	Profitability	Revenue per visitor
Liquidity	Sales to Working Capital: $\dfrac{\text{Annualized Net Sales}}{\text{AR + Inventory} - \text{AP}}$	Liquidity	Cost performance index
Efficiency	Accounts Receivable Turnover: $\dfrac{\text{Net Credit Sales}}{\text{Average Accounts Receivable}}$	Efficiency	Conversion rate
Solvency	Times interest earned: $\dfrac{\text{EBIT}}{\text{Interest expenses}}$	Solvency	Customer lifetime value

For companies that have both Brick and Click revenue streams, the question can arise as to whether these entities might be better run as a single integrated effort, or if there could be value to the businesses being treating separately. There is no one single correct response, and the considerations cited here may be helpful as guidance to draw out various considerations.

FIGURE 5.9 Financial metric categories and KPI corollaries

TABLE 5.3 KPI citations in 10-Ks

KPI	Company	URL
Chat sessions initiated	Snap, Inc.	https://www.sec.gov/Archives/edgar/data/1564408/000156459018002721/snap-10k_20171231.htm
Customer acquisition cost	The Priceline Group, Inc.	https://www.sec.gov/Archives/edgar/data/1075531/000107553116000084/pcln-20151231_10k.htm
Customer lifetime value	Constant Contact, Inc.	https://www.sec.gov/Archives/edgar/data/1405277/000119312513084678/d442306d10k.htm
Customer service chat count	Salesforce.com, Inc.	https://www.sec.gov/Archives/edgar/data/1108524/000110852416000053/crm-2016131x10k.htm
Customer service email count	Google, Inc.	https://www.sec.gov/Archives/edgar/data/1288776/000119312510030774/d10k.htm
Email click-through rate	Constant Contact, Inc.	https://www.sec.gov/Archives/edgar/data/1405277/000119312513084678/d442306d10k.htm
Mobile site traffic	Cvent, Inc.	https://www.sec.gov/Archives/edgar/data/1122897/000112289716000029/cvent10k.htm

KPI	Company	URL
Pay-per-click	Marchex, Inc.	https://www.sec.gov/Archives/edgar/data/1224133/000119312513103463/d445944d10k.htm
Revenue per visitor	Paychex, Inc.	https://www.sec.gov/Archives/edgar/data/723531/000072353117000023/payx-20170531x10k.htm
Texting subscribers	MetroPCS Communications, Inc.	https://www.sec.gov/Archives/edgar/data/1283699/000119312511051403/d10k.htm
Traffic source	Cvent, Inc.	https://www.sec.gov/Archives/edgar/data/1122897/000112289716000029/cvent10k.htm

Notes

1 Even in the nineteenth century there were evolving theories related to financial reporting, with two competing ideas on the central questions of who is to be the beneficiary of financial statements and for whom those financial statements are prepared; there were proponents of the "proprietary theory" (the financial statements of a corporation are prepared for the benefit of shareholders) and the "entity theory" (the financial statements are prepared for the benefit of common and preferred shareholders as well as bondholders). See A.C. Littleton (1933), *Accounting evolution to 1900* (New York: American Institute Publishing Co., Inc.), and W.A. Paton (1922), *Accounting theory, with special reference to the corporate enterprise* (New York: The Ronald Press Company).

2 S.A. Zeff (2014), The objectives of financial reporting: A historical survey and analysis, *Accounting and Business Research, 43*(4), 262–327.

3 G.O. May (1934) *Audits of corporate accounts*, 1934 (New York: AIA).

4 There are online research firms and data software companies that specialize in searching the text of financial statements, and CalcBench.com is one of the best (and offers a free trial as well).

5 Metadata is information that provides descriptions of other data. For example, metadata can include information about how the data was created, its purpose, the time and date of its creation, the entity who assembled the data, where on a device the data was created, the size of the data file, the data quality, the source of the data, and the process used to assemble the data. Many of these items are easily accessible on most electronic files, such as those in Word or Excel.

6 Your particular firm may not yet be large enough to appear on the radar of the various tools cited in this list, and if that's the case, the list can still be helpful with seeing where the competition is situated.

7 The cost of a particular Google AdWord is determined by an auction process whereby more popular search terms are bid higher. By monitoring which keywords become more or less expensive, insight can be gained into the type of business firms are seeking to build.

8 A more complete list of tracking solutions beyond Google Alerts would include Buzzbundle, Mention, Talkwalker Alerts, Hootsuite, Reputology, Awario, Brand24, Sendible, Postific, BoardReader, Icerocket, and Anewstip.

9 Many rating agencies provide industry profile updates for free, after a simple registration process.

10 Baruch Lev and Feng Gu (2016), *The end of accounting and the path forward for investors and managers,* Wiley Finance (Hoboken, NJ: John Wiley), pp. 36 and 41. In fact, Lev and Gu present evidence that the ratio between price variations and corporate news may be far less than 40–50%.

11 Vijay Govindarajan, Shivaram Rajgopal and Anup Srivastava (2018, February 26), "Why financial statements don't work for digital companies," *Harvard Business Review.*

12 Ibid. In research performed in the 1990s, Lev found that firms with a preponderance of intangible assets often outperformed firms reporting more tangible assets, owing to a greater propensity for innovations among the former.

13 Eddie Yoon (2012, October 17), "Demand and sales aren't equivalent," *Harvard Business Review.*

14 Jeff Maling, Rod Fertig, and Arun Muthupalaniappan (2017, September 7), "Are you accurately measuring your company's digital strength?," *Harvard Business Review.*

15 Although the basic Airbnb concept is lodging without amenities of room service, maid service, gym, concierge, and in-house shop for a newspaper and toiletries, Airbnb is looking to transform this as well with its Experiences program and other innovations.

16 Many website hosting sites offer analytic services at no extra charge, and Google Analytics is a freemium offering with many useful KPI metrics generated for no fee.

While it certainly could be said that "Average order size" is information that Bricks could collect via a customer's loyalty card/credit card data, not all Bricks have these sources of information, and even Bricks that do will also see purchases made in cash. By contrast, all online orders can be tracked to a particular user in a number of different ways including payment method, username, shipping address, and more.

Bibliography

Aho, J. (2005). *Confession and bookkeeping: The religious, moral, and rhetorical roots of modern accounting.* Albany, NY: State University of New York Press.

Ahrens, T. (1996). Styles of accountability. *Accounting, Organizations and Society, 21*(2/3), 139–173.

Bay, C., Catasús, B., & Johed, G. (2014). Situating financial literacy. *Critical Perspectives on Accounting, 25,* 36–45.

Catasús, B. (2010). Indicators as technology: Debates on the link between indicators and action (unpublished paper). Presented at the European Accounting Association Conference (EAA) in Istanbul, May 2010.

Catasús, B., Ersson, S., Gröjer, J.-E., & Wallentin, F. Y. (2007). What gets measured gets … on indicating, mobilizing and acting. *Accounting, Auditing & Accountability Journal, 20*(4), 505–521.

Catasús, B., & Gröjer, J.-E. (2006). Indicators: On visualizing, classifying and dramatizing. *Journal of Intellectual Capital, 7*(2), 187–203.

Erturk, I., Froud, J., Johal, S., Leaver, A., & Williams, K. (2007). The democratization of finance? Promises, outcomes and conditions. *Review of International Political Economy, 14*(4), 553–575.

Faÿ, E., Introna, L., & Puyou, F.-R. (2010). Living with numbers: Accounting for subjectivity in/with management accounting systems. *Information and Organization, 20,* 21–43.

Govindarajan, V., Shivaram Rajgopal, & Anup Srivastava (2018, February 26). Why financial statements don't work for digital companies. *Harvard Business Review.*

Lev, B., & Gu, F. (2016). *The end of accounting and the path forward for investors and managers.* Wiley Finance. Hoboken, NJ: John Wiley.

Littleton, A.C. (1933). *Accounting evolution to 1900.* New York: American Institute Publishing Co., Inc.

Maling, J., Fertig, R., & Muthupalaniappan, A. (2017, September 7). Are you accurately measuring your company's digital strength?" *Harvard Business Review.*

May, G.O. (1934) *Audits of corporate accounts.* New York: AIA.

Napier, C. (2006). Accounts of change: 30 years of historical accounting research. *Accounting, Organizations and Society, 31*(4–5), 445–507.

OECD. (2005). *Improving financial Literacy: Analysis of issues and policies.* Paris: OECD Press.

Paton, W.A. (1922). *Accounting theory, with special reference to the corporate enterprise.* New York: The Ronald Press Company.

Yoon, E. (2012, October 17). Demand and sales aren't equivalent. *Harvard Business Review.*

Zeff, S.A. (2012, draft). The objectives of financial reporting: A historical survey and analysis. *Accounting and Business Research, 43*(4), 262–327.

6

TANGENCIES

Creative ideas can appear online with amazing speed, and these often relate to innovative products and services. Bearing in mind the ease with which these digital creations can be made part of an existing firm's operations, it can benefit companies to be open to (or even actively seek out) these innovations. Ideas may be related to revenue-generation projects, or expense-reduction solutions. In light of the relative ease with which something new can often be grafted onto a business's existing platform or practices, we refer to these opportunities as tangencies. That is, the new feature is not treated as something that will materially transform a company's core operations (at least not initially), but rather is complementary with existing operations, and it can potentially assist with profitability or efficiency or even both. Further, tangencies are characterized by their neither requiring significant capital outlays nor the implementation of appreciably greater resources.

A tangency is an opportunity for a firm to explore a business venture complementary with its core business. A tangency does not necessarily need to involve a huge commitment of capital to be launched, though that could be the case. Over time, a tangency may well grow into a source of materially significant revenue streams, business leads, or other beneficial attributes, or might simply serve as a short-term opportunistic splash to highlight the creative or serendipitous talents of a company.

In 1919, General Motors (GM) formed the General Motors Acceptance Corporation (GMAC) to help dealers finance and maintain their inventories. Soon after, in the early 1920s, it made credit available to consumers as well. The idea was conceived by GM's then President, Alfred P. Sloan; early loans required a 35% initial payment with the remaining amount due in installments over 12 months so that GMAC could see a paydown in principal prior to car repairs becoming an added expense to the consumer after the first year.

Over the years GMAC experienced a number of transformations, such as financing locomotives during World War II, getting into the home mortgage business in the 1980s, establishing GMAC Bank in 2000, and then transforming that into Ally Bank in 2009. Today there is also GM Financial, which is the wholly owned captive finance subsidiary of General Motors. Over the years GM's involvement in financial aspects of the automobile industry has had its ups and downs, though more recently, GM President Dan Ammann stated that the finance arm of GM is central to sustaining profitability when auto sales stall or the economy dips.[1]

Recent examples of tangencies include the following:[2]

- Amazon explores the issuance of small business loans to its various supplier relationships

   o Amazon already has a good sense of what its small business relationships are capable of generating on a financial basis, and the loans would presumably tie businesses more closely to Amazon.

- Blackberry decides that the software underlying its hardware (mobile devices) has commercial value, and monetizes it as a separate line of business.
- Adobe decides to offer its software on a subscription basis to evaluate market response, then moves to an exclusive subscription-based model.
- Apple unveils Apple Pay, enabling MasterCard users to pay for items with various Apple devices.
- The introduction of for-profit online education and school loans.

   o These online schools may already have accumulated meaningful data on the relationship between a student's classroom performance and timely payment of tuition, or payment factors related to a student's age, course of study, or other.

- Insurance companies selling data online via Quandl or other data stores.

   o Quandl is a fascinating company that offers all manner of online data. For example, an auto insurance company might anonymize their sales of auto insurance policies, which when converted into an index can be used by economists or others as a coincident indicator of auto sales (or precursors of economic growth).

Other examples of tangencies might include the following:

- A refurbished mobile device company offers on-demand insurance.

- By offering consumers on-demand mobile device insurance (perhaps $1 a day over the duration of a beach vacation in case a phone is dropped in the ocean), an insurance payout of $50 could be made in exchange for the damaged device. The company could then sell the refurbished phone at a profit.

- A local movie theater offers its venue for corporate presentations.
- Server-intensive firms provide cloud storage services as a third-party offering.
- Clothing firms offer virtual-reality/augmented-reality experiences to help customers envision the look of potential purchases.
- An auto parts store explores 3D printers to generate obscure parts on demand.
- A school offers its facilities to organizers of a summer camp that teaches computer skills.
- A restaurant expands into the food truck business (or vice versa).
- Businesses selling data create software which optimizes how data is used (or vice versa).
- Firms in the software business create consulting arms to help others integrate solutions into existing platforms, or create new ones.

As indicated in the examples above, tangencies can be created organically (i.e., internally at a firm) as well as with an external point of attachment. Figure 6.1 presents a conceptual view of tangencies and points of attachment.

As to external considerations, these can arise when a firm decides to use the product(s) or service(s) of another firm (such as social media or a distribution company), but with that external resource linking with already existing touchpoints within the firm. Internally, firms can develop an aspect of a current business line that is presently rather small relative to existing revenue streams, or create an entirely new line of business that is in some way linked to an existing business endeavor. A tangency differs from an acquisition or merger in that it is an opportunity that can be captured on a collaborative basis. Table 6.1 helps to delineate these various approaches.

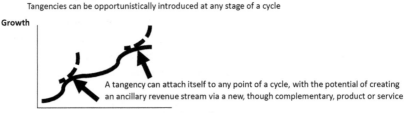

Tangencies can be opportunistically introduced at any stage of a cycle

Growth

A tangency can attach itself to any point of a cycle, with the potential of creating an ancillary revenue stream via a new, though complementary, product or service

Cycles of a core business, or economy

FIGURE 6.1 Tangencies and points of attachment

TABLE 6.1 Examples of tangencies

Internal: Internal

Idea	Point of tangency	Opportunity
Marketing department: Sales department	New advertising campaign	Closely coordinating the marketing message with the people who will be on the front lines with customers may result in a more optimal campaign.

Internal: External

Idea	Point of tangency	Opportunity
Insurance company: Sells repurposed internal data	Volume of new quote requests for auto insurance	New revenue stream from a market segment unrelated to the company's core business (data consumers versus insureds)

While the concept of tangencies in business has certainly been around for some time, the relative ease today of sourcing and opportunistically test-driving a given idea has perhaps never been greater. The proliferation of plug-and-play venues speak to this, with a considerable number of Fortune 500 companies offering app stores where users have access to myriad solutions that complement core functionality. Examples include the following:

- Salesforce.com and its "AppExchange" (Customer Relationship Management).
- Intuit QuickBooks and its QuickBooks Apps (accounting).
- Office 365 (Word, Excel, PowerPoint, etc.) apps and the Microsoft Store.
- And, of course, there is Apple's App Store, and Google's Google Play venue.

An important aspect of tangencies in the internet era also involves the consideration of speed, which can mean that an idea is quickly adopted and placed onto the path of success, but also that it can just as quickly be abandoned. If it is abandoned, this can perhaps happen with little internal expense or external notice due to the very nature of a tangency's low-key profile. With the hurdle of launching a business being appreciably lowered by the internet, which grants firms the ability to tap into an audience and distribution channel in fairly short order, more opportunities can surface, and failures can be easily discarded, all without consuming appreciable corporate resources in the process.

Although some, including some academicians, foresaw that the internet would enable the reduction of uncertainty by means of greater access to timely and complete information, it is not clear that this has yet been achieved. Accordingly, for a business environment characterized by uncertainties that may well not be dissipating anytime soon, a corporate strategy embracing the spirit of tangencies may be an appropriate opportunistic context in which to test-drive promising ideas.

Information flows can be a fundamental aspect of evaluating a Tangency opportunity, and if there is any industry where these are valued it would be finance, and if there is any market that could serve as a publicly observable laboratory for how information flows play out, it would be the stock market.

Volatility has long served as a proxy for uncertainty (or risk) in the financial markets. Indeed, it is commonly accepted that there is a trade-off between risk and reward with investments; the higher the potential return, then the greater the attendant risk associated with actually attaining that higher return. A portfolio of Treasury bills would be expected to have a lower return and smaller volatility than a portfolio of equities or a portfolio of commodities.

Market volatility can be calculated in a few different ways, and a helpful source of explanations of these is provided by the Corporate Finance Institute (CFI).[3] Consider the volatility time series presented in Figure 6.2.

Figure 6.2 shows volatility on a rolling eight-quarter average basis from 1990 to mid 2019, and provides us with the following insights:

- The average for volatility over this timeframe is 19.3%.
- There looks to be floor for volatility near 12%.

  o Despite advancements in the speed and ready availability of information flows over the past three decades, there appears to be a barrier to achieving lower thresholds of uncertainty as proxied by volatility.[4]

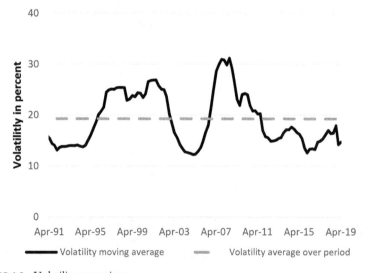

FIGURE 6.2   Volatility over time

- While a soft ceiling for volatility looks to exist just above 25%, it pushed above 30% during the Great Recession

  ○ While an increase in volatility during times of stress can be expected, it is of interest that such a bump occurred and lasted as long as it did (from Q1 2007 to Q3 2008) even with the maturity of the internet at that time as an established vehicle for information dissemination.

Perhaps we are discovering an Information Dichotomy: The idea that the ubiquity and ease of evaluating complex information helps with better understanding our past, yet these same information attributes pose a significant challenge with accurately forecasting the future (reflected in persistent volatilities as a proxy for uncertainty), due to the speed with which changes can be implemented in response to new information flows and the difficulties with parsing noise from substance. This Information Dichotomy may be contributing to the floor for how low volatility can go, and to the stickiness of volatility when it stays at upper bounds for prolonged periods.

As another perspective of stock market variability, consider Figure 6.3.

Figure 6.3 shows the number of days per year (going back to the 1960s) when there was a greater than 1% change (up or down) in the S&P 500 on a day-over-day basis.

A few observations related to Figure 6.3:

- First, after 1974, 25 years would pass before the market next had a year of more than 100 greater-than-1% days (this occurred again in the year 2000). Including 2000, there have been five such instances over the past 19 years. Something that had been a once-in-25-years event is now happening an average of once every 4 years.

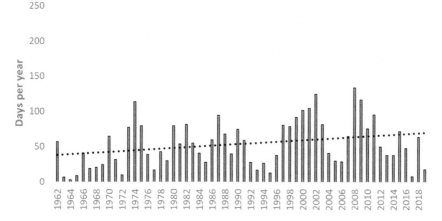

FIGURE 6.3 Number of days per year with market swings of more than 1% up or down on a day-over-day basis

- Second, since 1972 (when there were 10 swing days), 1995 exhibited 13 swing days and 2017 had a total of 8. The last bar in the chart takes us to mid-2019.
- Third, as the trend line shows, instances of larger one-day moves are clearly becoming more pronounced. In 2002 there were more than 120 days of large market swings, and in 2008 there were more than 130 days of such swings. To put these numbers in perspective, there are about 250 trading days per year; when the number of large-swing days accounts for half of the year's total trading activity, this is something of interest.

An information implication related to these observations could be that contrary to an expectation that greater speeds of information flows and proliferating online venues for disseminating information could make for a dampening effect of day-over-day swings in stock market prices, the opposite is occurring. A possible explanation for this might be that there is some type of market uncertainty which has been growing since the 1970s, and is contributing to the rise in day-over-day variability being observed. More on this later.

To provide another perspective of daily price action with the S&P 500, Figure 6.4 presents the number of days per year when there is a greater than 1% change (up or down) in the S&P 500 on an intra-day basis.

As shown, it was not until 1982 that the frequency of intra-day price moves of more than +/- 1% dropped below 200 trading days per year (measured from the low of the trading day to the high of the trading day). Considering that there are about 250 trading days each year, from the early 1960s up until the early 1980s an intra-day price move of more than +/- 1% was pretty much a daily event. In November 1982 a rather severe recession came to an end,

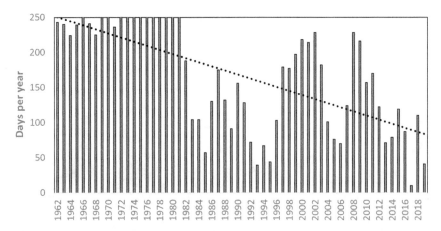

FIGURE 6.4 Number of days per year with market moves of +/-1% or greater on an intra-day basis

though it took until the year 2000 before the market again produced more than 200 trading days of intra-day price moves of greater than +/- 1%. Since 1981 there have been only five years in which the market traded in excess of +/- 1% on an intra-day basis for more than 200 days.

In summary, at minimum, we observe the following:

> The frequency of larger (+/- 1%) intra-day market swings has been steadily decreasing, while the frequency of larger (+/- 1%) day-over-day market changes has been increasing.[5]

Perhaps one way to characterize the observed dynamics between inter- and intra-day price variability dynamics is on the basis of tactical versus strategic trading. That is, maybe there is simply a market dynamic at play whereby a distinction exists between price variation attributes for intra-day (tactical) considerations, and attributes of inter-day (strategic) considerations, with the latter embodying a heightened uncertainty. As an example of the more transitory nature of intra-day price variability, many studies show that a stock's initial reaction to a quarterly earnings report is oftentimes reversed a rather short time later (even within less than 24-hours).[6]

Other factors today that are perhaps fueling a strong intra-day tactical trading orientation include: the trend of lower commissions for active trading; the proliferation of online trading sites with helpful tools and commentary; program trading; the growing number of day traders who purposely do not hold positions past the market close (day trading); the existence of so-called market circuit breakers that place limits on larger intra-day market moves; and the emergence of new and interesting products-cum-strategies via exchange-traded funds (ETFs) and other innovative products.[7]

From a distance, the characteristics of volatility seen in Figure 6.2 seem to have changed very little since 1990. Certainly, there have been times when volatility has spiked dramatically as related to the episodes inclusive of the dot. com bubble, and the 2008 financial crisis. With volatility being a reflection of heightened risk and uncertainty, there is certainly a dose of this present during times of market stress. However, despite massive improvements in the quantity, quality, and accessibility of information over the past few decades, the floor of volatility has not moved. Though the nature of market variations has evolved, as seen in the decline in the variability of intra-day market changes relative to an increasing choppiness of day-over-day market moves, the bigger picture trend of volatility has been to fluctuate within a fairly consistent band of 12% to 25% on a quarterly moving-average basis.[8]

***

The reason why all of this matters from a digital finance standpoint is that these topics highlight fundamental aspects of data's history, with its certainties and uncertainties, and help to inform the challenges and opportunities of data today. And a reason why this matters in the context of tangencies in particular is that for a marketplace where uncertainty (as proxied by volatility) is as pervasive as ever, although the speed of decision-making is increasing, the pursuit of strategies of a tangential and risk-sharing nature can be an attractive proposition. Risk sharing can take place in the context of profitability, regulatory considerations, reputation, and other factors.

In the sciences, there is something known as the Law of Conservation of Energy, and it is commonly referred to as the First Law of Thermodynamics. This law states that energy can neither be created nor destroyed. Perhaps there is a related paradigm within the financial markets. That is, perhaps there is a grand sum of volatility across all markets around the world inclusive of stocks, bonds, commodities, real estate, and all other assets, and with an ebb and flow as investing uncertainties rise and fall. Within such a construct, perhaps volatility is not easily created or destroyed, but continuously shifts and evolves, both with respect to how it manifests itself (as with intra-day price moves versus inter-day price moves), and with where it appears (New York versus London, the gold market versus the foreign exchange market, and so on).

Complementing the ideas advanced by Lev and the volatility findings shared thus far, there is the work of Anup Srivastava, published in the *Journal of Accounting and Economics* in 2014.[9] Srivastava finds progressively lower earnings-quality measures from 1970 forward, with growing intensities of intangibles being a major culprit affecting business performance and financial reporting. He specifically cites increasing volatility of revenues, expenses, and cash flows, arguably attributable to the immediate expensing of intangible investments and uncertainties surrounding the benefits of intangible investments. Srivastava observes comparable phenomena when referencing the cash components of revenues, expenses, and earnings, which he regards as being less likely to be affected by GAAP dynamics and more likely to reflect changes in the fundamentals of underlying transactions. He concludes that the observed trends of declines in earnings quality are strongly related to changes in the business activities of the publicly listed firms in his study. These observations would also seem to be consistent with the heightened market volatility dynamics previously cited.

***

Additional support for the notion of greater uncertainties associated with the particular strategic positioning of a stock's price is found in the work of Lev and Gu, and others. Specifically, as discussed in Lev and Gu's *The End of Accounting*, the relationship between stock prices and earnings has been weakening since the mid-1970s, when the knowledge effect first surfaced, and per Figures 6.2 and 6.3, this is about the time when earnings began to dampen as meaningful explainers of stock dynamics. With modern volatility being less of an intra-day and more of an inter-day factor, perhaps this signals that fundamental company considerations like earnings are giving way to more tactical trading biases, and that this stems in part from the decline of information content in earnings (and is reflective of the growing role of intangibles and the knowledge effect). Accordingly, when a more dominant driver of explaining fundamental company dynamics emerges, perhaps a slowing or reversal in intra- versus inter-day trends will surface.

Meantime, the dispersion (or differences) in forecasts of key economic releases has also not shown much improvement over the past few decades.

Even with the vast amount of publicly available information related to such economic fundamentals as how the economy is progressing (measured by Gross Domestic Product) or how prices are behaving (as proxied by the Consumer Price Index), obtaining forecasts that come close to actual results seems to be as elusive as ever. This notion of thinking about market volatility or uncertainty as ebbing and flowing, though with finite limitations related to how much it can be minimized, also seems to be something we can observe with economic fundamentals.

The concept behind tangencies is to promote a way of thinking about business for every stage of the business cycle. It is applicable across firm size, location, industry sector, and years in existence. There are insights applicable for every entity in the business of providing goods or services, including nonprofits.

The Greek philosopher Heraclitus taught that "The only thing that is constant is change."

Any strategy for business success needs to consider the realities of an ever-changing economic environment. Indeed, a fundamental aspect of tangencies is to embrace the uncertainty of commerce. A better understanding of this dynamic can open new vistas of clarity and understanding about emerging opportunities and how best to seize them.

There can be tremendous opportunities with strategies that seek to capture and ride the curving cycle of a business, industry, or economy, and a core element of success is directly attributable to applying different ways of approaching a particular challenge.

Parenthetically, financial analysts are not the only ones who have been frustrated by the transitory and elusive nature of uncertainty. Despite considerable advancements with forecasting techniques, statistical software, and the unprecedented availability of data in particular, the accuracy of economic predictions has not improved much recently. Again, what makes this an especially perplexing riddle is that basic economic theory tells us that information is meaningful, yet considering that we are in an age when information is more accessible than it has ever been, there looks to be a floor to just how low uncertainty can go.

In Figure 6.5 we show the statistical dispersion among professional forecasts for the US Consumer Price Index (CPI) since 1962.[10]

Here's an easy way to think about what dispersion is measuring: Are professional forecasters generally in agreement with one another with their expectations for a particular economic release? If yes, dispersion tends to be smaller. If no, dispersion tends to be larger.

Consistent with our observations concerning volatility in Figure 6.5, a floor for dispersion with CPI forecasts that has not moved lower over the past 60 years.[11]

Figure 6.6 presents differences (subtracted values) between actual versus forecast values of monthly CPI releases. The forecast values are taken from the Federal Reserve Bank of Cleveland's "Inflation expectations" dataset.[12]

As Figure 6.6 shows, an accurate CPI forecast continues to be an elusive goal, though certainly not for lack of trying. Even forecasting innovations that seek to leverage unique data attributes have a difficult time with consistently accurate forecasts.[13]

For example, the Federal Reserve Bank of Atlanta has launched "GDPNow," which is a "nowcast" of the government's official estimate of GDP prior to its release. The idea behind a nowcast is that it incorporates information into a continuously updated forecast on a real-time basis.[14]

At the Atlanta Fed's Frequently Asked Questions page dedicated to the GDPNow model, they state "Overall, these accuracy metrics do not give compelling evidence that the model is more accurate than professional forecasters."[15]

For many of us, it is the elusive nature of finance and market environments that makes them so wondrous. When real life is the laboratory, there are simply too many variables to pin down to obtain measurements as precise as we might like to have. We cannot shout "freeze" and then scurry around to collect the data we need to perform analyses. As social scientists we don't have the luxury, often available in the hard sciences, of conducting exacting experiments in controlled environments under ideal conditions. And yet it is this same reality that makes finance an intriguing multidimensional challenge that involves exigencies of human behavior, politics, natural phenomena, consumer sentiment, business cycles, and all the rest.

FIGURE 6.5 Dispersion in forecasts for the US Consumer Price Index, 1989 to present

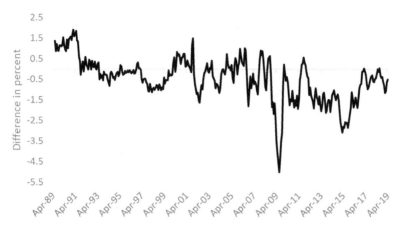

FIGURE 6.6 Difference between actual and forecast inflation (actual minus forecast) for monthly CPI

In January 2016 *The Economist* profiled an International Monetary Fund (IMF) study that delved into the forecasting of GDP.[16] Despite what many might consider to be their unique level of access to information relating to the global economy, the IMF's own Independent Evaluation Office concluded that the accuracy of IMF forecasts was "comparable to that of private sector forecasts." "But how accurate is that?" *The Economist* poignantly asked. "Not very," was its own reply. Examining forecasts from 1999 to 2014, *The Economist* found that there had been 220 instances when an economy grew in one year before contracting in the next, and not once did the IMF see the contraction coming in the following year. Making this all the more noteworthy is the fact that the forecasts were published in April, giving the IMF at least a three-month head start over many private sector economists, who announce their annual projections in December of the previous year or at the latest in January of the new year. As the subtitle of *The Economist* piece opines, "growth is devilishly hard to predict." Indeed.

***

Over the past 30 years or so, stock market volatility has transformed itself in a rather interesting way. Specifically, intra-day volatility of stock market prices has been steadily declining, while day-over-day stock market price volatility has been steadily rising. All the while, the floor level of volatility has been incredibly solid going back decades, rarely and only transitionally edging below 12% per Figure 6.2. Meantime, the seeming inability to generate more accurate economic forecasts as reflected in persistent dispersions is another fascinating phenomenon.

Despite huge advances with the speed and availability of data and tools, there looks to be an impenetrable floor of uncertainty (proxied by market volatility and dispersions) that may not ever edge below the lower bounds that have prevailed for decades.[17] While we have certainly learned a great deal thus far in this age of big data, there is so much more for us to discover.

***

A fundamental question with respect to any Brick or Click is "What business are you in?" The answer to this question can greatly help with obtaining clues related to identifying Tangency opportunities.

The answer to the question of what business a company is in can sometimes vary greatly depending upon who is responding.[18] For example, if this question were in relation to Google, the following answers might reasonably be provided:

> Consumer: Google is in the search engine business (Google Chrome).
> Equity analyst: Google is in the advertising business (Google AdWords).
> Student: Google provides tools (Google Docs, Google Scholar, Google Classroom).
> Small business owner: Google provides software solutions and insights (G Suite, Google Analytics).

In at least one sense, all of these responses are correct … these are indeed all businesses that Google is in. When viewed through a lens of "What Google businesses generate revenues?," a few insights can emerge.

For example, a consumer does not pay a fee to use Google Search to find a nearby retailer, yet that retailer may be paying Google for prominent page placement with search results. If Google were only in the search business, it would lose money, even though it is estimated to have about a 80% market share of the search market in the United States and about 90% in Europe. A way Google leverages Google Search to make money is via Google AdWords and AdSense, as marketing venues alongside other internet platforms as well as television, cable, and radio. In relation to other online advertising venues (Bing ads, LinkedIn ads, and others) AdSense has a market share of about 20%, and in relation to all forms of advertising it is very low.[19]

Meantime, Google is just one part of the larger company "Alphabet," and the following is excerpted from a piece authored by Larry Page at Alphabet's website:

> What is Alphabet? Alphabet is mostly a collection of companies. The largest of which, of course, is Google. This newer Google is a bit slimmed down, with the companies that are pretty far afield of our main internet products contained in Alphabet instead. What do we mean by far afield? Good examples are our health efforts: Life Sciences (that works on the

glucose-sensing contact lens), and Calico (focused on longevity). Fundamentally, we believe this allows us more management scale, as we can run
things independently that aren't very related.[20]

It seems that Alphabet wants to convey a sense that it is involved with many
different ventures, and it certainly is. But might there be a particular motivation
for it to convey this particular impression? Part of the answer may be found in
this additional statement from Larry Page:

> I should add that we are not intending for this to be a big consumer
> brand with related products—the whole point is that Alphabet companies
> should have independence and develop their own brands.[21]

One take on the narrative advanced by Larry Page is that while Alphabet is
indeed a large company, it is a large company comprised of many small firms
operating in a decentralized way.[22] To put a sharper point on it, Alphabet wants
to make the case that it is not a monopoly with monopolistic powers.

Five ways to address what business a company is in could include the following inquiries:

1.   What is the market share of its free products or services?
2.   What is the market share of its paid products or services?
3.   What is its free product or service, and what is its paid product or service?
4.   What is the industry segment of the product or service?
5.   Who are the competitors?
6.   Where are the users being sought, and where are they located?

Knowing what business you are in can help guide you to what tangencies can
be of the greatest potential benefit to you.

The business visionary and author Peter F. Drucker had the following to
say on this subject:

> Actually "what is our business" is almost always a difficult question which
> can be answered only after hard thinking and studying. And the right
> answer is usually anything but obvious.[23]

I remember my excitement as an undergraduate student, when one morning
a special announcement was made at the business school by the president of the
university. The school had just been awarded a special endowed chair in economics, and the benefactor was Buckhorn Incorporated. Among the remarks
made about Buckhorn was a key decision made by the company years earlier
relating to the kind of business it was in. In brief, Buckhorn had established
a strong brand for itself as a company capable of producing quality metal containers for a variety of products, but along came a new material for making

containers known as plastic. Hence, a key question arose: Was Buckhorn in the metal container business, or was it in the container business? Deciding upon the latter, Buckhorn retooled its operations for making containers from plastic, and business boomed as consumers increasingly preferred plastic products.[24]

Sometimes it takes a threat or crisis of some sort for a company to come to grips with its true core, but it doesn't have to be that way. If the determination can come prior to a crisis, there is certainly a greater chance of making more prudent decisions of consequence in a more deliberative fashion.

When things are going well for a company or industry, the focus is oftentimes on the product or service on a standalone basis, and this is probably as it should be. But as the product or service matures, and as opportunities open up for competitors, the landscape can change, and oftentimes rather quickly:

- Telegraph companies suddenly found themselves within a communications industry where persons could actually speak directly with one another via telephone; Morse code specialists became redundant, with telephones permitting people to communicate directly with one another in their own voices.[25]
- Telephone companies suddenly found themselves within a communications industry where persons could speak with one another via internet cable (or wirelessly) and for free.
- Television, radio, cable, and print media found themselves competing with cellphones and mobile devices as venues capable of providing users with access to music, news, shows, and movies, and even the ability to create and post their own content.
- The entertainment industry is adapting to a world where human-based reality is giving way to technological experiences; computer-generated holograms of rock stars, and crowd experiences of attending a concert or professional sports event that can be experienced while sitting at home with a high-tech headset.

Any firm in any industry can benefit from taking a quiet moment from time to time to think about the following questions in relation to evaluating what business it is in:

- Who are the competitors?
- Who are potential competitors, who has dropped away as a competitor, and who has been acquired or completed an acquisition?
- What are the new technologies that have been introduced into the industry?
- What are the new market segments that are emerging, or the older ones that are shrinking?
- What would be some examples of potential tangencies that could serve as venues to explore opportunities in the context of the industry's evolving landscape?

Tangencies might not only represent opportunities for firms to explore new revenue-generation opportunities, but perhaps also to tap into more efficient or
cost-saving solutions as well.[26]

***

Supply chains are another important part of the business model for many
firms, and are ripe for tangency considerations. Supply chains are connections
that businesses have to entities that provide goods or services necessary for operations. Professional sports teams have talent scouts to supply leads on promising
players. A surgeon is dependent on the single supplier of a unique medical
instrument. Walmart uses thousands of suppliers from all around the globe to
source its consumer products. A business can be in a situation where it is critically dependent upon one or two key suppliers, or may have so many suppliers
(and backups) that is rarely in a position of not having products to sell. In the
context of supply chains and tangencies, we can think of each supplier's goods
or services as being a potential revenue stream opportunity, either in terms of
supporting an important aspect of the business (for example, an employment
agency providing workers, or inputs for a final product), or a product that will
simply be passed along for sale (a cleaning product that a retailer places on their
shelf).[27]

For many companies the internet has served to create a direct line to key relationships. The historical roles of intermediaries are fading; for example, fewer
salespersons are engaging directly with customers, and purchasing agents are
negotiating terms and conditions with several potential suppliers as opposed to
obtaining products from electronic marketplaces where multiple vendors are put
into competition with one another.

For contexts where auctions are a viable alternative, what are the costs and
benefits to firms using auction venues to obtain the supplies it needs? Are auction processes conducive to firms building meaningful relationships, or do those
even matter? Is there perhaps value, from a risk-management perspective, to
using traditional and auction-based platforms to hedge against adverse disruptions
in critical supply-related needs? To what extent can existing platforms in these
regards, such as E2Open, help to ensure that supplier options are reliable and
reputable, or does due diligence fall entirely on the procurer of supplier
products?

There are no single correct answers to these questions that would be applicable
for every business model. Rather, these are questions that would be appropriate for
any supplier-dependent business to evaluate, and on a continuous basis.

Certainly one of the most fascinating case studies in the context of internet
supply management is Amazon.com. Amazon do not manufacture products, and
they do not have a traditional retail channel. Rather, Amazon is involved with
a large, complex, multidimensional supply chain that involves product manufacturers, and Amazon very carefully monitors how its pricing of products compares with that of independent online retailers.[28]

The online pricing strategy of many start-ups consists of offering goods or services at unsustainably low prices in order to capture market share, while the pricing strategy for many Bricks seeking an online presence has consisted of simply transferring their offline prices onto the internet. There are risks and opportunities involved with both of these approaches.

With Clicks, it is certainly the case that they generally do not have the same base of expense requirements of Bricks. Clicks do not require storefronts or onsite/nearby storage of inventories (and perhaps do not require any warehousing), and online customers can do their browsing and comparison shopping without the need of a sales clerk. There are also considerations related to competitive environment, as a user can simply click over to another website if prices are not seen as particularly compelling.[29]

***

As a parting context for the role of tangencies, let us consider the role of subscriptions as a fast-growing business model opportunity for many digital firms. The digital subscription economy is growing dramatically, with many businesses dating their start to when Adobe launched its subscription model in 2013. Since that time, innovative variations include Netflix memberships, the Dollar Shave Club, monthly Stitch Fix clothing, Amazon Prime, and monthly subscriptions for Microsoft Office, Amazon Web Services, and SaaS business apps.[30] Zuora CEO Tien Tzuo was the first to coin (and trademark) the term "the subscription economy," describing the trend of buying and using digital products and services on a pay-as-you-go (or grow) model. Today about 84% of net new software is offered in the form of software as a service (SaaS). While this model is dominant today, this was not quite the case in 2013.

Interesting scenarios of compare–contrast can arise when comparing subscription economy solutions involving Bricks versus those involving Clicks. For example, with the Netflix subscription model, one user who chooses to stream a particular movie does not prevent another user from streaming the same movie at the same time. However, with the MoviePass subscription model, a user who takes a seat in a theater might prevent another person (perhaps a full-price-paying user) from watching the same movie at the same time. At minimum, from a pricing model perspective, MoviePass would appear to have a more challenging problem to solve: selling the monthly pass at too low a price and risk movie-theater seats being unavailable for full-price customers, versus selling the pass at too high a price and foregoing sales to users who would otherwise be infrequent users of the monthly subscription. In one respect the modeling problem could be seen in the context of pricing an insurance product. MoviePass sells subscriptions (insurance policies) in the hope that revenues (insurance premiums) more than cover expenses (claims). To extend this analogy, here are additional similarities:

- Caps: Insurance companies often limit the claims dollars they pay for particular incidents, and MoviePass has a limit of three movie passes per month.
- Copays: Insurance companies may ask the user to pay a fee for particular types of healthcare visits, and MoviePass sometimes invokes "peak pricing" for certain releases.
- Cross-sells: Once an insurance company has a customer for one particular type of product, it may seek to sell them another; the mark-up for movie-theater snacks and beverages is well known.
- Deductibles: The base price of an insurance policy can increase with greater coverages, and a comparable situation exists with MoviePass, whereby surcharges exist for 3D productions and other special situations.
- Exclusions: Insurance companies often limit items that can be covered under a particular policy, or certain types of events that can give rise to claims; MoviePass limitations include select daily movie rotations, and not being able to see particular movies more than once.
- Seasonality: Just as there can be cyclicality with flood or hurricane insurance claims, there can be times of the year when moviegoing may be more or less popular (e.g., with timing of entertainment industry awards, holiday periods, and the "summer blockbuster," and so on).

In sum, tangencies can form a core part of a business or be a more opportunistic venue to evaluate a new idea. Tangencies can also be evaluated whereby a firm opens itself up (perhaps via API accessibilities) to be evaluated by a third party seeking a new opportunity. For each of these contexts, the internet is a readily accessible and adaptable venue for experimentation and implementation. Table 6.2 provides a comparison between the pursuit of tangencies versus that of acquisitions.

TABLE 6.2 Tangencies versus acquisitions

Tangencies	Acquisitions
Minimal capital	Capital commitment on some level
Outsourcing of build and maintenance	In-house build and maintenance
Culture preserved	Cultures may differ
Manageable to scale	Growth of resources is an in-house responsibility
Third-party dependencies	Dependencies are in-house
Ease of exit	Exit may be costly and time consuming
Arms-length risk exposure	Risk is brought in-house
Expansion of reach and expertise with minimal outlay	Commitment of capital and employee time can be considerable
Economized due diligence	Appreciable due diligence
Speed to implementation	Negotiations can take time
Boilerplate agreements	Tailored agreements

Notes

1 Mike Colias (2018, June 3), "GM's rebuilt finance arm: Profits minus the mortgage mess," *Wall Street Journal.*
2 For a historic tangency example, we could cite Carlsberg (yes, the brewery) and the decision by J.C. Jacobsen (Carlsberg's founder) to create the Carlsberg Laboratory in 1875, where leading-edge chemistry insights could be applied to making better beer; Jacobsen openly welcomed outside talent to join in with the research efforts (open-sourced solutions). Key discoveries were shared with others outside of the Carlsberg enterprise. Curiously, it was in 1908 that William Sealy Gosset of the Guinness brewery shared the value of t-distributions for small sample sizes (under the pseudonym "Student," in the publication *Biometrica*), and Guinness applied the insights to its own production runs.
3 "What is volatility?" (n.d.). Corporate Finance Institute. https://corporatefinanceinstitute.com/resources/knowledge/trading-investing/volatility-vol/.
4 With regards to the speed of information flows related to the financial markets in particular, consider the 2014 book *Flash Boys: A Wall Street Revolt,* by Michael Lewis (New York: W.W. Norton & Company).
5 The observation of higher inter-day price variations appears to be supported by other studies as well. For example, in *Anomalous Behavior of the Volatility of DJIA over the Last Century*, Working Paper No. 2006-03, Shaikh A. Hamid and Tej S. Dhakar find that daily percent changes in the DJIA for the first half of the twentieth century were lower than in the second half of the century. Further, they show that the pick-up in this volatility in the second half of the century appears in the mid-1970s, corresponding with Lev and Gu's observations related to the knowledge effect. Specifically, Hamid and Dhakar show that mean daily standard deviation values calculated a monthly spike from 0.67% in the 25-year period of 1950–1974, to 0.88% in the 25-year period immediately following (or nearly a third more volatility).

   In "Stock market volatility: 10 years after the crash" (1998; *Brookings-Wharton Papers on Financial Services*), G. William Schwert cites the largest daily percent increases and decreases in the DJIA from 1885 to 1997. In the 25-year period of 1950–1974 there are zero instances cited, while for 1975 to 1997 there are 7 instances catalogued. Following Schwert's stated methodology to continue calculations out to the end of 2018, there are several more instances that could be cited. Schwert also provides charts for other markets around the world, and it appears that outside of the United States there has generally been a more dampened volatility experience for the period of 1975 to 1997. This is of interest since these markets tend to treat knowledge differently from the United States: generally speaking, GAAP is applicable for the United States while IFRS is applicable for over 110 other countries and a company's development costs can be capitalized under IFRS as long as certain criteria are met (while with GAAP, development costs are expensed the year they occur and cannot be capitalized).
6 See Travis L. Johnson and Eric C. So (2018), "Asymmetric trading costs prior to earnings announcements: Implications for price discovery and returns," *Journal of Accounting Research 56*(1), 217–263; Xuan Huang, Alex Nekrasov, and Siew Hong Teoh (2018), "Headline salience, managerial opportunism, and over-and underreactions to earnings," *The Accounting Review, 93*(6), 231–255; and Patricia M. Dechow, Richard G. Sloan, and Jenny Zha (2014), "Stock prices and earnings: A history of research," *Annual Review of Financial Economics, 6*(1), 343–363.
7 As regards ETFs, these products can generally be regarded as portfolios of stocks and bonds. When purchases or sales of ETFs are made on a daily basis, their constituent parts must be bought and sold as well. Finally, while day traders may be contributing to the dampening of intra-day volatility as trades are reversed at the end of each trading session, they might also be contributing to the exacerbation of day-over-day volatility at the start of each new session as new rounds of trades are initiated.

8 To be sure, many significant transformations have affected turnover since 1950. For example, program trading emerged in the late 1980s, and some argue that this exacerbated the stock market crash of 1987. High-frequency trading (HFT) has more recently been cited as a culprit for market swings, and day-trading activity has most certainly grown into an important segment of the market. With the advent of Electronically Traded Funds (ETFs) in particular, it has become especially easy for professional investors and individual investors alike to actively move in and out of positions, often multiple times during the same day. Related to this notion of extreme short-term trading is the idea of "going home flat," or hedging (or completely unwinding) positions ahead of a market's close. This practice would seem to be consistent with a capping-off of daily returns, which are then revisited the following trading day.

9 Anup Srivastava (2014), "Why have measures of earnings quality changed over time?," *Journal of Accounting and Economics* 57 (2–3) (April 2014), 196–217.

10 The forecasts were collected from professional economists, and dispersion measures the statistical discrepancies with respect to that group. Specifically, the series shows the difference (dispersion) between the 75th and 25th percentiles of forecasts for growth at six months prior to the actual CPI release.

11 The rationale for referencing this data as opposed to some other forecast series is that the people at the Cleveland Fed have done outstanding work with respect to making strides with better understanding inflation dynamics.

12 See https://www.clevelandfed.org/our-research/indicators-and-data/inflation-expectations.aspx.

13 See https://www.clevelandfed.org/our-research/indicators-and-data/inflation-nowcasting/about-inflation-nowcasting.aspx. Academic studies have been performed to attest to other challenges of nowcasting, as with the value of waiting for data revisions. That is, many economic releases are subject to updates with new information after an initial release is announced; it's simply the case that certain things may not be known (or fully known) at the precise moment when the initial data is shared. See Dean Croushore (2008, March), *Frontiers of real-time data analysis*, Working Paper No. 08-4 (Philadelphia, PA: Research Department, Federal Reserve Bank of Philadelphia), https://philadelphiafed.org/-/media/research-and-data/publications/working-papers/2008/wp08-4.pdf?la=en.

14 There may not be updates every day, rather only on those days when the information content of a relevant economic variable is announced.

15 See "Frequently asked questions" (n.d.), GDP Now, *Federal Reserve Bank of Atlanta* [website]. https://www.frbatlanta.org/cqer/research/gdpnow.aspx?panel=2.

16 "A mean feat: Despite forecasters' best efforts, growth is devilishly hard to predict" (2016, January 9), *The Economist*.
     http://www.economist.com/node/21685480.

17 Similar dynamics seem to hold with the forecasting of key economic variables as well (GDP, CPI, etc.).

18 In the context of banking, a FinTech analyst might see the future of banking more in the context of a distribution platform, while a traditional analyst might see its future as being dominated more by the creation of products and services.

19 See Datanyze.com, as of rankings provided on January 21, 2019.

20 Larry Page (2015, August 10), "G is for Google," *Alphabet* [website], https://abc.xyz.

21 Ibid.

22 In June 2018, Forbes published a list of the top 2000 global companies ranked by market capitalization, and Google was ranked 23rd.

23 Peter F. Drucker (2004, February), "Defining business purpose and mission," *The Daily Drucker*.

24 I would like to thank Joe Borer, Marketing Operations Manager at Buckhorn Incorporated, for assisting with recalling the particulars of this seminal moment in the company's evolution.

25 It was also at about the same time as the telegraph's proliferation that public compan-
    ies began to publish their financials more widely, and modern-day rating agencies
    emerged. Indeed, Moody's began publishing in 1900, S&P in 1906, and Fitch in
    1913.

26 The question of "What business are you in?" is something that has been subject to
    significant academic interest as well. For example, in "Industry window dressing"
    (*Review of Financial Studies*, *29* (12), February 2016, 3354–3393), Huaizhi Chen,
    Lauren Cohen, and Dong Lou state:
    "A firm's primary industry classification is determined by the segment with the
    majority of sales. We find evidence that investors overly rely on this industry classifica-
    tion in their investment decisions without sufficiently factoring in firms' underlying
    economic operations." The authors then go on to discuss their research findings that
    suggest certain company managers may take specific actions in order to take advantage
    of being classified into "favorable" industries (i.e., those with high valuations). Indeed,
    firms that operate in favorable and non-favorable sectors and are close to industry
    assignment cutoffs are significantly more likely to be just over the 50% classification
    tipping point in terms of percentage sales from the favorable segment. These industry
    window-dressers also seem to devote a disproportionate amount of earnings conference
    calls to the favorable industry. (p. 3389)

27 In the case of Apple, their suppliers may sometimes see their equity price decline
    when Apple itself is perceived as being weaker or more vulnerable in the market-
    place; see Lauren Feiner (2019, January 3), "Apple's suppliers are getting crushed by
    its lowered revenue guidance," *CNBC*, https://www.cnbc.com/2019/01/03/apples-
    suppliers-are-getting-crushed-by-its-lowered-revenue-guidance.html.

28 One interesting dimension of Amazon's future will be observing the evolution of
    how other large retail venues such as Alibaba feed product into Amazon (e.g.,
    buying cheaper on Alibaba and selling for more on Amazon), and vice versa. In
    this fashion perhaps a global arbitrage-free marketplace will eventually materialize
    within a fascinating laboratory environment for observing the Law of One Price at
    work.

29 For evaluating ideas in the context of competitive forces, a variety of frameworks are
    available, including SWOT analysis (strengths, weaknesses, opportunities, and threats),
    PEST analysis (political, economic, social, and technological factors), PESTEL analysis
    (political, economic, social, technological, environmental, and technological), and
    Porter's Five Forces (competition in the industry, potential of new entrants, power of
    suppliers, power of customers, and threat of substitute products). Some view the pro-
    gression of SWOT to the other frameworks as an evolution from more micro con-
    siderations to more macro factors.

30 Of course, some business models are, and have always been, subscription-based,
    such as newspapers and magazines. Many of those publications that exist in Click
    formats offer a freemium opportunity, whereby an initial number of articles are
    free.

Bibliography

Ahuja, G., & Lampert, C. M. (2001). Entrepreneurship in a large corporation:
    A longitudinal study of how established firms create breakthrough inventions. *Strategic
    Management Journal*, *22*, 521–543.

Almeida, P., Song, J., & Grant, R. M. (2002). Are firms superior to alliances and markets? An
    empirical test of cross-border knowledge building. *Organization Science*, *13*(2), 147–161.

A mean feat: Despite forecasters' best efforts, growth is devilishly hard to predict. (2016,
    January 9). *The Economist*. http://www.economist.com/node/21685480.

Colias, M. (2018, June 3). GM's rebuilt finance arm: Profits minus the mortgage mess. *Wall Street Journal*.

Croushore, D. (2008, March). *Frontiers of real-time data analysis*. (Working Paper No. 08–4). (Philadelphia, PA: Research Department, Federal Reserve Bank of Philadelphia). Retrieved from https://philadelphiafed.org/-/media/research-and-data/publications/working-papers/2008/wp08-4.pdf?la=en.

Das, T. K., & Teng, B. (2000). A resource-based theory of strategic alliances. *Journal of Management, 26,* 31–61.

Dechow, P.M., Sloan, R.G., & Zha, J. (2014). Stock prices and earnings: A history of research. *Annual Review of Financial Economics, 6*(1), 343–363.

Drucker, P.F. (2004, February). Defining business purpose and mission. *The Daily Drucker*.

Dushnitsky, G., & Lavie, D. (2010). How alliance formation shapes corporate venture capital investment in the software industry: A resource-based perspective. *Strategic Entrepreneurship Journal, 4*(1), 22–48.

Dushnitsky, G., & Lenox, M. J. (2005). When do incumbents learn from entrepreneurial ventures? *Research Policy, 34*(5), 615–639.

Feiner, L. (2019, January 3). Apple's suppliers are getting crushed by its lowered revenue guidance. *CNBC*, https://www.cnbc.com/2019/01/03/apples-suppliers-are-getting-crushed-by-its-lowered-revenue-guidance.html.

Frequently asked questions. (n.d.). GDP Now, *Federal Reserve Bank of Atlanta* [website]. https://www.frbatlanta.org/cqer/research/gdpnow.aspx?panel=2.

Goerzen, A., & Beamish, P.W. (2005). The effect of alliance network diversity on multinational enterprise performance. *Strategic Management Journal, 26,* 333–354.

Gulati, R., & Singh, H. (1998). The architecture of cooperation: Managing coordination costs and appropriation concerns in strategic alliances. *Administrative Science Quarterly, 43*(4), 781–814.

Haans, R.F.J., Pieters, C. and He, Z.-L. (2016). Thinking about U: Theorizing and testing U- and inverted U-shaped relationships in strategy research. *Strategic Management Journal, 37*(7), 1177–1195.

Hamel, G., Doz, Y.L., & Prahalad, C.K. (1989). Collaborate with your competitors and win. *Harvard Business Review, 67*(1), 133–139.

Hamid, S.A., & Dhakar, T.S. (2006). *Anomalous behavior of the volatility of DJIA over the last century*. (Working Paper No. 2006–03). Manchester, NH: Southern New Hampshire University.

Hoang, H.T., & Rothaermel, F. T. (2005). The effect of general and partner-specific alliance experience on joint R&D project performance. *Academy of Management Journal, 48*(2), 332–345.

Huang, X., Nekrasov, A., & Teoh, S.H. (2018). Headline salience, managerial opportunism, and over-and underreactions to earnings. *The Accounting Review, 93*(6), 231–255.

Hoffmann, W.H. (2007). Strategies for managing a portfolio of alliances. *Strategic Management Journal, 28,* 827–856.

Johnson, T.L., & So, E.C. (2018). Asymmetric trading costs prior to earnings announcements: Implications for price discovery and returns. *Journal of Accounting Research 56*(1), 217–263.

Kale, P., Dyer, J., & Singh, H. (2002). Alliance capability, stock market response and long-term alliance success: The role of the alliance function. *Strategic Management Journal, 23,* 747–767.

Katila, R., & Ahuja, G. (2002). Something old, something new: A longitudinal study of search behavior and new product introduction. *Academy of Management Journal, 45*(6), 1183–1194.

Keil, T. (2004). Building external corporate venturing capability: Initial conditions, learning processes and knowledge management. *Journal of Management Studies*, *41*(5), 799–825.

Lavie, D., Kang, J., & Rosenkopf, L. (2011). Balance within and across domains: The performance implications of exploration and exploitation in alliances. *Organization Science*, *22*(6), 1517–1538.

Lavie, D., & Miller, S.R. (2008). Alliance portfolio internationalization and firm performance. *Organization Science*, *19*(4), 623–646.

Leten, B., Belderbos, R., & Van Looy, B. (2016). Entry and performance in new technology domains. *Journal of Management Studies*, *53*(8), 1257–1291.

Lewis, M. (2014). *Flash boys: A Wall Street revolt*. New York: W.W. Norton & Company.

MacMillan, I., Roberts, E., Livada, V., Wang, A. (2008). Corporate venture capital (CVC): Seeking innovation and strategic growth. Gaithersburg, MD/Washington, DC: National Institute of Standards and Technology-US Department of Commerce 08–916.

Narayanan, V.K., Yang, Y., & Zahra, S. A. (2009). Corporate venturing and value creation: A review and proposed framework. *Research Policy*, *38*(1), 58–76.

Page, L. (2015, August 10). G is for Google. *Alphabet* [website]. https://abc.xyz.

Sampson, R.C. (2007). R&D alliances and firm performance: The impact of technological diversity and alliance organization on innovation. *Academy of Management Journal*, *50*(2), 364–386.

Sarkar, M.B., Aulakh, P.S., & Madhok, A. (2009). Process capabilities and value generation in alliance portfolios. *Organization Science*, *20*(3), 583–600.

Shi, W., Sun, J., & Prescott, J.E. (2012). A temporal perspective of merger and acquisition and strategic alliance initiatives: Review and future direction. *Journal of Management*, *38*(1), 164–209.

Schilling, M.A. (2009). Understanding the alliance data. *Strategic Management Journal*, *30*(3), 233–260.

Schilke, O., & Goerzen, A. (2010). Alliance management capability: An investigation of the construct and its measurement. *Journal of Management*, *36*, 1192–1219.

Schwert, G.W. (1998). Stock market volatility: 10 years after the crash. *Brookings-Wharton Papers on Financial Services* (January).

Srivastava, A. (2014). Why have measures of earnings quality changed over time? *Journal of Accounting and Economics 57* (2–3) (April 2014), 196–217.

Sykes, H. (1990). Corporate venture capital: Strategies for success. *Journal of Business Venturing*, *5*(1), 37–47.

Wadhwa, A., Phelps, C., & Kotha, S. (2010). Creating exploratory innovations by learning from entrepreneurial ventures. In D.B. Audretsch, G.B. Dagnino, R. Faraci & R. E. Hoskisson (Eds.), *New frontiers in entrepreneurship* (pp. 147–173). New York: Springer.

What is volatility? (n.d.). Corporate Finance Institute. https://corporatefinanceinstitute.com/resources/knowledge/trading-investing/volatility-vol/.

7

CYBER RISK

While a convenience of digital data is that it is easily stored and readily accessible, that also represents one of its greatest risks; namely, the threat of a database being hacked, with all manner of personal or corporate proprietary data being stolen and compromised in some way. Another risk is that a hacker might gain access to a database, and then demand a ransom for not wreaking havoc in one way or another. Because of the potential for abuse, both within a company (intentional or otherwise) and from outside it (intentional or otherwise), a plethora of laws and regulations have been promulgated by governmental (and quasi-governmental) agencies around the world to help safeguard consumer information, with fines payable if companies are deemed to have failed to ensure proper privacy and other protections are in place.

With the proliferation of data comes a great responsibility to protect privacy matters in relation to it, and this is especially true when it comes to particularly sensitive information with financial or medical significance. In recognition of this, finance sector regulatory bodies around the world are signaling a clear intention to monitor privacy practices.

The Chinese word for "crisis" is composed of two characters; one that signifies danger or risk, and another that denotes opportunity. Within this context, the notion of risk management for a firm can be thought of as identifying metrics that can assist with preserving and growing opportunity while minimizing failure.

Risks of failure can emanate from many sources, though broadly speaking these may be either internal or external, and can evolve from either anticipated or unanticipated circumstances. For example, the senior management of a firm (internal) may elect to pursue development of a new product with a clear understanding of the risks involved, yet the new product may simply not catch on due to its high price point (an anticipated outcome). In another scenario, a firm's competitor (external) might suddenly exit the marketplace (an unanticipated event) and hence permit a greater-than-expected level of success for a new product.

***

Certainly an important differentiating factor between nondigital and digital companies and processes is the ease of collecting and storing information with the latter. The desirability for a company to have its key customer data in one well-organized and detailed central repository also serves as an enticement for hackers (external) to illegitimately take that data, either to use it themselves or to resell it to others who will exploit it for their own gain. It can also be an enticement for a disgruntled or rogue employee (internal) to compromise their firm.

Personal data can be quite valuable; not only data pertaining to credit card numbers and the like, but also information that reveals behavior, spanning buying habits and health records. When regulators express concern and impose fines in relation to privacy violations, they are addressing all of these areas of potential risk.

Any company may have both internal and external data that it has collected. Further, in both contexts the data can be either personal or non-personal. For example, a company's internal data might include each employee's personally identifiable information (e.g., social security numbers for payroll) as well as any company trade secrets. Meanwhile, a company's external data might include the credit card numbers of its customers. Generally speaking, privacy laws have more recently tended to be centered on the adequate safeguarding of consumer data.

Some broad categories of possible cyber violations in relation to consumer privacy could include the following:

- Internal: A company misuses external data it has collected.
- Internal: A company fails to properly protect external data it has collected.
- Internal: A rogue employee compromises internal data, or data collected from outside third-party customers or other sources.
- External: A company is subject to an attack whereby its own internal data is compromised, or its holdings of external third-party data are compromised (from customers or other).
- External: A company is forced to pay ransom in exchange for not having its external data stolen, or is otherwise compromised.

Fines pertaining to the above can be related to the following:

- Failure to report the incident in a timely fashion, or not at all
  (Yahoo in 2018: fine of $35 million for failure to report a data breach).
- Failure to have implemented proper safeguards that could have prevented an incident

(Target in 2017: fine of $18.5 million for its failure to attend to proper safeguards and warnings, which resulted in an incident).
- Making payments to cover up an incident
  (Uber in 2018: Fine of $148 million for paying hackers to cover up a breach).
- Data breach by a rogue employee
  (Morrisons supermarket chain in 2018: significant legal and defense expenses were incurred in this closely watched UK case, and corporate liability was established for the data breach made by a person under the company's employ).
- Misuse of personal data
  (Allegations that Facebook exposed up to 87 million users' information to Cambridge Analytica, violation of a prior agreement with the commission, and misuse of phone numbers obtained for account security purposes).

While there are certainly many things about cyber risks that are new from a technology standpoint, there are business and political considerations that are equally novel in these contexts as well. For example, until 2019 with Facebook, the largest fines related to privacy violations were levied by European authorities against United States–based companies. Cyber risk and accountability transcends just about every kind of boundary. Figure 7.1 provides a framework for thinking about cyber risk contexts.

A variety of principles related to the importance of privacy have been promulgated around the world, and a sampling of these include the following:

- Transparent management of personal information.
- Anonymity.
- Treatment of solicited personal information.
- Handling of unsolicited personal information.
- Notification of the collection of personal information.
- Use or disclosure of personal information.
- Cross-border disclosure of personal information.
- Security of personal information.
- Access to personal information.
- Correction of personal information.

What's more, nuances in what is most important about privacy can vary from country to country, and it has been estimated that over 80 countries have privacy laws today. In the USA, many states have promulgated their own privacy laws, and in some global jurisdictions a website is required to obtain the implied consent of users when browser cookies are used. In other locations a user has the right to demand that their personal data be deleted at any time. Aside from differences in what is reflected or not within privacy laws, there are also varying views on what personal information consists of (e.g., an IP address). Even within countries, privacy laws can differ by industry. In the United States, healthcare is governed by the Health Insurance Portability and

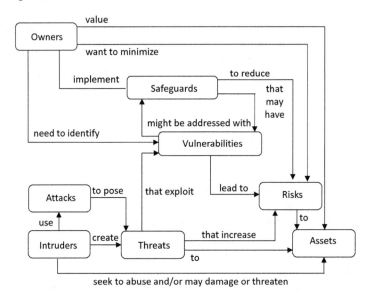

The above framework is with reference to schematic ISO 15408:2005,
and multiple variations can be created

FIGURE 7.1   Framework for thinking about cyber risk contexts

Accountability Act of 1996 (or HIPAA), while banking is governed by the
Gramm-Leach-Bliley Act of 1999. And in Europe, the General Data Protection
Regulation (GDPR) is applicable across many industries including healthcare
and banking, but a challenging wrinkle exists with the latter.[1] That is, Europe
also has the Markets in Financial Instruments Directive II (MiFID II), and this
has a strong element of know your customer (KYC), which involves the collection and retention of a large volume of client and counterparty information
including electronic communications, data which must be made available to
regulators within 72 hours of a request. Meantime, GDPR mandates the protection of rights related to data erasure. Understanding and safeguarding privacy
may be more of a journey than a destination for some time to come. In the
meantime, with the significant risk and potential costs to business of being in
breach of a privacy protection, or of having security pierced, it behooves every
company with digital data to take continuous precautions to adequately protect
all information in its possession.[2]

***

Table 7.1 presents a variety of corporate fines and penalties of various types
issued against companies in the United States and Europe. The range of amounts
involved is rather wide, from $12 million to $20.8 billion. Certainly one consideration that helps to explain the disparity in these numbers would be the particular alleged offenses.[3]

TABLE 7.1 Larger fines and penalties imposed against corporations, United States and Europe, 2012 to July 2019

	Company	Fine/ Penalty	Year	Jurisdiction	Company HQ	Reason
Data and Privacy						
	Facebook	$5B	2019	US	US	Security
	Uber	$148M	2018	US	US	Security
	Google	€50M	2019	France	US	Data infraction
	Apple	$32.5M	2014	US	US	Choice and consent
	Tyco	€30M	2019	France	Ireland	Data infraction
	AT&T	$25M	2015	US	US	Security
	Google	$22.5M	2012	US	US	Collection
	Tesco Bank	$21M	2018	UK	UK	Security
	Google	$17M	2013	US	US	Collection and notice
	Anthem Blue Cross	$16M	2018	US	US	Security
Antitrust						
	Google	$5.0B	2018	Europe	US	Requiring mobile phone to pre-install Google Search and its browser app
	Google	$2.7B	2017	Europe	US	Google shopping being given an illegal advantage
	Qualcomm	$1.2B	2018	Europe	US	Unfair payments arrangement
	Citicorp	$925M	2017	US	US	Foreign currency exchange
	Barclays, PLC	$650M	2017	US	UK and Northern Ireland	Foreign currency exchange
	Servier and other pharmceuticals	$582M	2014	Europe	France	Colluding to delay introduction of a drug so as to purchase competitors
	JPMorgan Chase & Co.	$550M	2017	US	US	Foreign currency exchange

(Continued)

TABLE 7.1 (Cont.)

Company	Fine/Penalty	Year	Jurisdiction	Company HQ	Reason
AU Optronics Corporation of Taiwan	$500M	2012	US	Taiwan	Liquid Crystal Display (LCD) panels
Yazaki Corporation	$470M	2012	US	Japan	Automobile parts
Bridgestone Corporation	$425M	2014	US	Japan	Anti-vibration rubber products for automobiles

Corporate crimes

Company	Fine/Penalty	Year	Jurisdiction	Company HQ	Reason
British Petroleum	$20.8B	2016	US	UK	Several violations inclusive of environmental damages
Bank of America	$16.65B	2014	US	US	Inadequate risk disclosure of complex securities
Volkswagen	$14.7B	2016	US	Germany	Anomalies with emissions tests
JP Morgan Chase	$13B	2013	US	US	Inadequate risk disclosure of complex securities
BNP Paribas	$8.9B	2014	US	France	Improper channelling of international funds
CitiGroup	$7B	2014	US	US	Mortgage related issues
Anadarko Petroleum	$5.15B	2014	US	US	Environmental considerations
GoldmanSachs	$5B	2010	US	US	Issues with complex securities
GlaxoSmithKline	$3B	2012	US	US	Misbranding and hiding safety information
Credit Suisse	$2.88B	2014	US	Switzerland	Tax evasion assistance

Sources: https://digitalguardian.com/blog/hilton-was-fined-700k-data-breach-under-gdpr-it-would-be-420m; https://learn.censible.co/risky-business-top-ten-corporate-crackdowns/; https://www.businessinsider.com/the-7-biggest-fines-the-eu-has-ever-imposed-against-giant-corporations-2018-7#7-telefnica-fined-207-million-in-2007-10; https://www.computerworld.com/article/2487796/data-privacy/jay-cline--u-s--takes-the-gold-in-doling-out-privacy-fines.html; https://www.csoonline.com/article/3316569/data-breach/biggest-data-breach-penalties-for-2018.html; https://www.esecurityplanet.com/network-security/att-hit-with-record-breaking-25-million-data-breach-fine.html; https://www.theverge.com/2018/4/24/17275994/yahoo-sec-fine-2014-data-breach-35-million

To help protect us from becoming unnecessarily distracted by various nuances of corporate law, for our purposes here we cite the following three areas of potential wrongdoing, ranked by increasing fine amounts:

• Data/privacy matters.
• Antitrust matters.
• Criminal matters.

With each of the above categories, there can be instances whereby an alleged violation was intended by a firm, and situations where it was unintended. For example, a credit card company may not have intended to have its sensitive data be stolen, yet nonetheless failed to adequately safeguard against this. Or a pharmaceutical company may not have intended for its new drug to cause harm, but missed something in a testing phase. And a company may have thought it was acting in good faith with acquiring a company, only to have the government decide that it was somehow acting in an anticompetitive fashion. Sometimes these considerations are cast in the context of a company being the "victim" rather than the "aggressor," as with their being hacked (victimized) as opposed to making unauthorized use of personal data (proactive wrongdoing). This seems to be borne out in Table 7.1 in relation to penalties and fines, with Uber being required to pay $148 million in 2018 for alleged efforts to withhold information about a data breach from drivers and authorities, versus a $12 million fine for LifeLock in 2010 for allegedly boasting that it had protection safeguards that were not as strong as it had claimed.

In 2015 Lifelock was ordered by the Federal Trade Commission (FTC) to pay a $100 million fine for alleged violation of terms pertaining to LifeLock's 2010 court order. This record FTC fine for an order enforcement action places the dollar amount of a non-data breach situation into the upper reaches of fines where a breach occurred.[4]

The $5B size of the Facebook fine is such that it's tempting to view it not so much as a fine within a new upper-tier of data violations, but as a fine that has been pushed into the lower-tier of the next category of corporate malfeasance: antitrust. In this vein, perhaps it is not a coincidence that the $5B amount matches the antitrust fine imposed by Europe against Google a year earlier in July 2018.[5]

As another insight into deciphering corporate fines and penalties, we can look at the size of monetary payments in relation to a year of income for that particular firm. For example, in 2012 British Petroleum's fine related to their oil-spill episode amounted to 110% of the company's annual income, while in that same year Johnson & Johnson's fine for improper drug marketing was 23% of its income, and Barclays Bank's fine for charges of manipulating interest rates was 5% of its income.

As a normative matter, a legal message here seems to be that while privacy and data violations are bad, they have not risen to a level of criminality in terms of upper-level fines. Perhaps part of the reasoning behind this is an element of understanding related to how very challenging it can be to effectively manage enormous amounts of information, and that there can be a meaningful distinction between being passively guilty of perhaps not doing enough to ensure safeguards are in place, and proactively seeking to do evil.

What will be of great interest to watch in the next couple of years is how fines are levied for data and privacy breaches around the world, and particularly in Europe with the implementation of the GDPR. At the time of writing, there are cases pending that are being closely monitored for potential record-breaking fines.

For one particular take on all this, there is a rather unique modern development here in that a company might find itself liable for monetary damages relating to activities that historically had not been regarded as core elements of its business operations. The furthest back that there seems to have been a data or privacy breach of much consequence in the United States, at least in relatively recent history, would be 1984.[6] Prior to the 1980s it would certainly have made sense to a banker that their firm's customer data had tremendous value, though the notion of someone stealing it would not likely have been a strong consideration. An even more remote thought would have been the threat that they could be fined because someone else had illegally taken something from them. It would perhaps be analogous to the suggestion today that someone who has been mugged should be fined for permitting themselves to be robbed. But things have changed. Due to the ease of loading a USB key with a volume of

TABLE 7.2 Factors that can moderate and exacerbate cyber episodes

Factors that can moderate cyber episodes	Factors that can exacerbate cyber episodes
Board-level involvement	Artificial intelligence usage
Data classification schema effectuated	Cloud usage
Employee training	Compliance failures
Existance of a Chief Protection Officer	Extensive use of IoT venues
Frequent changing of passwords	Integrations with mobile devices
Incident response team in place	Lost or stolen devices
Insurance in place	Third-party relationships
Involvement of business continuity management (BCM)	Use of consultants
Participation in threat sharing	
Speed of notification with breaches	
Strength of ID protection	
Use of data loss protection software (DLP)	
Use of encryption	
Use of security analytics	

TABLE 7.3 Types of cyber acts and perpetrators

Acts	Perpetrators
Botnets	Competitors
Cyber espionage	Corporations
Data breaches	Cybercriminals
Denial of service	Cyberfighters
Disruptions	Cyberterrorists
Exploit kits	Hacktivists
Identity theft	Insiders
Information leakage	Malware
Insider threat	Nation states
Outages	Non-malicious users expose a weakness
Phishing	Script kiddies
Physical manipulation/damage/theft/loss	
Ransomware	
Spam	
Web application attacks	

data that at one time would have been stored in rows of filing cabinets, the world has changed rather dramatically. Now it is the entity that has been robbed that may find itself being fined, and rather expensively so; and it may be fined for something related to a more tangential aspect of its business (books and records) rather than to its core revenue-generating activities (making loans, taking in deposits, providing financial advice, and so on).

In addition to all that a firm can realistically do to protect itself against cyber harm, there is the availability of cyber insurance, and this is something that any firm with a digital presence ought to at least look into having.

Table 7.2 presents a listing of factors that may exacerbate or moderate possible cyber episodes, and Table 7.3 shows types of cyber acts and perpetrators.

Cyber risk is probably more of a journey than a destination, in which continuous efforts are paramount to helping reduce, though perhaps not ever perfectly eradicating, the threat of a breach. In this context, regulatory authorities around the world are making it quite clear that firms involved in any way with data, and especially data in digital form, absolutely must be diligent in regard to every aspect of their relationship to it.

***

Notes

1 A companion set of laws for Europe alongside the GDPR are the Privacy and Electronic Communications (EC Directive) Regulations 2003 (PECR).
2 As this is being written, the outcome of the Brexit negotiations is very much uncertain. The United Kingdom has laws governing its financial sector (the Financial

Services and Markets Act 2000) and data (United Kingdom Data Protection Act 2018), though how these will evolve in the coming months and years remains to be seen. A sampling of more recent cases in the UK includes the following:

- £100,000 fine for AMS marketing (August 2018), for sales calls made without checking the Telephone Preference Service (TPS) register.
- £60,000 fine for STS Commercial Ltd (July 2018) after sending spam texts (also referred to as "unsolicited direct marketing") without receivers' consent.
- £200,000 fine for revealing the names of child-sexual-abuse victims in a mass email (July 2018)
- £140,000 fine for Lifecycle Marketing Ltd (August 2018) for selling personal data records to Experian.
- £2,000 fine for Noble Design and Build of Telford (July 2018) for failing to respond to an information request regarding use of closed-circuit televisions.

3 No judgment is intended to be reflected here, as in some instances the cases cited are under review in one way or another.
4 Specifically, the FTC's 2015 filing alleged LifeLock violated various elements of the 2010 order.
5 Variations of privacy and data protection themes seem to be evolving on a regular basis as well. For example, in February 2019 it was announced by Germany's Federal Cartel Office (antitrust) that it would seek limitations against Facebook being able to gather and use information collected about people from websites other than Facebook. com (apparently via Facebook "Like" and "Share" buttons and others). It seems Facebook was also to be discouraged from using information gleaned from other business venues owned by Facebook, such as WhatsApp.
6 In 1984 a global credit information company called TRW, and today known as Experian, was subjected to a hacking in which about 90 million records were stolen.

In what is admittedly a stretch of sorts to what may have been history's first-ever data theft, we can cite the appropriation of books and manuscripts by Norman Crusaders in the year 1204 when they ransacked the Imperial Library in Constantinople. Some historical scholars even believe that some of this stolen information may have been sold to Italian buyers, who greatly valued the insightful content (see historyofinformation.com).

If we were to define data theft in the context of activities intended to collect valuable information in a clandestine way, we could go back to at least the time of Sun Tzu in around 500 BC, when he wrote *The Art of War* and spoke of the use of spies, the five classes of spies, and the "divine manipulation of the threads."

In terms of electronic data security breaches, we could look to the telegraph. In fact, there is a story that a wavelength Marconi had intended to use for a demo of his new wireless invention was hacked by someone wanting to show that the messages could not be sent privately. In time, encryption methods were developed.

Bibliography

Betterley, R. (2010). *Understanding the cyber risk insurance and remediation services marketplace: A report on the experiences and opinions of middle market CFOs*. Sterling, MA: Betterley Risk Research. http://www.casact.org/community/affiliates/CANE/0412/Betterley2.pdf.

Betterley, R. (2013). *Cyber/privacy insurance market survey*. Sterling, MA: Betterley Risk Research. Retrieved from http://betterley.com/samples/cpims13_nt.pdf.

Cyber attack statistics. (n.d.). *Hackmageddon* [website]. Retrieved from http://hackmageddon.com/. Regularly updated. Last accessed June 18, 2019.

ENISA. (2012). *Incentives and barriers of the cyber insurance market in Europe.* Retrieved from https://www.enisa.europa.eu/publications/incentives-and-barriers-of-the-cyber-insurance-market-in-europe/.

European Commission. (2012). *Proposal for a regulation of the European parliament and of the Council on the protection of individuals with regard to the processing of personal data and on the free movement of such data (General Data Protection Regulation).*

Gordon, L. A., Loeb, M. P., & Sohail, T. (2003). A framework for using insurance for cyber-risk management. *Communications of the ACM, 44*(9), 70–75.

Government Communications Headquarters (GCHQ). (2012). *10 steps to cyber security.* White Paper of the Information Security Arm of GCHG. London: GCHG.

Harvard Business Review Analytic Services. (2013). *Meeting the cyber risk challenge.* Boston, MA: Harvard Business School Publishing.

Healey, J. (2013). *A fierce domain: Conflict in cyberspace, 1986 to 2012.* Vienna, VA: Cyber Conflict Studies Association.

Hofmann, A., & Ramaj, H. (2011). Interdependent risk networks: The threat of cyber attack. *International Journal of Management and Decision Making, 11*(5/6), 312–323.

Kesan, J. P., Majuca, R. P., & Yurcik, W. J. (2004). *The economic case for cyberinsurance.* University of Illinois Law and Economics Working Papers.

McAfee. (2013). The economic impact of cybercrime. https://www.mcafee.com/enterprise/en-us/assets/executive-summaries/es-economic-impact-cybercrime.pdf.

National Association of Insurance Commissioners (NAIC). (2013). Cyber risk. Retrieved from http://www.naic.org/cipr_topics/topic_cyber_risk.htm. Last accessed June 18, 2019.

Nierhaus, F. (1986). A strategic approach to insurability of risks. *Geneva Papers on Risk and Insurance – Issues and Practice, 11*(2), 83–90.

Ponemon Institute. (2013b). Managing cyber security as a business risk: Cyber insurance in the digital age. Retrieved from https://www.experian.com/innovation/thought-leadership/ponemon-study-managing-cyber-security-as-business-risk.jsp.

Shetty, N. S. G., Felegyhazi, M., & Walrand, J. (2010). Competitive cyber-insurance and internet security. In T. Moore, D. Pim, & C. Ioannidis (Eds.), *Economics of information security and privacy* (pp. 229–247). New York: Springer.

Wang, Q.-H., & Kim, S. H. (2009). Cyberattacks: Does physical boundary matter? ICIS 2009 Proceedings, Paper 48. Proceedings of 30th Annual International Conference on Information Systems, Phoenix, AZ, December 15–18, pp. 1–18.

The White House. (2013). Executive Order: Improving critical infrastructure cybersecurity. Exec. Order.

Willis. (2013). *Willis Fortune 500 cyber disclosure report.* http://blog.willis.com/downloads/cyber-disclosure-fortune-500.

PART III

The future of digital finance

8

BECOMING DIGITAL

For many companies today it is not so much a matter of being digital on some level or other, but rather a case of deciding which degree of digitalization is perhaps the most appropriate, or how to better manage current digital venues. For some firms, becoming more digital may be a matter of being more proactive with marketing campaigns that tap into social media venues, while for other companies, a stronger digital presence may be defined as aggressively seeking to optimize channel integrations (such as between Click and Brick operations). For still others, becoming more digital may mean launching an artificial intelligence project, or a new app. Regardless of where a firm may be, and whether it has realized it or not, the chances are very good that it is already using powerful digital functions. Even basic email functionality today has automated decision rules built in, ranging from the identification of spam to autocomplete for words and phrases, and even reminders to attach a file, reply to an unopened message, or place a meeting into a calendar. The digital world is here and now, and the open-ended nature of the question of what is the best next move can be daunting. Playing it safe may contribute to FOMO (Fear of Missing Out), and justifiably so if a competitor steps up with a compelling innovation. But being on the leading edge could be a risky proposition as well if a new technology leapfrogs the one your company is presently developing, or if the reality of it does not quite correspond to your original vision. Most firms today at least have a website, and thereby have access to helpful (and free) metrics that can be captured with online analytical tools to identify visitors and their behavior and to create strategies for converting visits into purchases. In brief, large budgets and grand schemes are not required to tap into the power of digital, and you can start from wherever you are right now.

It can be daunting to think about what it can mean for a firm to simultaneously manage for near-term results, position for longer-term growth, and strategically channel challenges of digitization into a value creation opportunity, and all while operating under the constraints of limited investment bandwidth and perhaps, even, with little knowledge of what all this means. Figure 8.1 provides an illustration of layers to channel integration for Bricks and Clicks.

In many respects, "digital" represents opportunities for a firm to differentiate itself. This differentiation can come about by using digital resources in order to: better understand current and potential customers so as to sell them even more; identify gaps in current offerings as regards customer interests and then filling those; reaching new customers; providing goods and services more quickly; or providing altogether new customer experiences. Firms that do not at least have some kind of digital strategy, however basic it might be, run the risk of not only missing out on a chance to improve and grow, but of failing to retain (or onboard) talented individuals who very much want to be a part of a digital future.

There can be value in looking at what a variety of industries are doing beyond your particular firm's sphere of interest. This is not only for the ideas you might see that relate to your own operations, but because your customers live in the same world you do, and the advancements they benefit from in one area could eventually become standards that they also expect your company to fulfill.[1]

A case could perhaps be made that departments within firms evolved over the years as separate entities because of delineations imposed by the nature of the data itself; for example, accounting data being distinct from marketing data and operations data, and so forth. With increasing available methods today which allow us to collate and report all types of data elements on a single dashboard, distinctions on the basis of data types may be fading in favor of differentiations on the basis of skillsets in order to take data streams and turn them into deliverables for value-added decision-making. That is, to evolve from reporting to interpreting, analyzing, recommending, and implementing. In this new context, the lines separating the traditional functions of sales, marketing, accounting, and so forth may become increasing blurred, to be replaced by an organizational culture in which department labels mean less than collective results.

Against this backdrop, partnerships, alliances, third parties, and vendor relationships can be expected to become very important. Indeed, relationship building has

FIGURE 8.1 Layers to channel integration, Bricks (offline) and Clicks (online)

never been as important in business as it is today. At the very least, it is a good idea to take advantage of opportunities to attend vendor presentations, industry workshops, and trade shows/conferences. Use these venues to not only hear what presenters have to say, but what your colleagues from other firms are talking about as well, whether on a panel discussion or during a coffee break.

One way to think about organizing one's thoughts around digitization can be with respect to the following:

- Customer engagement – using online, social media, and mobile apps to strengthen existing customer relationships and identify new business.
- Data and analytics – using big data, real-time analytics, and cognitive computing to better understand sources of existing business and evaluate market opportunities.
- Ecosystem dynamics – electronic information exchanges, Internet of Things (IoT), and evaluating how the firm's digitization efforts fit into the bigger picture.
- Operations – straight-through processing and robotic process automation (RPA), and considering nondigital practices that might be better performed if digitization were involved.
- Enhancements – unified digital platforms, digital solution development methodology and processes, and evaluating current digital solutions in the context of how they can be improved.
- New offerings – plans to generate value from a new digitization initiative, use process improvement methods, and measure expected revenue enhancements or expense mitigations.
- Intel – deliberative efforts to use publicly accessible digital (and other) data to evaluate a firm's positioning relative to competitors.
- Culture – having a corporate environment in which stakeholders can feel supported if they raise ideas related to digitalization.

There are a few ways in which a firm might see itself in the context of digitization:

- All-in digital – Embracing a digital theme across every area where it could possibly be applied.
- Opportunistic digital – Applying digitization to areas where value is perceived, and oftentimes operated in-house.
- Digital aspirations – At the beginning stages of a commitment to digital projects.
- Targeted digital – A near-term and narrowly defined application of digital, perhaps with reference to a third-party platform.
- Currently uncertain – Thinking there could be value in using digital, but uncertain how to proceed.
- Non-digital – Making a deliberate decision that digital is not to be pursued for at least the time being, for any number of reasons.

Figure 8.2 presents a view of the intensity of technology in relation to business models, and Figure 8.3 shows a perspective of user involvement by type of financial activity.

The motivation for digitization can be multifold, including factors related to strategic positioning, revenue enhancement, expense minimization, marketing, operations and legal. Various considerations that could fall under these headings might include:

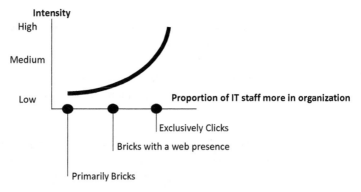

FIGURE 8.2 Intensity of technology in relation to business models

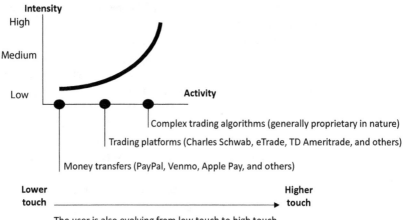

FIGURE 8.3 Intensity of direct user involvement by financial activity

- Customers: Is there market potential that could be opportunistically tapped via digital venues (social media)?
- Agility: Could a digital approach provide for a more expedient offering in the marketplace (Click versus Brick)?
- Products and services: Is it possible to provide the firm's offerings via digital means (app)?
- Existing markets: Are there market segments that might be especially receptive to a new digital approach (millennials)?
- Expenses: Could digitization help to lower the costs of doing business in some way, as with risk mitigation (blockchain)?
- New markets: Are there untapped users that could be accessed, within local markets or by using more far-reaching campaigns (going global)?
- Decision-making: Could digitization help streamline or facilitate decision-making or communication processes (Slack)?
- Revenue: Is there a digital dimension to a business that might lend itself to becoming a revenue stream in some way (such as the sale of internally generated data)?

Questions that businesses might ask themselves when evaluating a digital strategy include the following:

- Vision: This identifies what the proposal is all about, and why it is important. How does the digital strategy align with the overall corporate strategy, and why is this particular initiative so important to achieve?
- Imperatives: Clear goals must be identified, and with success criteria well defined, particularly those related to strategic positioning, revenue enhancement, and expense mitigation. The question might be: Who are the beneficiaries, what are reasonable revenue and expense expectations, how is success measured, and who is accountable?
- Plan versus reality: In brief, this is a candid assessment of where the firm is, and what is required for the strategy to be successful. What are the gaps, how does the plan address those, and what are the required resources?
- Resources: Is the talent (full-time, part-time, consultants) required for success presently with the firm, and if not, would it be best acquired by hiring, acquisition, or a partnership/alliance?
- Touchpoints and revenues: Is the nature of the strategy such that an agile and iterative approach could be used, whereby well-defined sprints could be implemented to begin achieving revenue prior to final project completion?[2]
- Refine and modify: The goals and success criteria identified under the imperatives step should be routinely reviewed for benchmarking purposes, with any adjustments made along the way. Would any goals benefit from being pushed forward or back, or removed altogether? Might there be any new goals that have emerged? KPIs that could be relevant to this might include:

- Customer KPIs: net promoter scores, repeat business, and conversion rates.
- Employee KPIs: onboarding time, turnover, and revenue per employee.
- Process KPIs: average resolution time, rejection or return rates.
- Financial KPIs: revenue per customer, time customers spend at the improved venue.

***

Silos and synergies

There is an important distinction to be made between the situation of a company that was not digital previously wanting to move in that direction, and that of its originating as a digital company. One way to characterize this distinction is in the context of silos.

A silo within a firm can be defined in a variety of ways, and one of those would be as a particular department (usually of more than one person) that in one regard or another has come to see itself (or to be perceived by others) as being more of an entity unto itself. In some situations it can be a matter of a particular department answering more unto itself or a select few than to the organization as a whole; more a matter of accountability, than hierarchy.

For traditional companies seeking to make digital more of a centerpiece of their business, digital initiatives may look to some individuals in the organization to act like the tip of a spear intended to pierce a particular silo's outer shell. Sharing the digital strategy with the organization can help with buy-in and support of the initiative.

For companies that stand out as digital, that can often mean that from day one the functions of sales and marketing are already bound together in a natural alliance (with online products and services being sold via online marketing campaigns), and accounting and finance are not too far removed from online payment collections, processing, and reporting. For a firm with regulatory or compliance obligations, these roles might be subsumed as ancillary functions of the previously cited functions on an ad hoc basis, or absorbed by an individual handling miscellaneous tasks.

Depending upon the firm's leadership and their particular roles (as founding programmers, fundraisers, or other), the functions they take on might either augment the centralized role of digital in the company, or complement it around the immediate periphery.

For Bricks looking to add on digital functions, the process of sorting out where those ought to live can be fraught with angst. One way to approach it is with a mindset of a strategic acquisition, though with the difference that this is a process of working creatively to integrate a new business partner embodied as a technology rather than as people and products. As such, this might naturally serve to bubble up conversations in a more positive and constructive way

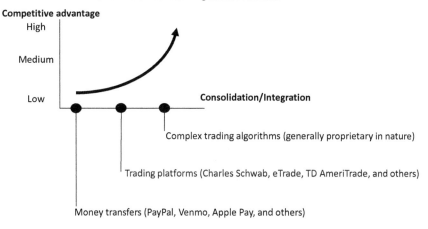

FIGURE 8.4 Evolution of consolidating finance functions

around matters such as who has ownership of new accountability or deliverables in the evolving corporate ecosystem. Figure 8.4 presents a perspective of a potential evolution of consolidating finance functions.

The accounting function in particular is often seen as a silo within many Bricks, and this can become stressed with the introduction of digital add-ons.

When a silo can be re-engineered to become a more integral part of an organization, synergies of scale and efficiency gains are often realized.

Not all solutions need to come from within, and for some data needs, a third-party vendor may be a good solution.[3]

Things to consider when evaluating a third-party data vendor would include the following:

- Vision: Does the vendor see itself as simply ticking the boxes with having certain types of data available, or is there a real commitment to integrity?
- Experience: Are there people with the vendor who know the industry well, and who have been around for some time?
- Culture and values: Does the vendor convey a sense of its dedication to excellence in what it is doing?
- Ability to execute: Is the vendor able to accommodate a variety of ways in which to create and provide deliverables?
- Technology adaptability and support: Is there a sufficient level of service to ensure that questions are resolved in a timely manner, whenever they might arise?
- Cost: Is the vendor competitive?
- Company viability: Does the company appear to have a strong business model and presence, which give some assurance that it will be around for some time?

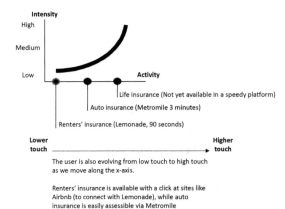

There is also a unique role for aggregators to play in this process. That is, online solutions that offer users the opportunity to enter their information once, with a search commenced for all available solutions ranked by cost.

Life insurance (Not yet available in a speedy platform)

Auto insurance (Metromile 3 minutes)

Renters' insurance (Lemonade, 90 seconds)

The user is also evolving from low touch to high touch as we move along the x-axis.

Renters' insurance is available with a click at sites like Airbnb (to connect with Lemonade), while auto insurance is easily assessible via Metromile

FIGURE 8.5 Intensity of technology in relation to types of insurance offerings

Figure 8.5 provides an illustration of technology in the context of types of insurance offerings.

***

Though the word "digital" may evoke a sense of something done electronically that replaces or makes easier a process that was previously more manual, this may not always be the case. Digital transitions rarely occur on their own, and may at times require at least an initial investment of time and effort to be launched. Over time, digital innovations can certainly assist with achieving economies of scale, process agility, and efficiencies.

When a company identifies a digital opportunity and decides to pursue it, there can be a few different ways to proceed. A few possibilities consist of the following:

External:

With an external approach, a new venture is created as a separate unit from the base company, and the rationale for this might include the following considerations:

- The business idea stands a real chance of perhaps reaching a point of credibly competing with the base company; rather than run the risk of the venture cannibalizing the base company, steps can be taken to keep it at arm's length and have it create its own distinct user base and value proposition, and energy.
- The venture does indeed become successful and the base company wishes to bring it in-house in a methodical way that is complementary with current business practices. Conversely, if the base company has evolved to a point at which it might prefer the sell the venture, it can more easily do so with a detached external structure.[4]

Internal:

Where there is low channel conflict, it could be a reasonable decision to embed the venture. Benefits to this might include:[5]

- Leveraging the existing organizational structure to achieve cost savings, as well as to facilitate the input, guidance, and experience of base company employees.
- If the venture would mostly involve a particular department or group of people within the base company, keeping it internal could be an easier process to manage.
- If agility and timeliness are seen as desirable, an internal launch could be valuable as a way of tapping into known employee talents and established processes.
- If cultures and compensation structures related to the venture and base company are compatible, this could ease acceptance and implementation.

External/Internal:

As a hybrid approach, an external/internal strategy is one whereby the base company sets up a venture as a separately operating unit, while retaining up to 100% ownership. A separate set of books is maintained for the new venture, but with revenues (or losses) fully accruing to the base company. One way to achieve this would be via a tracking stock approach. Some considerations associated with this might be:[6]

- The tracking stock venture may have a unique business culture associated with it, and making it into an internal-facing operation might dilute its creative or entrepreneurial spirit.
- Keeping the venture internal could divert management focus from core business activities, and run the risk of having a small revenue stream consume a very large portion of C-level time and energy.
- If the venture were to have a particularly anemic or spectacular takeoff phase, this could impact core business financials in a confusing way. Stakeholders of the core company might not readily understand or appreciate how the venture is serving as a drag or boost to operations, with a knock-on effect for KPIs and financial goals.
- When the venture reaches a more mature phase, it can perhaps be more easily folded into the core company, or sold.

Figure 8.6 provides a checklist of sorts to help evaluate whether an XTech opportunity might be better placed outside of a firm or inside.

Place inside		Place outside
• Opportunities to improve, enhance, or motivate existing lines of business	**Growth**	• A greater potential for growth, with more freedom to experiment and develop
• Low potential of channel conflict	**Channel**	• High potential of channel conflict
• Serves as a natural extension of an existing internal business segment	**Placement**	• A brand new product
• Is related to a target market of a current line of business	**Market**	• A brand new segment of the market
• Is more symmetrical with existing business priorities		• Is more asymmetrical with existing business priorities
• Potential to impact the entire firm	**Penetration**	• Impact of success or failure is likely to be contained to the venture (without knock-on effects on the entire firm)
• Existing resources are well positioned to help leverage the venture in terms of operations, distribution, marketing, or other	**Timing**	• Speed of getting up and running is key
		• Value of operating quickly under a new structure is paramount
• The internal culture is aligned with the culture of the new business	**Culture**	• A unique culture is associated with the new idea
• Considerations related to compensation, flex-time, benefits, and other are consistent	**Organization**	• The way in which people are to be compensated and the work environment expectations all differ from the existing firm

FIGURE 8.6 Criteria for evaluating when to place an XTech outside of the firm versus inside

In a study performed by ACORD and Salesforce, it was found that insurance companies who had embraced digitalization witnessed materially better performance in terms of share price, premiums generated, and earnings growth relative to their peer group. An area of interest for future study may be what actual contributions to performance were attributable directly to digitization itself, rather to the culture of these firms that embraced innovation generally. Curiously, the study also found an outperformance cohort that it termed the "Digital Laggards," or insurance companies that were ignoring digitization. The study seemed to attribute these positive results to near-term share price-boosting activities such as dividend payouts, share buybacks, and price competition, and with longer-term digitization benefits being sacrificed for short-term gains. Perhaps part of the answer also relates to the context of low-touch and high-touch insurance products, where auto insurance could reasonably be expected to be closer to a low-touch paradigm and with a life insurance annuity product being closer to high touch.[7]

Figure 8.7 presents a perspective of low touch and high touch in the context of Clicks and Bricks, and services and products.

***

The hiring process is another area where digitalization is permitting some interesting developments. Not only are online job postings the dominant venue for sourcing employment, but online recruiting processes often ask prospective employees to take an online personality or aptitude test of some sort as part of an overall hiring assessment process. Test results can be compared with the responses of previous applicants who were hired and performed well (or not so well). In some selective instances there is also an evolving de-emphasis of academic degrees in favor of experience. For a top-notch computer programmer, there may be more interest in the rather practical consideration of how much coding they have done in Python or C++ than in which schools they attended. Someone needing Java-Script might have an easier time finding a well-qualified and inexpensive programmer on an online coding forum than by posting an ad on Craigslist or LinkedIn.

***

So how best to proceed from wherever you or your firm may currently be in the context of things digital? From a practical standpoint, you can simply start

	Clicks		Bricks	
Lower touch	Services	Products	Services	Products
	• Orbitz	• Amazon	• Drive-thru car wash	• Gas/charging station
	• Airbnb	• 1 800 FLOWERS	• Bank ATM	• Fast food drive-thru
Higher touch	Services	Products	Services	Products
	• Education	• Insurance	• Spa treatment	• Tailored suit
	• Taxes	• Loan	• Auto repair	• Pets

FIGURE 8.7 Low touch – high touch: Clicks and Bricks, services and products

from wherever you are now. That is, embrace being at the very beginning, or intermediate level, or whichever other stage where you may be at in this moment, and plan your next move using the tools and guidelines provided throughout this text.

Whether you are already involved in digital finance in some way or other, or simply want to be in the loop, here are some things you can do:

- Stay abreast of industry news for the sectors of interest to you, and venture into what's happening in other fields from time to time for crossover ideas.
- Identify and follow websites, blogs, and tweets from businesses and individuals who have interesting things to say on digital finance topics.
- When new tools, apps, or features are released (and especially when they are free, as a trial or on a freemium basis), give them a try.
- Check out crowdfunding sites from time to time, and see what new offerings are being developed. Perhaps even think about investing in one or two if a nominal amount might provide you with unique insights.
- Listen in on podcasts that seem interesting, and attend a conference or seminar, not just for the presentation but the opportunity to pick up on sidebar conversations and network with others who have similar interests.
- If you have an idea, share it with others for their input, or see about putting it into practice.
- Carve out time in your weekly schedule (even if just a couple of hours each week) to dedicate to creative thinking. Go to the folder on your mobile device where you've saved articles during the week that you didn't have time to read, and ponder their ideas in a quiet setting. As part of this process, routinely ask yourself what your own particular value-add can be in the areas of interest to you, and how you can further grow into a helpful resource in your particular domain.
- Never stop asking questions, including those about whether things that have been done one way for years might possibly be transformed into something new. And be open-minded as to where those insights may surface, whether they come of individuals who are young or old, experienced or novice, and within your field or far removed from it.
- Think about digital companies that you find interesting, and apply the ideas of P*Q: In what ways is the company using digital to generate revenues, or to attract users who will in turn help to generate revenues?
- What businesses are at risk today, and how might their decline give rise to a new opportunity?

Another important consideration for firms is the type of culture they promote, and a number of surveys have been carried out to try to better understand this dynamic. Every firm is unique, though some generalities have been identified. For example, in an article entitled "InsurTech vs. Incumbents: What's Really Different About Their Cultures?", it was noted that in survey results only established carriers made specific mention of supporting communities as a cornerstone of their culture or stressed "purpose-driven" aspects of their mission. Meantime, nearly all InsurTech executives cited their culture as one where "everyone has a voice" and where information is shared. Finally, leaders of established companies stated they have active roles in shaping and transforming their cultures, while InsurTech executives were more likely to say their cultures simply evolved or that their teams created their own cultures.[8]

Certainly a key element of any positive culture environment involves a commitment to ethical standards. Using a term he originated, Steven Minsky refers to the "see-through economy," and discusses how the internet is increasingly an environment in which transparency empowers the general public to impact a company's reputation, and in which companies are evolving into powerful positions as guardians of public data. In this context, risk management, regulatory compliance, and ethical standards are paramount. Ethical behavior is a cornerstone of building trust, and trust in the digital age will become an increasingly important attribute sought by users in their online and other dealings, particularly when it comes to personal data and privacy protections. A key component of all this is education; it can be a challenge to determine the best ethical path to follow in the context of a blockchain-distributed ledger if that very concept is not well understood. To that end, to those reading this now, at the end of this last chapter of the text, well done! You are well on your way in your proactive journey to better understanding the world of digital finance, with all of its challenges, solutions, detail, and ambiguity.

Follow the energy!

Notes

1 Deloitte has published several excellent pieces on a variety of digital topics, and has made them freely available online on its website.
2 A "sprint" is when a relative short span of time (usually a week or two) is dedicated to completing a particular set of critical tasks.
3 For a helpful guide to questions enterprises can ask of themselves to better understand internal views on data and technology, see *HBR Pulse: An inflection point for the data driven enterprise* (2018, November), *Harvard Business Review*, https://hbr.org/sponsored/2018/11/an-inflection-point-for-the-data-driven-enterprise.
4 The term "cannibalizing" refers to how a new venture might somehow minimize an existing venture, such as by taking away its customers, market share, profitability, or other.
5 "Channel conflict" is a reference to one venue of conducting business (for example, online) somehow competing against the interest of another venue (offline). It might also be a reference to how firms need to be mindful of how messages with one channel (website, mobile app, social media) match up with messages across other channels for consistency and effectiveness. In these contexts, "omni-channel" strategies are often coordinated.
6 A definition of tracking stock (or targeted stock) is that it's a specialized equity offering based on the carved-out operations of a wholly owned subsidiary of a firm. The tracking stock trades at a price related to the operations of the specific division of the company being "tracked." Prior to the dot.com bubble many companies created tracking

stocks for their internet operations (as with Disney and go.com), and today tracking stocks are commonly associated with higher-growth segments of firms.
7 ACORD and Salesforce, (2017, October), "Digitization, automation, and value creation in the insurance industry," ACORD and Salesforce, Part 1 of 3.
8 Susanne Sclafane (2018, November 15), "InsurTech vs. incumbents: What's really different about their cultures?" *Carrier Management.*

Bibliography

ACORD and Salesforce. (2017, October). Digitization, automation, and value creation in the insurance industry. *ACORD and Salesforce*, Part 1 of 3.

Baker, S.R., Bloom, N., & Davis, S.J. (2016). "Measuring economic policy uncertainty." *Quarterly Journal of Economics, 131*(4).

Bloom, N., Jones, C.I., Van Reenen, J., & Webb, M. (2017). *Are ideas getting harder to find?* NBER (Working Paper No. 23782).

Brynjolfsson, E., Rock, D., & Syverson, C. (2017, November). *Artificial intelligence and the modern productivity paradox: A clash of expectations and statistics.* (NBER Working Paper No. 24001).

Bughin, J., & van Zeebroeck, N. (2017). *Getting digital bucks: How the interplay of disruption and types of strategic responses shapes digital investment payoffs and solves the Solow paradox.* (Working Paper). Brussels: ULB Institutional Repository, ULB/Université Libre de Bruxelles.

Bughin, J., & van Zeebroeck, N. (2017). The right response to digital disruption. *MIT Sloan Management Review* Summer 2017 Issue, *58*(4) (April).

Bughin, J., LaBerge, L., & Mellbye, A. (2017). The case for digital reinvention. *McKinsey Quarterly.* (July/August 2017), 4–17.

Comin, D., & Hobijn, B. (2010). An exploration of technology diffusion. *American Economic Review, 100*, (5), 2031–2059.

Davis, S.J. (2017). Regulatory complexity and policy uncertainty: Headwinds of our own making. Paper prepared for Hoover Institution Conference on Restoring Prosperity, February 9, 2017, Hoover Institution, Stanford University.

Flamm, K. (2017). Has Moore's Law been repealed? An economist's perspective. *Computing in Science & Engineering, 19*(2), 29–40.

HBR Pulse: An inflection point for the data driven enterprise. (2018, November). *Harvard Business Review.* Retrieved from https://hbr.org/sponsored/2018/11/an-inflection-point-for-the-data-driven-enterprise.

McKinsey & Company. (2017). How digital reinventors are pulling away from the pack. McKinsey.

Remes, J., Manyika, J., Bughin, J., Woetzel, J., Mischke, J., & Krishnan, M. (2018). *Solving the productivity puzzle: The role of demand and the promise of digitization.* Brussels: McKinsey Global Institute. Retrieved from https://www.mckinsey.com/~/media/McKinsey/Fea tured%20Insights/Meeting%20societys%20expectations/Solving%20the%20product ivity%20puzzle/MGI-Solving-the-Productivity-Puzzle-Report-February-22-2018 .ashx/MGI-Solving-the-Productivity-Puzzle-Report/\-February-22-2018.ashx.

Sclafane, S. (2018, November 15). InsurTech vs. incumbents: What's really different about their cultures? *Carrier Management.*

INDEX

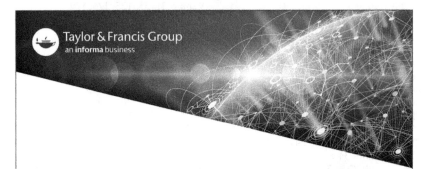

For Product Safety Concerns and Information please contact our EU
representative GPSR@taylorandfrancis.com
Taylor & Francis Verlag GmbH, Kaufingerstraße 24, 80331 München, Germany